PSYCHOLOGY AND HEALTH SERIES

Series editor:
Donald Marcer
Department of Psychology, University of Southampton

During the last 20 years the behavioural sciences have come to play an increasingly important part in the training of doctors, nurses and other health professionals. Not surprisingly this shift of emphasis in education has been accompanied by a minor deluge of textbooks, all concerned with the relationship of psychology to health. Though many of these books are excellent, the range of subject matter that most of them seek to encompass necessarily means that many complex issues cannot be covered at anything other than a superficial level.

This series consists of individual texts, each dealing in some depth with a particular issue in which health professionals and psychologists have a shared interest. Though most are written by psychologists with an established academic record, they are aimed primarily at practising professionals. With this in mind the contributing authors have all had experience in teaching students or members of the medical and other health professions and with very few exceptions have worked in a clinical setting. Thus they are well suited to fulfil the brief that is common to all the books in this series. That is, while the theoretical basis of the issue under discussion must be spelt out, it must be done in such a way that it enables readers (be they doctor, nurse, physiotherapist, etc. or student) to practise their professions more effectively.

1. Biofeedback and Related Therapies in Clinical Practice
   Donald Marcer
2. Psychological Problems in Primary Health Care
   Eric Button
3. Psychology and Diabetes
   Psychosocial factors in management and control
   Richard W. Shillitoe
4. Communicating with Patients
   Improving communication, satisfaction and compliance
   Philip Ley
5. Understanding Stress
   A psychological perspective for health professionals
   Valerie J. Sutherland and Cary L. Cooper
6. Psychosexual Therapy
   A cognitive-behavioural approach
   Susan H. Spence

Psychosexual Therapy

A COGNITIVE–BEHAVIOURAL APPROACH

Susan H. Spence

Senior Lecturer in Psychology,
University of Sydney, Australia

CHAPMAN & HALL
London · New York · Tokyo · Melbourne · Madras

Published by Chapman & Hall, 2–6 Boundary Row, London SE1 8HN

Chapman & Hall, 2–6 Boundary Row, London SE1 8HN, UK

Chapman & Hall, 29 West 35th Street, New York, NY10001, USA

Chapman & Hall Japan, Thomson Publishing Japan, Hirakawacho Nemoto Building, 7F, 1–7–11 Hirakawa-cho, Chiyoda-ku, Tokyo 102, Japan

Chapman & Hall Australia, Thomas Nelson Australia, 102 Dodds Street, South Melbourne, Victoria 3205, Australia

Chapman & Hall India, R. Seshadri, 32 Second Main Road, CIT East, Madras 600 035, India

First edition 1991

© 1991 Chapman & Hall

Typeset in 10/12 Times by Mew Photosetting, Beckenham, Kent
Printed in Great Britain by Page Bros (Norwich) Ltd

ISBN 0 412 35450 0

A catalogue record for this book is available from the British Library

Library of Congress Cataloging-in-Publication data Spence, Susan, H.
        Psychosexual therapy : a cognitive–behavioural approach / Susan H. Spence.
        p. cm. – (Psychology and health series : 6)
        Includes bibliographical references and index.
        ISBN 0–412–35450–0 (Pb)
        1. Sex therapy. 2. Psychosexual disorders—Treatment.
        3. Cognitive therapy. I. Title. II. Series.
        [DNLM: 1. Cognitive Therapy—methods. 2. Psychosexual Dysfunctions—therapy. WM 611 5744p]
        RC557.S64 1991
        616.85′830651—dc20
        DNLM/DLC
        for Library of Congress   91–15744
                                                                              CIP

Contents

Preface

The increasing number of individuals and couples seeking help for psychosexual difficulties presents a challenge to the helping professions. Although considerable progress has been made over the past twenty years in the development of therapy approaches, there remains a significant proportion of cases who fail to respond to treatment or whose improvement in sexual functioning is short-lived. It is suggested that such limitations of therapy reflect our lack of understanding of the psychosocial determinants of sexual responding. Whereas the biological determinants are now well understood, much less is known about the psychosocial factors which influence sexual responding.

The aim of this book is to examine in depth some of the psychosocial factors which must be considered during the assessment and treatment of psychosexual dysfunction. It has been written for those helping professionals who already have expertise in cognitive–behavioural assessment and therapy. Although much of the text focuses on practical issues, reference is made to empirical evidence regarding the determinants of sexual functioning and effectiveness of therapy methods. A scientist-practitioner approach is followed wherever possible, combined with practical illustrations from the author's own clinical work.

The early chapters of the text provide a detailed review of the biological and psychosocial determinants of sexual functioning. A model is produced which emphasizes the importance of cognitive and general relationship factors in satisfactory sexual responding. Although the role of cognitive and relationship factors has been stressed elsewhere, there has been a paucity of literature concerning ways in which psychosexual therapy can be combined with recent cognitive–behavioural approaches designed to modify maladaptive cognitions or to enhance the quality of the couple's general relationship. The middle chapters of the text therefore describe how assessment may be designed to consider the contribution of cognitive and general relationship factors to the presenting problem. The volume then examines ways in which traditional psychosexual therapy may be integrated with marital and cognitive interventions in order to maximize the effectiveness of treatment. Methods to increase positive experiences between the couple and to improve communication and problem-solving skills are given particular consideration in the marital therapy section. Cognitive techniques, such as the training of attention focusing and fantasy skills or restructuring of maladaptive thoughts and attitudes related to sexual functioning, are also described in detail.

This type of approach to therapy is suggested to be equally relevant for all client groups, irrespective of age, sexual orientation or handicap. Nevertheless, it is acknowledged that specific populations such as elderly, homosexual or physically handicapped clients have unique needs and characteristics of which the therapist must be aware and which must be considered in the implementation of therapy. Such issues are discussed in the later chapters of the book.

The final chapter explores the professional and ethical aspects of psychosexual therapy. The complexity of human sexual responding demands that therapists have a high level of understanding of the biological and psychosexual determinants. It is important for the non-medical practitioner to understand the information provided by medical and physiological examinations and to be able to integrate such information with that produced from the cognitive-behavioural assessment. It is also important for adequate education to be provided concerning the many ethical and professional issues which arise within the context of the treatment of sexual problems. Overall, there is a need for a high level of training for those involved in the treatment of psychosexual difficulties.

Many people made this volume possible. In particular, I would like to thank my family and friends for their support during the months of research for, and preparation of, this manuscript. My colleagues, in particular David Kavanagh, also require a mention for their constructive comments concerning earlier drafts. Louise Sharpe and Tracey Larkin should be congratulated on their enthusiastic proofreading. Finally, I would like to thank the many clients from Badham Clinic at the University of Sydney whose case material forms the basis for the case examples provided here.

SHS

1

Introduction

WHY IS THERE AN INCREASING DEMAND FOR THE TREATMENT OF SEXUAL DIFFICULTIES?

It is clear that sexual difficulties are extremely common and there is a considerable need for therapy services to help the large number of couples or individuals who experience such problems. Although it is difficult to estimate the exact incidence of sexual disorders, studies suggest that between 30% and 50% of couples experience some form of sexual dysfunction (Stuntz, 1988). For example, Frank *et al.* (1978) reported that 63% of wives and 40% of husbands in their sample of US couples experienced at least one type of sexual dysfunction. An even higher percentage reported sexual difficulties such as difficulty relaxing during sex and inadequate amounts of foreplay before intercourse. A study caried out in Sweden by Nettelbladt and Uddenberg (1979) also found that 40% of men in their sample reported a 'tendency' towards sexual dysfunction. Garde and Lunde (1980a) found that 35% of a random sample of 40-year-old women in Denmark reported current sexual problems. It seems therefore that studies suggest a remarkably high frequency of sexual dysfunction in the general population.

The number of couples seeking help in dealing with their sexual problems appears to have increased markedly over the last twenty years (Kaplan, 1987). It seems unlikely that this trend actually reflects an increase in the incidence of sexual problems and is more likely to have resulted from changes in social attitudes and availability of services. In the past, couples with sexual difficulties tended to opt to continue their relationship in the absence of a sexual component or to seek alternative sexual partners. As social attitudes towards sex and sexuality have changed, it has become increasingly acceptable to request the help of a therapist in order to deal with sexual difficulties. The general public have become aware that services and techniques are available which can be highly successful. Media communications convey the message that sex is an important part of a relationship, that everyone (even women!) should be able to enjoy sex and achieve arousal and orgasm. The general public therefore hold higher expectations from their sexual relationships. The advent of AIDS is also likely to encourage couples to rectify their sexual difficulties, rather than seeking sexual relationships elsewhere (Kaplan, 1987). The overall result is an increasing number of couples who wish to develop a successful sexual relationship.

Although we tend to be bombarded with media advertising of the importance of sexual activity, we should stop to wonder why people tend to perceive sexual competence as being so important. There are no simple answers to this question. From a biological perspective, sexual activity provides the mechanism by which conception and reproduction may occur. Sexual behaviour may therefore be perceived as a response to a biological drive state which benefits the survival of the species. For many couples, however, sex serves a very different function. For some it may provide a source of expression of affection and intimacy. Indeed, there is considerable evidence to demonstrate the close relationship between sexual and marital satisfaction (Halgin *et al.*, 1988). In practice, this is likely to reflect a two-way influence in which sexual disharmony may produce marital dissatisfaction and marital discord may lead to sexual difficulties. Hence, a satisfactory sexual relationship appears to be important in the maintenance of marital relationships generally. It should be pointed out, however, that many couples have extremely good relationships without the involvement of any sexual activity. For other couples sexual activity may provide a source of general tension reduction. Irrespective of the reason, we are left with the position that satisfactory sexual relationships are a highly valued goal for many couples. Whether or not this is an over-valued goal is debatable.

The increasing number of couples seeking help for sexual difficulties may also reflect the greater emphasis on sexual functioning amongst older people. Many people over the age of 65 today have lived through the era of increased focus on sexual performance. The majority of older couples now expect to continue to have a satisfying sexual relationship and are more prepared to seek help if sexual difficulties occur. Hence, a wider range of the adult population is likely to seek help for sexual difficulties than was previously the case. This is also true of individuals with specific disabilities, such as spinal injuries or physical handicaps, who now may also expect to receive help to enable them to achieve satisfactory sexual relationships. As a result, therapists need to extend their knowledge in order to develop ways of assisting a wide range of client groups with their sexual functioning. This book attempts to go beyond the traditional married couple, in order to explore the application of sex therapy techniques to a wide range of special populations.

WHAT ARE SEXUAL DYSFUNCTIONS?

The term dysfunction implies some form of breakdown in normal functioning. This type of approach to the definition of dysfunction requires knowledge as to what is normal in relation to sexual functioning. An enormous number of problems exist in establishing what 'normal' sexual behaviour consists of. It is very difficult to obtain samples that are truly representative of the general population. Most research has been conducted with samples that are special in some way, such as students or university staff members. Even those studies that have attempted to examine the 'general' population run into problems. It is very difficult to get all people in the sample to respond to surveys of a sexual nature and it is likely that the people who agree are somewhat different from those who refuse. We must even question whether the responses of those people who do agree to take part in the survey are accurate, given that their answers may be influenced by memory limitations and the desire to impress the examiner. Furthermore, the way that questions are phrased may influence the results that are produced. Hence if the investigator asks 'How often do you have intercourse with your partner?' one may obtain a very different picture of human sexual functioning than if the investigator asked 'How often do you try to avoid having intercourse with your partner?'

These limitations must be borne in mind in interpreting the findings of surveys such as those of Hite (1976) and Kinsey *et al.* (1948, 1953). Hence, it is not really appropriate to suggest that there is a set range for the frequency of sexual behaviours, such as intercourse or orgasm, within which humans should operate in order for their sexual functioning to be classed as normal. A further

3

problem with the studies of Kinsey and colleagues is that they occurred so long ago as to make the use of the data highly questionable in relation to today's population. Indeed, recent surveys of sexual behaviour suggest considerable changes in patterns of sexual activity since the Kinsey studies were conducted (e.g. Wyatt *et al.*, 1988).

It is clear, therefore, that enormous problems exist in determining what is 'normal' in terms of frequency of sexual activity or the intensity or duration of a response. For example, what is the 'normal' time taken for a woman to become sexually aroused/lubricated following the commencement of stimulation? Similarly, what is the 'normal' duration for a male to hold back ejaculation once coitus begins? Such questions are extremely difficult to answer and have led to a host of different criteria being used in the classification of specific sexual dysfunctions, usually involving some arbitrarily set cut-off point.

It is suggested that the concept of 'normality', in the sense of comparison with data which is of dubious validity, should be used cautiously in determining whether a sexual dysfunction exists. Instead it is proposed that the concept of distress to the couple should be taken as the primary criterion for the decision as to whether a sexual dsyfunction exists. It is obviously easier to establish that a dysfunction is present when the target response is totally absent, such as lack of orgasm, lack of ejaculation or lack of intercourse. Whether or not this situation is then viewed as a sexual problem depends upon whether a change is desired by the client(s). This is also true for instances in which the frequency/ intensity/duration of a sexual response or activity is significantly different from normal, but it is not a cause for concern to the couple. For example, rapid ejaculation or low levels of sexual arousal would only be viewed as a sexual difficulty if the issue is perceived as a problem by the couple.

The concept of normality does need to be taken into account for clients who hold unreasonable expectations as to their performance, and for whom education as to what is 'normal' sexual responding is required. For example, some couples may have unrealistic expectations as to the length of time the male may hold an erection before ejaculation occurs. Others may believe a sexual problem to exist if the male is unable to attain an erection on the third or fourth occasion of intercourse and ejaculation on the same evening. Obviously, some reference to sexual behaviour of the general population would be warranted here in counselling the couple and in reducing unrealistic expectations.

WHAT TRIGGERS INDIVIDUALS TO SEEK HELP FOR SEXUAL DIFFICULTIES?

By the time a couple seek help with a sexual problem, the problem will often have persisted for several months, if not years. Various attempts at self-help may have been made and these will not have been helpful in the long term. Presentation at a clinic with a request for therapy for a sexual difficulty is generally anticipated as an embarrassing and/or stressful event which many couples would rather avoid. Hence, there is usually some trigger that generates enough motivation to push clients into seeking help. This is often a crisis in their relationship or a failed attempt at self-help. Events of this type typically mean that individuals seeking help will be feeling rather despondent and lacking a strong belief that the problem can be successfully overcome. One of the first steps of the assessment and therapy process is therefore to begin to increase motivation and self-efficacy regarding the client(s)' ability to rectify the problem.

THE CASE FOR THE MULTI-SKILLED COGNITIVE-BEHAVIOURAL ASSESSOR/THERAPIST

Over the past twenty years, our knowledge of the biological and psychological variables which influence sexual functioning has progressed dramatically. As a consequence, a great deal of success has been achieved in the development of medical and psychological treatment programmes for sexual dysfunctions. Much of the credit for the development of behavioural approaches must go to Masters and Johnson (1970). Their techniques for the treatment of a variety of sexual problems continue to be widely used throughout the world. Gradually, people have come to realize that sexual difficulties can be successfully treated and it is acceptable to seek help for such problems. Prior to the pioneering work of Masters and Johnson, sexual difficulties tended to be suffered in silence and professional help was rarely available.

In any new book related to the treatment of sexual dysfunctions one must ask: what progress has been made since the work of Masters and Johnson? what is new? how can the technology of sex therapy be improved? Several criticisms may be made of the state of sex therapy as developed following the work of Masters and Johnson. Throughout the 1970s and 1980s an 'epidemic' occurred of therapists who specialized in the treatment of sexual problems. These 'sex therapists' came from a variety of professional backgrounds and some were purely lay persons who read and trained themselves through attendance at workshops and so on. Many of these therapists practised as technicians in which the technology was applied, based on the detailed therapy outlines reported by Masters and Johnson. The technology was very much a package approach in which certain standard treatment methods were administered, such as a ban on intercourse and sensate focus exercises, followed by specific methods for specific disorders, e.g. the squeeze technique for premature ejaculation. Although detailed structured interviews were normally conducted, the content of treatment rarely made full use of the data produced. There was a marked absence of a behavioural analysis and little attempt to develop individually tailored programmes based on the outcome of the assessment. The skills of the sex therapist-technician tended to be in the application of the Masters and Johnson technology with minimal concern for individualized assessment, aetiology and prognosis. The underlying assumption of this approach is that sexual behaviour can be considered in isolation from other psychological, health, social or family influences (Meyer, 1983). The major aim of the present text is to outline a cognitive-behavioural approach to assessment and intervention that takes into account the contribution of factors from the individual, the couple, the system and the environment. The aim is to move away from the concept of the sex therapist-technician to the skilled cognitive-behaviour assessor and therapist who is able to tackle sexual behaviour in the same way as other aspects of human behaviour. It is acknowledged that many multi-skilled therapists do already exist who either specialize in the treatment of sexual disorders or who are able to deal with sexual dysfunctions within a wide range of human psychological disorders.

There is a current tendency for general therapists, such as the clinical psychologist in a community health setting, to refer sexual problems on to a specialist, rather than conducting the treatment themselves. Furthermore, few therapists ask routinely about sexual functioning of clients and are likely to miss many instances of sexual problems that are a source of distress to clients and could easily be tackled. We must ask why this is the case. Undoubtedly, it partly reflects the inhibitions of the therapist which, in turn, reflect the lack of openness about sex which continues in our culture today. Many therapists feel uncomfortable about discussing sexual matters, while others feel they would be prying unnecessarily into the client's personal life. Given that many clients are hesitant to present initially for help with regard to sexual difficulties and are often reluctant to admit to them, a request for help with regard to some other problem may mask a sexual dysfunction for which the client would like assistance. Indeed, Croft (1982) cited evidence to suggest that many persons with sexual problems seek help for other difficulties rather than initially divulging their sexual difficulties to a health professional.

A further explanation for the reluctance of many general thera-pists to involve themselves with sexual dysfunctions is the assump-tion that sexual behaviour is far more complex than other forms of behaviour, given the multitude of biological and psychological variables which influence sexual responding. Meyer (1983) sug-gested that the concept of the 'sex therapist' tends to create the impression that sexual disorders are intrinsically different from other behavioural problems. It is suggested here that sexual behaviour should not be viewed as intrinsically different from other forms of behaviour, as many other forms of behaviour are also found to be influenced by a multiplicity of psychological and biological influences (e.g. anxiety, fears or depression). The adequately trained cognitive-behaviour therapist would not be so likely to refer cases involving anxiety or depression on to 'depression' specialists or 'anxiety' therapists. The majority of therapists who are trained in the skills of cognitive-behavioural assessment and therapy should be capable of applying these skills to the treatment of sexual difficulties. This book is therefore designed for those who already have the basic skills of cognitive-behavioural assessment and therapy but who require the additional knowledge to enable them to apply their skills effectively to the treatment of sexual dysfunctions. It is suggested that further reading, practical case supervision and workshop experience would form an important adjunct to the knowledge and skills gained through this text. Such additional educa-tion, however, should be considered in relation to the treatment of any psychological difficulty and this recommendation should not be taken as an indication that sexual behaviour is in any way special or 'too difficult' for the general cognitive-behaviour therapist to tackle.

There are several benefits of encouraging general therapists to take on the task of dealing with sexual difficulties. First, many practitioners work in localities in which there is a lack of specialists to refer to and referral on is not an option for them. Second, it is hoped that by increasing the knowledge of general therapists with regard to sexual functioning they will become less inhibited about routine questioning regarding sexual difficulties. This should result in easier access to therapy for many clients who are reluctant to make a direct request for assistance with a sexual problem. Third, it is suggested that many clients prefer to receive help for sexual problems within a generalist setting rather than being referred to a specialist 'sex' clinic, where the nature of their presenting difficulties is more obvious to others.

Finally, it is suggested that a therapist who possesses the skills of cognitive-behavioural assessment and therapy should be able to apply these skills to cases of sexual difficulty in a way that enables an individually tailored programme to be developed. This method is likely to be more effective, particularly with complex cases, than the package treatment approaches used by many sex therapist-technicians who frequently do not possess the skills required to conduct an adequate cognitive behavioural assessment or to design individualized therapy programmes. Furthermore, the generalist is likely to be highly skilled in other areas of assessment and therapy which are often relevant in cases of sexual dsyfunction, such as marital distress, child management problems, generalized anxiety and depression. There is a danger in the package-type approach to dealing with sexual difficulties of overlooking such areas and this in turn may limit the long-term effectiveness of treatment. This is particularly important given that the majority of referrals for sexual dysfunction tend to experience additional problem areas. For example, Halgin et al. (1988) cited evidence to suggest that 70% of counsellees for sex therapy also had significant marital problems. The multi-skilled therapist is in a better position to deal effectively with additional psychopathology than the practitioner whose skills are limited to the area of sexual problems. Obviously, the ideal therapist should be competent in the application of cognitive-behaviour assessment and therapy to a wide range of problems, including sexual dysfunctions. It is this goal that the present book aims to meet. In many respects this reflects my own interest in sexual problems, coming from the perspective of a clinical psychologist who deals with a wide range of psychological problems, amongst which sexual dysfunctions are likely to emerge. I do not write from the position of a practitioner who specializes in sexual problems, but rather a multi-skilled, cognitive-behaviour therapist who has no hesitation in conducting therapy programmes for clients who present with sexual difficulties. Evaluation of the effectiveness of intervention for the treatment of female orgasmic dysfunction, conducted by the author at the University of Sydney, demonstrated the positive results that may be obtained by generalist practitioners working within a generalist clinic (Spence, 1985).

The need for a detailed cognitive-behavioural assessment and carefully tailored intervention programme is emphasized by Halgin *et al*. (1988). These authors concluded that recent empirical investigations of the effectiveness of psychological treatments of sexual dysfunctions indicate a much lower level of efficacy compared to the extremely positive results reported in early studies, such as the work of Masters and Johnson (1970). Halgin *et al*. (1988) suggested that this reflects a change in the type of client seeking help for sexual difficulties. They suggested that early studies included many clients in whom lack of sexual knowledge was a primary causal factor and for whom a simple psycho-educational approach was sufficient to enhance sexual functioning. As the general public has become increasingly knowledgeable about sexual matters and basic self-help techniques, the cases that remain tend to involve much more complex interpersonal and intrapersonal problems. Such cases are much harder to treat and require a multi-faceted intervention programme which tackles the accompanying interpersonal and intrapersonal problems. Halgin *et al*. (1988) stress the danger of the specialist who acquires the skills of the sex therapist in the absence of more broad-based assessment and therapeutic skills.

Our knowledge of the determinants of sexual behaviour has progressed remarkably over the part thirty years and it has become increasingly clear that a complex interaction is involved between psychological and biological variables. Although clients who are referred for psychological intervention should generally be referred to a medical specialist for consideration of biological factors, it is also essential that the cognitive-behaviour therapist has a detailed understanding of the biological processes involved. There is a marked need to integrate medical and psychological approaches to intervention. For many individuals, it is difficult to determine whether biological and psychological causes are responsible for the difficulties. In many instances there will be need for the therapist to work in conjunction with medical specialists in order to tackle both the psychological and biological aspects of the disorder. This text provides information about those physical and psychosocial factors which determine sexual functioning, which will enable the practitioner to operate within a multidisciplinary team and to liaise more easily with medical colleagues.

THE CONTENT OF THIS BOOK

The underlying philosophy of this text is one of cognitive-behaviourism. Such an approach proposes that sexual behaviour consists of cognitive, physiological and overt components, which are influenced by biological and environmental variables in the same way as occurs for any other form of human behaviour. The interaction between biological and environmental factors must be taken into account in order to understand the development and maintenance of sexual problems. Biological factors include circulating hormone levels, neurological functioning, drug effects or other physiological and/or biochemical processes which influence sexual functioning. Environmental influences include events which shape the person's learning history, such as antecedent situations that trigger particular behaviours, the consequences of behaviour (reinforcing or punishing experiences) and learning through observation. The approach taken to understanding human sexual behaviour also highlights the reciprocal nature of sexual activity, given that it generally involves two people. This makes matters somewhat complex, as the couple constantly influence each other and act as stimuli and consequences for each other's behaviour. The role of cognitive events as triggers for sexual behaviour, as part of the sexual behaviour and as consequences of sexual behaviour, is also emphasized. Our thoughts, attitudes, beliefs and values are therefore acknowledged as being important parts of sexual behaviour and also important sources of influence over sexual responding.

The following text assumes an adequate understanding of the underlying principles of cognitive-behaviour assessment and therapy. For those who are not familiar with such approaches some preparatory reading from texts such as Bellack and Hersen (1988) would be beneficial. Given that the aim of the text is to encourage a more global view of sexual problems within the context of other inter- and intrapersonal problems, the book is focused towards the multi-skilled therapist who is already able to tackle problems such as marital distress, parenting problems, depression, anxiety and interpersonal skill deficits.

In addition to outlining a cognitive-behavioural approach to the assessment and treatment of sexual difficulties, the text aims to provide an up-to-date coverage of the literature. It attempts to go beyond previous texts that provide a basic summary of sexual history taking and psychological treatment components. Wherever possible the content is based upon empirical evidence, rather than being limited to therapist intuitions, with a critical stance being taken towards evaluation of the literature. With an emphasis on empirical data, Chapter 2 provides a detailed discussion of the major psychological and biological factors which influence sexual functioning. Chapter 3 then summarizes the classification of sexual disorders, with details concerning the characteristics of specific sexual problems. The assessment process is covered in Chapter 4, with an emphasis on the clinical interview and use of data from self and partner questionnaires and self-monitoring. A detailed format for the cognitive-behavioural interview is provided.

Chapter 5 introduces a cognitive-behavioural approach to therapy which also takes into account the context of the couple's general relationship. A model of intervention is outlined in which therapy is designed to meet the needs of each individual or couple, based upon the outcome of the assessment. The content of therapy may require a focus on marital enhancement techniques, cognitive therapy methods or sexual task assignments, as appropriate. General points regarding therapy are covered, such as when to accept clients for therapy, the content of preparatory sessions, the structure of sessions, programming for generalization, general therapist skills and deciding where to start in therapy. The second half of the chapter then provides detailed discussion of the techniques and practical issues involved in the application of cognitive and marital therapy methods, as applied to the treatment of couples who present with sexual dysfunctions. Case examples are used to illustrate the major points. Chapter 6 progresses to outline the development of sexual skills using a variety of behavioural techniques. The first section describes those methods which are applicable to a wide range of sexual problems, whereas the second part of the chapter examines different forms of psychosexual dysfunction and appropriate sexual skill development techniques.

Chapter 7 provides a detailed review of the literature and highlights inadequacies in much of the existing research. Suggestions for future studies are made. Chapter 8 then explores the sexual problems of special populations, such as elderly, mentally handicapped, physically ill or disabled, and homosexual clients. Specific suggestions are made for the adaptation of the cognitive-behavioural approach to meet the special needs of each client group. Finally, Chapter 9 discusses some of the professional issues which apply in the assessment and treatment of psychosexual dysfunctions. Particular consideration is given to ethical issues and the training of therapists.

2

The Determinants of Sexual Behaviour

In order to understand why sexual problems develop, it is first necessary to have a sound knowledge of how people normally respond sexually and the biological and psychosocial factors which regulate our sexual behaviour.

A SUMMARY OF THE HUMAN SEXUAL RESPONSE

Various models have been used to describe the human sexual response, most of which derive from the observational studies of Masters and Johnson (1966). Stuntz (1988) provided a detailed review of the processes involved in what he termed the DEPORD model of the human sexual response cycle. This is an acronym for desire, excitement, plateau, orgasm, resolution and desire, which are suggested to form separate phases of sexual responding in both the male and the female.

The desire phase

Desire refers to the cognitive and affective components of the appetitive aspects of sexual behaviour. As such, desire refers to thoughts or fantasies about sex or 'urges' to engage in sexual activity, which typically trigger sexual arousal responses. In many respects the desire phase can be seen as a drive state in which a need is created to engage in a particular behaviour, in this case sexual behaviour, in order to reduce the 'need' or drive state. It must be borne in mind that desire is a cognitive activity which cannot be observed directly. Although the person's level of sexual activity (both self-stimulatory or with a partner) is likely to be greater with high levels of desire, activity should not be equated with 'desire' given that desire may occur in the absence of sexual arousal or overt activity. We must therefore rely on the person's subjective reports of desire rather than using frequency of sexual activity as a measure of desire, despite the inherent problems of self-reports of cognitive events.

Desire may be triggered by a range of stimuli. These may be external cues (sight, sound, taste or smell), such as the sight of a partner, or may be internal or cognitive events such as a thought about a particular stimulus (e.g. a partner) which in turn triggers off thoughts or fantasies and/or subjective feelings of sexual desire. Although the current trend is to emphasize the distinction between sexual arousal and desire, the relationship between these two components of sexual responding is unclear. For example, how do the subjective feelings of desire differ from those of sexual arousal? Does sexual desire always have to precede sexual arousal or can sexual desire occur in response to the physiological responses of sexual arousal? These questions remain unanswered and it is possible that the distinction between sexual desire and arousal is not as clear-cut as some authors would have us believe.

The excitement phase

From a biological perspective, the aim of sexual excitement is to produce changes within the male and female body that will enable intercourse and conception to take place. In the unaroused state, the penis is flaccid, the vagina is not well lubricated and insertion of the penis into the vagina would be difficult. Sexual arousal therefore brings about the changes required for erection of the penis, lubrication of the vagina and preparation for the orgasmic response. In the male, the excitement or arousal phase involves a combination of penile arterial dilatation, increased arterial blood flow, active relaxation of the smooth muscles of the tissue of the corpora cavernosa (a sponge-like tissue, see Figure 2.1) and constriction of venous outflow (Williams, 1987). These processes result in an engorgement of blood within the corpora cavernosa which causes the penis to become erect and the foreskin to retract. The general process of arousal is also accompanied by a tightening of the scrotal sac, raising of the testicles within the scrotum, nipple erection and general bodily reactions such as increased muscle tension, blood pressure, heart rate and respiration rate.

14

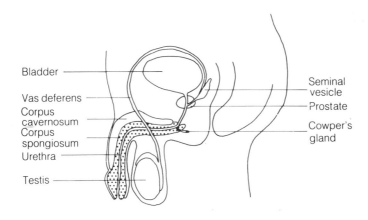

Figure 2.1 A side view through the male genitalia.

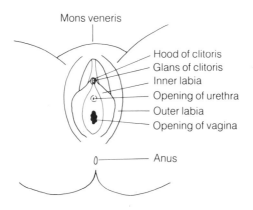

Figure 2.2 The external anatomy of the female genitalia.

In the female, a similar vasocongestive response occurs during sexual arousal, causing vaginal lubrication, vaginal lengthening, and formation of the orgasmic platform around the base of the vagina. Clitoral engorgement also tends to occur, resulting in the raising of the clitoris towards the area of the mons venis (see Figure 2.2). The labia may become darker in colour as the result of increased blood flow. Similar general body responses occur during this phase to those found in the male.

Although the physiological changes of sexual arousal may progress in a steady manner, given appropriate stimulation, the subjective feelings of excitement are not necessarily continuous and may occur in waves of increasing and decreasing arousal (Hawton, 1985). People also differ in the rapidity and intensity with which the different aspects of sexual arousal occur, hence sexual arousal may present as a different pattern of responses for different people.

The plateau phase

Masters and Johnson (1966) described the plateau phase as a period in which the responses of the excitement phase continue, up to a point of ejaculatory inevitability in men and just prior to orgasm in women. Other authors have suggested that the plateau phase is merely a continuation of the excitement/arousal response with no clear-cut neurophysiological mechanisms to distinguish it from the arousal stage and which therefore does not warrant separate reference (Jehu, 1979).

The orgasmic phase

Various attempts have been made to define the term 'orgasm'. Rosen and Beck (1988) suggest that orgasm is best viewed as a complex interaction between peripheral and central processes which are the result of a process of synchronous afferent discharge. A range of genital, skeletomuscular, cardiovascular and respiratory responses then occur in conjunction with higher-level cortical activity which is reflected by electroencephalographic (EEG) changes.

During the orgasm/ejaculation phase for the male, two separate components can be identified: emission and expulsion. Emission involves contractions of the vas deferens, seminal vesicles and ejaculating ducts as semen is placed at the entrance to the urethra.

Simultaneously, the internal sphincter of the urethra contracts which prevents ejaculation backwards into the bladder. The result is the formation of a pressure chamber in which the system prepares for expulsion of the ejaculate. At this point most males report a feeling which is usually described as 'ejaculatory inevitability'. This is then followed by expulsion, in which rhythmic contractions of the penile urethra and muscles at the base of the penis occur at around 0.8-second intervals, propelling the ejaculate through the penis. In the woman the orgasm phase involves similar rhythmic contractions, but of the muscles around the base of the vagina and pelvic floor. This is usually preceded by a retraction of the clitoris under the clitoral hood. Debate still continues as to whether the physiological responses involved in orgasms which are triggered by clitoral stimulation are the same as those resulting from vaginal stimulation (Rosen and Beck, 1988). Whilst the basic physiological responses appear to be the same, it may be that the subjective feeling created by stimulation to different genital areas may be experienced differently for some women, depending upon the area being stimulated.

At this point it is worth mentioning the 'G' spot, which you may be asked about from time to time. The 'G' spot refers to an area in the anterior wall of the vagina which was proposed by Grafenberg (1950) to trigger orgasm and to produce a release of fluid through the urethra. This fluid was suggested to be similar in content to the prostatic secretions of the male, rather than containing urine. Several researchers have since tried to identify the physiological and anatomical basis of the 'G' spot and to determine whether females are capable of releasing a fluid which is distinct from urine. A review of empirical studies by Quadagno (1988) suggested that some women do have a pressure-sensitive area on the anterior wall of the vagina which may lead to orgasm when stimulated. This area, however, does not appear to be a discrete anatomical entity with well-defined boundaries and orgasm may similarly be triggered by strong rhythmic pressure to other areas of the vagina in some women. Quadagno (1988) also concluded that women who produce fluid at the time of orgasm are releasing urine and not fluid resembling male secretions. As such, there appears to be little support for the existence of the 'G' spot as proposed by Grafenberg (1950).

The resolution phase

Finally, the resolution phase occurs which, in the male, involves a refractory period where gradual detumescence occurs and little response results from further sexual stimulation. The length of this period varies according to the individual and the age of the man involved. Females typically have a much briefer resolution phase, but general detumescence occurs in much the same way as for the male.

BIOLOGICAL DETERMINANTS OF SEXUAL DYSFUNCTION: THE ROLE OF DISEASES, ILLNESS AND INJURIES IN SEXUAL DYSFUNCTION

Human sexual behaviour is determined by a host of biological, environmental and psychological influences. As a result, there may be numerous causes for a breakdown in normal sexual responding. The assessor needs a sound understanding of these determinants in order to identify areas which may be tackled during the therapy process. Although the focus here is on behavioural assessment and intervention, a competent knowledge of biological factors is particularly important for those working with sexually dysfunctional clients.

A variety of diseases, illnesses and injuries which interfere with hormonal, vascular or neural systems may directly impair sexual responding, as may physical damage to the sex organs. Other health problems may have an adverse effect on sexual functioning, not through the direct effects upon the body but through psychological influences. For example, individuals with health problems such as myocardial infarction may be capable theoretically of adequate sexual responding but may fail to do so for fear of further injury. Many serious illnesses also result in a reduction in sexual desire because of general feelings of ill health and fatigue. Furthermore, some illnesses cause severe disfigurement of the body and may cause the client to develop concerns as to their physical attractiveness to their partner. These issues were highlighted by Anderson and Wolf (1986) in an interesting paper which discusses the psychological consequences of serious illness which may interfere with sexual functioning.

Even when there is direct involvement of an illness in sexual difficulties, the degree of impairment may exceed that caused specifically by the illness. For example, Whitehead et al. (1983) suggested that a significant contribution to erectile failure amongst men with diabetes mellitus is made from the adverse psychological experiences of the disorder, such as anxiety, depression, fear and lethargy. Although diabetes mellitus is thought to impair erectile responding in some males due to damage to the peripheral nerves and small blood vessels caused by chronic, high blood glucose levels (Anderson and Wolf, 1986), it seems likely that erectile problems are exacerbated by the adverse psychological consequences of the condition.

In terms of direct influences on sexual responding, any illness or injury which impairs the neural, vascular or endocrine systems controlling the various aspects of sexual responding may result in sexual dysfunction. The nature of the problem, whether it be in the desire, arousal or orgasm phase, will depend on the physiological stage affected.

The role of neurological mechanisms in sexual functioning and dysfunction

Neurological involvement in normal sexual functioning

The responses of arousal and orgasm involve a complex network of neurological mechanisms. At a basic level, arousal and orgasm may result from reflex processes triggered by physical stimulation of the genitals. These systems operate through the spinal cord and lower brain stem, but are typically modified and controlled by higher cortical activity. Hence activity in either of these higher or lower neural pathways may influence the arousal or orgasm components. Overall, a complex interaction of physical stimulation and cognitive activity are important in determining how a person responds sexually.

The neurological mechanisms concerned with sexual responding involve a sensitive interaction of sympathetic, parasympathetic and somatic divisions of the nervous system. The arousal phase of erection in the male and lubrication/swelling in the female involves parasympathetic networks through the sacral region of the spinal cord (sacral roots S2, S3 and S4). This response is influenced by psychogenic processes from the cortex through sympathetic (noradrenergic) pathways which leave the spinal cord at the thoracolumbar region (T12–L1). Interestingly, recent studies have found evidence of a high concentration of noradrenaline in the corpora cavernosa, suggesting that adrenergic receptors in this area are important in keeping the penis flaccid. Blocking of these receptors by injecting drugs such as papaverine hydrochloride

19

directly into the corpus cavernosum may result in chemically induced erections (Nellans *et al.*, 1987).

The process of emission in the male and contraction of the uterine tubes and uterus in the female are then controlled by sympathetic (noradrenergic) pathways through the thoracolumbar spinal cord region. Finally, the process of expulsion in the male and rhythmic contractions of the vaginal sphincter and pelvic floor muscles in the female are under somatic nerve control and some degree of para-sympathetic mediation.

The separate control of different phases of the sexual response explains why, for some clients, only the arousal phase may be disturbed but the orgasm phase may be adequate. With other clients arousal may occur but the orgasm component is not achieved, and in some instances both arousal and orgasm may be affected. Drugs, illnesses and biological processes which differentially affect para-sympathetic and sympathetic pathways may produce different influences on the arousal and orgasm components of sexual functioning. A more detailed outline of the neurological mechanisms involved in sexual responding can be found in Boller and Frank (1982).

Most of our knowledge about the neurological influences over sexual functioning relate to subcortical pathways. To date, very little is known about the role of different neural pathways in the cortex and midbrain in humans. Although considerable research has been conducted with non-human species, it is not appropriate to generalize these findings automatically to humans. Some evidence concerning the neural pathways of the brain which regulate sexual behaviour can be obtained from the effects of injuries to specific regions of the brain. In many cases, the damage sustained affects more than one area, which makes it difficult to determine exactly which areas are responsible for the sexual behaviour observed. There is some evidence that the amygdala and septal regions of the brain are involved in the feeling of sexual pleasure (Boller and Frank, 1982). There is also some suggestion that the temporal lobes may be involved in sexual arousal, given that a sexual arousal response is occasionally found in association with epileptic seizures that have a focus in the temporal lobes. More often, however, temporal lobe epilepsy is associated with low sexual desire, particularly if onset precedes puberty, hence the relationship with sexual responding is unclear (Boller and Frank, 1982). In terms of frontal lobe involvement, lesions of the prefrontal–orbital surface have sometimes been found to result in disinhibition of sexual behaviour. Again the exact mechanisms involved are unclear and may reflect a general disinhibition of behaviour, rather than a specific influence on sexual behaviour.

Neurological involvement in sexual dysfunction

Any drug, illness, biological process or cognitive event which influences the neurological processes regulating human sexual responding has the potential to disrupt sexual behaviour, leading to sexual dysfunction. Damage to neural structures in the region of the brain, spinal cord or peripheral pathways may result from a variety of problems including physical traumas, surgical procedures, tumours, infections, multiple sclerosis, other degenerative diseases and congenital defects (e.g. spina bifida). The type of sexual difficulty produced will depend on the location and extent of the damage, as these factors determine which neural pathways are affected. Basically any disorder which affects any of the following aspects of neural functioning may impair sexual responding:

1. The afferent (sensory) nerves carrying input from the genitals to the spinal cord;
2. Those parts of the spinal cord in which the neural pathways of arousal and orgasm pass (thoracolumbar and sacral regions);
3. Their ascending and descending fibres to and from the brain;
4. The efferent pathways that carry neural messages from the spinal cord to the sex organs to trigger the sexual responses;
5. Those parts of the brain which regulate sexual behaviour (Jehu, 1979).

Sexual dysfunction resulting from neural impairment at a cortical level is relatively rare, but certain lesions within the hypothalamus or limbic system may interfere with sexual functioning (Kaplan, 1974). Neurological damage within the spinal cord is a more frequent cause of sexual problems. (The majority of research into the effects of illness and drugs upon sexual responding has been carried out with males. Hence, discussion here will refer primarily to the effect upon erectile functioning and ejaculation.)

Because different aspects of sexual responding are controlled by different neural pathways in the spinal cord, the effect of a spinal lesion may be to impair either the erectile response, the ejaculation component, or both, depending on its location and completeness. The location of the lesion may also determine the type of stimulation to which the person is able to respond sexually. For example, if the neural damage occurs in the thoracic or cervical region of the spinal cord, a reflex erectile response may be achieved from tactile stimulation, such as stroking (assuming the sacral region remains intact). Erections will not occur, however, in response to forms of stimulation, such as fantasy, involving higher cortical control through the thoracolumbar pathways which have been put out of action. These erections tend to be short-lived and orgasm is rarely achieved if the lesions are complete. When lesions occur in the lumbar region, the effect depends on the extent of the lesion. Boller and Frank (1982) reported that 8/20 men with lumbar lesions were able to attain psychogenic erections and 7/20 were able to take part in coitus and to ejaculate, suggesting that the sympathetic pathways at the thoracic/upper lumbar region (which control the emission stage) remained intact for these individuals. These authors suggest that the consequences are most severe if the lesion occurs in the sacral region, particularly if the lesion is complete. In such cases it is generally not possible to achieve reflex erections to tactile stimulation (which involve sacral pathways) or through fantasy or visual stimulation (which involve thoracolumbar pathways, but these must pass through the sacral region of the spinal cord on their way from the cortex).

The effect of spinal injuries on ejaculation is less clearly understood. Basically, any spinal injury which effects the thoracolumbar pathways involved in the control of ejaculation may impair ejaculation. Cases have been reported in which ejaculation has been maintained in the absence of erectile responding, reflecting the separation of pathways involved in the two functions.

The effect of spinal injuries on women's sexual functioning is even less clear. If the lesion occurs in the sacral regions, then a loss of sensation during intercourse is typically experienced. Unlike the male, for whom an intact arousal response is required in order that erection and intercourse can take place, the woman is generally able to take part in intercourse as a passive recipient of the process. The neural lesion may, however, disrupt the process of lubrication and orgasm is frequently impaired, particularly if the lesion is complete.

Various diseases and tumours which disrupt neural functioning in areas other than the spinal cord may also impair sexual behaviour. For example, multiple sclerosis results in the breakdown of myelin around the neural structures of the brain, brain stem and spinal cord. A high proportion of males with multiple sclerosis are found to experience sexual difficulties, with between 26% and 43% reporting erectile problems, which become more likely as the duration of the disorder increases (Boller and Frank, 1982). These authors also reported that around 50% of women with multiple sclerosis report problems of decreased libido, orgasmic dysfunction and poor lubrication, and the problems occurred even early on in the course of the disease. Typically the sexual problems tended to be variable, reflecting the cyclical nature of multiple sclerosis.

The consequences of cerebrovascular accidents (CVAs, strokes) also warrant a mention here. The effect of a CVA on sexual responding depends on the extent and location of the damage in the brain, and the length of time since its occurrence. There is some evidence of greater impairment of sexual arousal following left hemisphere CVAs but it is unclear whether this is a reflection of the greater incidence of depression following left hemisphere CVA. Frequently, a loss of sexual desire and coital frequency occurs following any type of CVA but this may reflect an overall decline in activity levels, rather than being a direct result of the CVA (Boller and Frank, 1982).

Diseases and injury to local neural pathways, rather than cortical or spinal areas, may also impair sexual responding. Diabetes mellitus has been found to have a variety of effects on the neural and vascular aspects of sexual responding. Neuropathy may occur at both peripheral and central nervous system levels, but the exact cause of this phenomenon is unclear. Neuropathic effects, combined with vascular degeneration, may lead to deficits in arousal and orgasmic responding in both men and women. Between 30% and 60% of males with diabetes mellitus are found to experience erectile difficulties (Jehu, 1979) and in some instances may exhibit retrograde ejaculation, in which semen is sent backwards into the bladder, resulting in dry ejaculation (Kaplan, 1974).The effects of diabetes mellitus on female sexual responding have been less well researched and evidence concerning the effect on arousal and orgasm is conflicting (Anderson and Wolf, 1986). However, there is some suggestion that females with this condition are more prone to vaginal infection and dyspareunia, which may have a secondary effect on sexual activity (Pietropino and Arora, 1989). Furthermore, Boller and Frank (1982) reported that 35% of previously orgasmic women experience complete absence of orgasm in the year following the onset of diabetes, an effect which was not evident for a non-diabetic comparison group. It is unclear whether this effect was the result of psychogenic reactions triggered by the diagnosis of the disorder, or whether it reflects genuine biological changes. Unfortunately, the impact of diabetes mellitus on sexual functioning is not always reversed upon control of the disorder with insulin or dietary methods, and sexual problems seem to increase with the duration of the diabetes (Boller and Frank, 1982).

Vascular diseases

Any illness, drug or surgical procedure which disrupts penile blood flow or pressure, resulting in inadequate build-up of blood within the penis, will impair the erectile response. Deficits in the penile arterial blood supply or excessive drainage of blood result in inadequate pressure and erection is impaired. Similar disorders in women may impair the lubrication/swelling phases. Local thrombotic diseases are implicated here and diabetes mellitus has also been found to result in vascular deterioration, in addition to neural impairment. Certain forms of vascular reconstructive surgery may also disrupt the vascular responses necessary for sexual arousal, as may certain types of medication. Drug effects will be dealt with below.

In some cases, kidney transplants have been suggested to impair erectile ability, particularly if two transplants have been conducted (Boller and Frank, 1982). This may not necessarily be the result of blood flow problems, as treatment frequently involves antihypertensive medication and dialysis. Psychogenic reactions are also highly probable, further interfering with sexual functioning. Any one or all of these factors could play a role in any sexual dysfunction which results.

Sexual dysfunctions such as loss of sexual desire, erectile problems or inhibited orgasm are not uncommon following myocardial infarction (Schover and Jensen, 1988), with decreased frequency of sexual activity being extremely common. In some instances, sexual difficulties may reflect the effects of antihypertensive medication. In others, the influences may be primarily psychogenic, such as fears of triggering a further heart attack.

Hormonal/endocrine disorders

Considerable research has demonstrated the importance of hormonal influences on the sexual behaviour of non-human species. With human subjects, however, much less is known and it is likely that cognitive factors play an overriding influence over hormonal determinants of

atrophy, and congenital defects such as Klinefelter's syndrome are examples of disorders which may affect the endocrine system so as to impair sexual functioning.

Genital impairment

Physical injury, inflammation or infection of the genital structures may interfere with sexual responding. Structural defects such as clitoral adhesions or poor episiotomies in women and excessively tight foreskin or excessive penile curvature in males may inhibit satisfactory sex. Infections such as urethritis, cystitis and prostatitis are examples of the many infections which may also produce pain during intercourse (Masters and Johnson, 1970). As with all forms of physical disorder or disability that are associated with impaired sexual functioning, the physical impact is frequently exacerbated by the pyschosocial consequences of the condition. It is often difficult to determine the relative contribution of the physical disorder and psychosocial factors to the development and maintenance of the sexual problem.

Cancer

Balducci *et al.* (1988) outlined the anatomical, physiological and psychological complications of cancer that may interfere with sexual functioning. Complications may result from the direct effects of the cancer upon anatomical structures, or from the effects of surgery, as may be the case for some men following radical prostatectomy operations. This operation was traditionally associated with severing of the neural pathways involved in erection, resulting in erectile difficulties for many men. Recent advances in the ability to identify the relevant neural pathways, and to conduct surgery without severing them, now permits this operation to be conducted in many cases without resulting in erectile problems. Radiation treatment and chemotherapy may also result in sexual difficulties. Both these procedures are associated with loss of vaginal lubrication and, for some women, may produce vaginal atrophy. For some men, repeated pelvic irradiation may lead to vascular defects and/or neuropathy, which in turn may impair sexual functioning. Surgical removal of the testes in testicular cancers may also result in sexual difficulties, through an influence on the endocrine system, as may surgical removal of the ovaries. The treatment of prostatic cancer by antiandrogenic therapy has also been reported to produce sexual problems, with a marked decrease in sexual interest and functioning being found in around 80% of patients. Balducci *et al.* (1988) suggested that the anatomical and physiological effects of cancer and its treatment cannot account for all the negative influences upon sexual functioning. These authors highlighted the psycho-social influences which impair sexual functioning for many cancer patients. For example, self and partner reactions to changes in physical appearance, such as hair loss, skin alterations, or weight changes resulting from the disorder or therapy, may play an important contributory role.

DRUG EFFECTS

A wide range of chemical substances may interfere with sexual functioning, the exact nature of which will depend on the biological action of the drug involved. Any drug which affects the neural, endocrine or vascular systems involved in sexual functioning may impair sexual responding. Particular attention must therefore be paid during assessment to any substance use by the client, whether it be prescribed medication, illicit drugs or alcohol.

Alcohol and other sedatives

Sedative compounds such as alcohol or barbiturates are known to have a depressing effect on brain functioning which may impair sexual functioning (Jehu, 1979). At low dosages, sedatives may have a disinhibitory effect which may enhance subjective feelings of desire and sexual arousal for some individuals, although laboratory studies with men suggest that even low doses of alcohol may reduce the degree of erection, despite subjective reports of increases in sexual arousal (Boller and Frank, 1982; Rosen and Beck, 1988). The increase in sexual desire, subjective arousal and sexual behaviour that accompanies low levels of alcohol consumption are thought to reflect a general disinhibitory effect that is not specific to sexual behaviour. Generally, a clear dose-related inhibition of the physiological responses of sexual arousal is found for both men and women, with impairment of ejaculation in men and decreased intensity of orgasm for women being found at high alcohol levels. At higher doses, a general depressant effect on cortical functioning occurs and this may suppress the erectile response in males. With prolonged alcohol abuse, a wide range of sexual difficulties may occur which are the result of various forms of vascular, endocrine or neural impairment (Rosen and Beck, 1988). The deterioration in interpersonal functioning which also accompanies prolonged alcohol abuse may also contribute to sexual difficulties.

Antihypertensives

Certain drugs which are used to control blood pressure may have an adverse effect on sexual functioning. Such drugs may effect the desire, arousal or orgasm phases, depending upon the neural pathways affected. This is not surprising given that most antihypertensive agents influence the activity levels of the sympathetic or parasympathetic nervous systems, both of which are involved in sexual functioning, and may also produce vascular effects which impede the vascular requirements of the sexual response. Most of the literature available to date has focused on the effects of antihypertensives on male sexual functioning and less is known about the effects on women.

Boller and Frank (1982) and Rosen and Beck (1988) provided useful summaries of the effects of hypertensive drugs. Drugs containing clonidine, reserpine, guanethidine, methyldopa, alpha-adrenergic antagonists (peripheral vasodilators) and beta-adrenergic blocking agents have all been found to produce impairment of erection or ejaculation in some males. Different studies have typically reported different estimates of the proportion of patients who experience adverse effects upon their sexual functioning as a consequence of antihypertensive medication. Many studies have failed to include untreated hypertensive control groups and it must be remembered that a proportion of untreated patients may also show sexual dysfunctions. This should be borne in mind when interpreting the results of studies which investigate the effects of antihypertensives on sexual functioning. Rosen and Beck (1988) in a review of empirical studies cited evidence to suggest that a particularly high incidence of sexual problems occurs following treatment with propranolol (a beta-blocker) or a combination of beta-blockers and diuretics. These authors reported a study from their laboratory in which a range of beta-blockers were found to produce significant reductions in plasma

29

and free testosterone and a trend towards decreased tumescence during nocturnal penile tumescence (NPT) recordings in normal volunteers, in comparison to their response to a placebo drug. Propranolol was found to produce the largest reductions in plasma and free testosterone. Generally it seems that sexual side effects may occur with the majority of the antihypertensive medications, if dosage levels are high and use is prolonged (Boller and Frank, 1982).

Antipsychotic drugs

There is evidence to suggest that some drugs within the phenothiazine and butyrophenone groups and their derivatives may interfere with sexual functioning. Amongst the phenothiazines, thioridazine has been particularly noted to result in erectile difficulty, reduced ejaculate and retrograde ejaculation in some males (Kotin *et al.*, 1976) and anorgasmia in some women (Segraves, 1988). Within the butyrophenones, haloperidol compounds have occasionally been reported to produce arousal and erectile problems (Kaplan, 1974). High dosages of any form of antipsychotic medication tend to produce drowsiness and decreased libido, which is part of a general reduction in activity levels.

Antianxiety drugs

Minor tranquillizers, such as chlordiazepoxide, diazepam, oxazepam or other benzodiazepine derivatives, are not generally associated with sexual dysfunction unless used in high dosages or for prolonged periods. Short-term use at standard dosage is frequently found to enhance sexual responding as the result of anxiety reduction and general disinhibition of behaviour. At higher dosages or with prolonged use, this group of drugs may lead to orgasmic failure in women and reduced desire in both males and females (Petri, 1980; Segraves, 1988).

Antidepressants

It is often difficult to assess the effects of antidepressants on sexual functioning as interest in sex may increase as positive mood increases, hence masking any direct effects on sexual responding. Bearing this

30

limitation in mind, evidence suggests that monoamine re-uptake inhibitors and the monoamine oxidase inhibitors may occasionally lead to erectile and ejaculatory problems for some males (Silverstone and Turner, 1982) and anorgasmia in some women (Segraves, 1988). Certain tricyclic antidepressants may also result in impairment of orgasm in women (Segraves, 1988) but Petri (1980) suggests that there is minimal evidence of sexual difficulties associated with the use of tricyclic antidepressants in males. Various mechanisms have been proposed to explain why some antidepressant medications may interfere with sexual functioning but the exact explanation remains to be elucidated.

Oral contraceptives

Evidence concerning the influence of oral contraceptives on sexual functioning is conflicting but there is suggestion that, for some women, the use of oral contraceptives may reduce sexual arousal levels (Trimmer, 1978). Different studies have produced conflicting findings, however, and it is difficult to draw conclusions from the results available. In order to assess the effects of oral contraceptives on sexual responding in women, it is necessary to make comparisons between women who are using oral contraceptives and a valid control group of women who use other forms of birth control. Taking oral contraceptives tends to produce greater security against pregnancy, compared to other methods of contraception, which may increase the frequency of sexual activity and make arousal more probable. Other forms of contraception do not provide such security against pregnancy or may require pausing during sexual activities to put the contraceptive device in place (eg. condom or diaphragm). These subtle differences in contraceptives may influence sexual functioning, therefore making it difficult to interpret the results of studies which have investigated the effects of oral contraceptives on sexual desire and arousal.

Marihuana

Several studies have shown that marihuana is associated with reports of increased sexual desire and pleasurable sensations (Rosen and Beck, 1988). The mechanisms underlying this effect are unclear and studies have tended to rely on subjective reports rather than physiological evidence. Conflicting findings have been reported concerning the long term effects of marihuana use on endocrine functioning, with some studies finding suppression of testosterone levels whereas others have not. Rosen and Beck (1988) concluded that studies have generally found evidence of reduced sperm counts in association with frequent marihuana use but this effect tends to reverse quickly upon cessation of use of the drug.

Illicit drugs

Evidence concerning the effects of drugs such as heroin, cocaine or amphetamines tends to be conflicting and will not be covered here. Interested readers are referred to texts such as Rosen and Beck (1988), which provides a detailed review of the effects of such drugs on sexual functioning.

AGEING

The vast majority of people are capable of sexual activity, sexual desire, arousal and orgasm throughout their lives but, as people get older, subtle changes in sexual responding begin to occur. These changes must be taken into consideration when deciding whether a sexual problem is present, or whether a person's current sexual functioning is consistent with the normal ageing process. A more detailed outline of the effects of ageing on sexual behaviour is provided in Chapter 8. In the male, ageing is generally accompanied by an increase in the time taken to attain an erection, a decrease in the force of the propelled ejaculate and a greater time taken to regain an erection once it has been lost (i.e. increased refractory period). Some subjective changes may also be experienced, such as reduction in the feeling of inevitability which is associated with the emission phase. Despite these changes, males are generally able to achieve erection and ejaculation from puberty throughout their life-span. Erectile and ejaculatory failure are not part of the normal ageing process.

Females also show changes in sexual anatomy and responding with age. The vagina wall may thin and its elasticity may become reduced. The intensity and rapidity of vasocongestion also declines, and there may be some reduction in the amount of lubrication. There may be a decrease in the number of contractions during orgasm in later life but, as with the male, women can generally continue to achieve orgasm throughout their lives. Menopause may produce difficulties for some women, particularly if lubrication is reduced or takes longer to occur. A more detailed outline of age related changes in sexual responding for women is provided in Chapter 8.

PSYCHOSOCIAL CAUSES OF SEXUAL DYSFUNCTION

Having outlined the major biological influences upon sexual responding, it is important to consider some of the psychosocial causes of sexual dysfunction. It must be stressed that, even when biological influences are found, these may be confounded by psychosocial factors which must also be dealt with during the therapy phase. Hawton (1985) suggests that psychological causes for sexual dysfunction may be classified into three types:

1. predisposing factors which have occurred earlier in life and have created a vulnerability to developing sexual difficulties in later life (such as restrictive upbringing, disturbed family relationships, inadequate sexual information or traumatic early sexual relationships);
2. precipitants which are events or experiences associated with the initial appearance of the problem (such as childbirth, marital disharmony, infidelity, ageing, depression, anxiety, a traumatic sexual experience or reaction to organic factors);
3. maintaining factors which result in persistence of the problem (such as performance anxiety, guilt, anticipation of failure, fear of intimacy, sexual myths, restricted foreplay, poor communication with the partner or marital disharmony).

Whilst such a classification of causal factors is appealing, it is very difficult in practice to determine whether a factor was a precipitating event or is currently maintaining the problem. For this reason, the following outline of causal factors does not attempt to make a distinction between precipitants and maintaining variables. Rather, it attempts to categorize aetiological factors into those that relate to the characteristics of the individual and those that involve external or environmental factors. Such a distinction is somewhat misleading, in that many external factors, such as the quality of the marital relationship, are strongly influenced by the characteristics of the individuals involved.

External and environmental factors

Physical environment factors

A variety of external environmental factors may influence sexual responding. Lack of opportunity, lack of privacy, or a cold, uncomfortable setting are typical examples of events which may be associated with an unsatisfactory sexual relationship, hence the need to consider such factors during assessment.

Life events

A wide range of life events may increase the chance that a sexual problem will develop. Factors such as loss of employment, death of a family member, excessive work demands, unwanted pregnancies, abortion or childbirth may trigger psychological reactions for some individuals which are associated with sexual dysfunction. It is important to emphasize that it is generally not the event itself which results in a sexual difficulty, but rather it is the person's appraisal of the event and subsequent emotional reaction to it that may lead to disruption of sexual functioning. For example, following childbirth the woman is usually rather sore for several days and sexual intercourse is typically avoided. Sexual activity may then be infrequent over the next few weeks as the result of fatigue following sleepless nights. A short-term loss of sexual desire has also been reported in men following attendance at childbirth (Gurian, 1988) which is suggested to result from the exposure to a situation in which their partner is often in extreme pain and in which the sight of blood is common. Longer-term sexual difficulties following childbirth are relatively unusual but may result as a symptom of postpartum depression or a general problem of adaptation to the changed role in life.

Sexual abuse in childhood and more recent sexual trauma may also be associated with the development of sexual difficulties. It is particularly important to consider early or more recent sexual abuse/trauma in view of the relatively high lifetime incidence of such events. It is becoming increasingly clear that a much higher proportion of the population experiences some form of sexual abuse or trauma than was traditionally thought to be the case. Although current studies do not permit an accurate estimate to be made as regards the incidence of sexual abuse in childhood or rape in adulthood, it seems likely that at least 10% of the adult female population will experience one of these events during their lives (Ellis, 1983; Fritz *et al.* 1981). Given that a significant number, albeit a minority, of individuals who are subject to such experiences tend to develop sexual difficulties, it is highly likely that clinicians will encounter women who have been previously sexually abused or raped.

Fortunately, not all people who are subject to potentially traumatic sexual experiences will develop subsequent psychological and sexual problems. Fritz *et al.* (1981) explored the incidence and effects of sexual abuse in childhood amongst 952 US college students. Their results showed that 7.7% of female and 4.8% of males had experienced some form of molestation in childhood. Of those that had been 'molested' only 23% of women and 19% of males reported problems of sexual functioning. The extent of sexual problems amongst adults who were sexually abused as children is dependent upon the population studied. Sexual problems are found more often amongst clinical samples of sexually abused persons who have typically sought help as the result of unresolved difficulties. For example, Jehu (1989) reported that 94% of previously sexually abused women who entered therapy were found to show sexual difficulties. These problems most commonly involved sexual phobias/aversion and impairment of satisfaction, desire, arousal and orgasm. Although the results of this study suggest high levels of sexual and adjustment problems amongst women who were sexually abused as children, it must be borne in mind that many individuals who are subject to similar experiences do not show such prolonged or marked psychological consequences. Tsai *et al.* (1979) attempted to determine why some women show such prolonged and severe reactions, whereas others appear to adapt better after child sexual abuse. These authors reported that problems of adjustment tended to be associated with longer and more frequent abuse, with an older age (particularly after age 11) and with the ability to recall more negative emotions regarding the experience, such as pressure to participate, pain and dislike for the abuser.

The experience of rape may also result in sexual difficulties, although again evidence suggests that the majority of women do not suffer long-term sexual or emotional problems after such an event. Ellis (1983) reviewed the empirical evidence concerning the long-term and short-term effects of rape. Immediately after the event, victims typically showed a range of global symptoms that can be categorized as post-traumatic stress reactions to the rape, such as sleep disturbance, nightmares, fears, anxiety, depression, interpersonal and sexual difficulties. Within three months, the vast majority of women tend to show a marked reduction in these symptoms, although sexual difficulties appear to be amongst the last problems to go. Unfortunately, a minority of women continue to show marked and prolonged adjustment problems which typically include sexual difficulties, particularly related to intercourse and intimacy with a male partner. Self-stimulation appears to be less affected.

It appears therefore that adverse sexual experiences, both in childhood and adulthood may result in later sexual difficulties for a minority of victims and the possibility should be investigated during the assessment process.

Partner's reaction to the sexual dysfunction

Sexual interaction involves a dyadic situation in which two people provide a constant source of influence over the other's behaviour. Partner stimulation, communication, feedback and response obviously play an essential role in the development of a sexual problem. In particular, the partner's response to the occurrence of sexual difficulties is important in determining whether such difficulties are likely to recur. Partners may react in a variety of ways to the occurrence of a sexual problem. The reaction may range from lack of any comment, to an affectionate cuddle and statement that the problem is not of major importance within the relationship, to comments that the problem reflects the lack of love or care from the partner or even that the problem reflects a general inadequacy in life! The response of the partner is likely to have a marked impact upon the other person's response to their sexual difficulty. The complex reciprocal nature of sexual interactions has led many practitioners to suggest that sexual problems should generally be viewed as belonging to the couple, rather than either individual.

General quality of the relationship

Marital and sexual difficulties are frequently found to coexist; indeed the majority of couples presenting with sexual problems report marital dissatisfaction and the majority of referrals for marital therapy report dissatisfaction with their sexual relationship (Zimmer, 1987). This is probably not surprising, as it is difficult to imagine having a satisfactory sexual relationship with a person with whom one does not have a good overall relationship. Furthermore, a problematic sexual relationship may also have an adverse effect on a couple's general interaction. In practice, it is likely that a vicious cycle of influence occurs, in which marital disharmony interferes with successful sexual functioning and sexual dysfunction generates further marital disharmony. Occurrence of either marital or sexual difficulties may adversely affect the other domain. In many cases there is therefore a need to integrate sexual and marital therapy during intervention. In cases where the marital discord is secondary to the sexual dysfunction then treatment of the sexual problem alone may enhance the general relationship. If marital disharmony is severe and accompanied by hostility, then attempts to rectify the sexual problem are unlikely to be successful and marital therapy should precede the treatment of the sexual problem (Lobitz and Lobitz, 1978). In practice, it is often difficult to establish whether the marital dissatisfaction is secondary to the sexual problem or a causal factor (Hawton, 1985). Greater discussion of the interaction between sexual and marital satisfaction is provided in Chapter 5.

Characteristics of the individual

Psychopathology

Various forms of psychopathology are associated with sexual dysfunction, in particular problems associated with anxiety and depression. The exact mechanism by which the various forms of psychopathology influence sexual behaviour may vary considerably. In some cases there may be a direct relationship between the psychological disorder and the sexual problem. For example, it seems likely that the biochemical imbalance associated with some forms of depressive disorder may also act to impair sexual functioning (Schreiner-Engel and Schiavi, 1986). These authors reported a marked association between low sexual desire in women and the lifetime prevalence of depressive disorder, which almost always preceded the onset of inhibited sexual desire. A higher level of premenstrual symptoms was also evident for the inhibited sexual desire group, compared to women who reported normal levels of sexual desire, but who were attending a sex therapy clinic for other reasons. Schreiner-Engel and Schiavi (1986) suggested that these results indicate a common biological aetiology for depressive disorder and low sexual desire amongst some women.

There is also evidence to suggest an association between impaired erectile functioning and depression in males (Thase *et al.*, 1988). Significant reduction in nocturnal penile tumescence responses were found amongst male outpatients with major depressive disorder compared to an age-matched sample of non-depressed, healthy controls. This effect was evident even when sleep time and rapid eye movement time were taken into account, indicating it not to be the result of disturbed sleep patterns. Such results provide further support for a link between the physiological aspects of sexual functioning and depression.

For other individuals, the psychological disorder may be associated with deficits in behaviour, such as poor interpersonal skills, which in turn lead to problems in the sexual relationship. The sexual difficulty is not therefore seen as being directly related to the psychopathology, but is associated with the cognitive or behavioural deficits which contribute to the person's psychological problems.

Evidence certainly suggests that sexual problems are more likely to be found in association with some forms of psychopathology. Indeed loss of interest in sexual activity is one of the accepted behavioural characteristics of depression. Loss of desire, decreased frequency of coitus and incomplete erections are frequently found amongst depressed samples (Petrie, 1980), the level of which is found to correlate with the severity of other symptoms of depression. Anxiety may also exert an inhibitory effect and has traditionally been suggested to result in sexual dysfunction, particularly if the anxiety relates specifically to sexual activities (Masters and Johnson, 1970). Generalized anxiety, in which thoughts are likely to be focused elsewhere and the person is likely to feel tense and irritable, is also likely to interfere with the person's ability to relax and focus their attention on sexual pleasure. Many aspects of psychopathology will be dealt with under subsequent headings, such as maladaptive cognitions, attention focusing and communication skills.

It has been suggested by many authors that sexual anxiety and fear play a major role in the inhibition of desire, sexual arousal and orgasm. The suggested importance of anxiety in the aetiology of sexual dysfunctions has been reflected in the central role accorded to anxiety reduction in intervention programmes. This has occurred despite the lack of empirical data to suggest that sexually dysfunctional clients typically experience either general or sexual anxiety or that anxiety has the effect of reducing sexual functioning (Barlow, 1986). Indeed, as Barlow pointed out, the limited evidence available tends to suggest that anxiety can facilitate sexual arousal as indicated by physiological assessment. This is supported by a recent study reported by Beggs *et al.* (1987) in which sexual anxiety stimuli were found to generate sexual arousal for sexually functional women, albeit less so than sexually pleasurable stimuli. Similarly, Barlow *et al.* (1983) found that male subjects showed increased sexual arousal responses during anxiety generated by the threat of an electric shock.

The results of studies such as those cited above, however, do not necessarily reflect the response of sexually dysfunctional individuals to anxiety. This led Barlow and colleagues to attempt to replicate the above study with sexually dysfunctional males (reported by Barlow, 1986). The results indicated that sexually dysfunctional males showed significantly less arousal during shock threat conditions compared to no threat, an effect which was not evident for non-dysfunctional males. Abrahamson *et al.*(1989) also reported that a high sexual performance demand condition reduced the penile response to erotic stimuli of males with erectile dysfunction. The high-demand condition required the men to observe feedback concerning the extent of their erections and to comment upon their quality. Non dysfunctional males were not found to be adversely affected by the high-demand condition but both groups showed some decline in erectile response during a neutral distraction demand task compared to a no-demand condition. This demonstrates that even neutral distraction activities can lead to some inhibition of arousal. Most importantly, it appears that sexually functional and dysfunctional males are differentially affected by sexual performance demand and the result is inhibition of sexual arousal for sexually dysfunctional males. This supports the position of therapists such as Masters and Johnson (1970), who place a strong emphasis on the role of anxiety and performance demand in the development and maintenance of sexual dysfunction.

Barlow (1986) pointed out the need to consider the different effects that the separate components of anxiety may have on sexual functioning. The physiological components of anxiety, such as increased heart rate and blood pressure, are also found in sexual arousal. Anxiety may therefore facilitate the physiological component of sexual arousal in some instances. The cognitive components of anxiety, however, may inhibit sexual responding, probably through the cognitive mediation pathways that influence sexual arousal.

Barlow's research team then set out to determine whether the cognitive influences over sexual arousal operate through the mechanism of cognitive interference or distraction. Hence, cognitive responses such as 'spectatoring' or performance demand would be suggested to inhibit sexual arousal because of the interference of distraction effects produced. Barlow (1986) reviewed several studies which demonstrated that this explanation is clearly not the case. Barlow concluded that sexually dysfunctional males are not generally bound to be adversely affected by neutral distraction or non-performance-related, self-focus situations, but their arousal responses tend to be inhibited by sexual performance demands. This pattern of responding differs from sexually functional males, whose arousal tends to be impaired by neutral distractors and yet enhanced by sexual performance-related demand conditions. Barlow (1986) proposed an alternative model to explain the differential effect of sexual perform-ance demand on sexually functional versus dysfunctional individuals. He suggested that sexually dysfunctional males tend to exhibit certain personality characteristics which pre-date the onset of the sexual problem. These include tendencies towards negative affect and expectancies, perceived lack of control and inaccurate/underestimated evaluation of performance. In sexual performance demand situations these characteristics result in an increased focus on non-erotic stimuli, which produces a lower level of focus on erotic cues. The increase in autonomic arousal produced then causes an even greater focus on the non-erotic stimuli (e.g. consequences of not performing). The final result is an inhibition of sexual responding and avoidance behaviour. Sexually functional individuals, who do not possess the predisposing personality characteristics, experience increased focus of attention to erotic cues in sexual performance demand situations and consequently increased sexual arousal.

The evidence available to date does, therefore, suggest that dysfunc-tional individuals tend to react to anxiety situations in a way that inhibits their sexual performance. This effect is suggested to be mediated by the degree to which cognitions produce a focusing of attention away from erotic cues towards negative cognitions con-cerning topics such as the consequences of failure or inability to perform.

Fatigue

Although fatigue is frequently a characteristic of depression and various forms of ill-health, it also deserves a separate mention here. Obviously, sexual desire and arousal are likely to be reduced if a person is tired or exhausted from other activities. It is therefore important that fatigue is excluded as a cause of a couple's sexual difficulties. Most couples begin their sexual activities at the end of the day, following a great deal of physical and mental exertion at work, home or recreation. Perhaps it is not surprising to find that for many couples desire is low and arousal is hard to achieve.

Sexual knowledge, sexual skills and communication skills

A person's knowledge of sexual anatomy and sexual techniques has important implications for a successful sexual relationship. In particular, a knowledge of appropriate means of stimulating the partner is necessary and lack of knowledge or skill may account for a partner's lack of arousal and/or orgasm. It is also important for the person to have satisfactory knowledge and skill about ways of producing arousal in their own bodies. This area has been emphasized in relation to primary inhibited female orgasm, with education regarding masturbatory techniques being a major focus of therapy (Heiman *et al.*, 1976). Although couples who seek help for sexual dysfunctions are reported to have a significantly lower level of sexual knowledge compared to non-dysfunctional couples (Derogatis and Meyer, 1979), this difference is not great and accounts for only a small proportion of the variance between samples. It seems likely that many couples have a good knowledge of sexual matters and techniques, but are less skilled when it comes to putting these into practice. As yet, we do not have satisfactory methods of assessing practical skills and are forced to rely on the subjective reports of the couple.

Practical skills can be said to involve two primary areas: physical stimulation skills and communication skills. Each person needs to be able to stimulate their partner appropriately and to achieve positions during sex from which they can obtain the greatest amount of arousal and pleasure themselves. From the communication perspective, the couple need to be able to initiate sexual interactions, to give feedback appropriately, to request certain activities and to turn down requests for sex in an acceptable manner. Each sexual encounter involves a complex series of interactions, each of which demands a range of social skills as well as sexual skills. Inappropriate communication by either member of the partnership may interfere with successful sexual responding (Spence, 1983).

It is worth spending a few minutes to think of how people acquire practical sexual skills. Most academic knowledge is gained through reading, talking to peers and occasionally watching films. Practical skills are then learned by trial and error, by putting knowledge into practice with one's own body or with a partner. Expertise in arousing the partner and bringing them to orgasm will depend on the receipt of appropriate feedback. Expertise in arousing oneself and attaining orgasm with a partner will depend on the cooperation of the partner and the couple's ability to 'trial-and-error' together. It is perhaps not surprising that some couples fail to develop satisfactory sexual skills as the optimal conditions, for learning, namely observation, discussion, practice, feedback and reinforcement, are frequently not met.

Cognitive events: the role of thoughts, attitudes and beliefs

Sexual responding in humans is not just determined by a series of reflex actions that are controlled by direct stimulation. Cortical influences play an important part in mediating these responses through neural pathways which descend from the brain, through the spinal cord, to the genitals. Cortical activity is thought to be influenced by hormonal factors and also by the specific cognitive activity that people engage in. Basically, we know very little about the biochemical and physiological processes that permit our thoughts to influence our sexual functioning. There is some evidence, however, to suggest that certain types of thoughts, attitudes and beliefs about various aspects of sexuality may have a considerable influence over the type of sexual activities people engage in and over their response in terms of desire, arousal and orgasm.

Before looking at these areas in more detail, it is important to clarify the terminology to be used. Specific thoughts, cognitions or self-statements are taken to refer to the internal dialogue of silent talk that people engage in throughout their waking lives. Imagery is taken to refer to visual or pictorial activity which enters people's awareness. Attitudes and beliefs do not refer to specific cognitive events, but to styles of thinking or biases in the interpretation of information, which tend to influence the content of our cognitive activity.

In the sexual domain, people tend to hold beliefs or attitudes concerning a wide range of subjects concerning:

- Sexual activities – what sexual activities are normal, pleasurable, acceptable; when; where; with whom; why.
- Sex roles – who may do what to whom; when; where; why.
- What good sex consists of: the role of orgasm; the role of spontaneity; the role of passion; the role of physical affection; the role of romance; the role of mutual orgasm.

Much has been written about the influence of thoughts, attitudes and beliefs upon sexual behaviour, most of it based on supposition rather than empirical evidence. Considerable importance has been paid to the role of maladaptive cognitions in the development and maintenance of sexual dysfunctions. For example, Zilbergeld (1978) proposed ten major myths which are common in Western societies regarding male sexual functioning which can be summarized as follows:

1. Physical contact *must* always lead to sex.
2. Sexual activity involves a steady and fixed path which *must* always end in orgasm.
3. Sexual activity *should always* involve intercourse.
4. The male *should* take charge and make the first moves in sex.
5. Men *should* know instinctively how to be sexually competent and enjoyable sex *must* be natural and spontaneous.
6. Sex *always* requires an erection.
7. Men are no longer influenced by traditional myths about the male role regarding sex.
8. Men *must* perform successfully in sex, as in other areas of their lives. It is performance that counts.
9. Men *must* always desire sex and be capable of responding sexually.
10. Real men *should not* express certain emotions to their partners.

Recent evidence suggests that sexually dysfunctional males show significantly greater acceptance of Zilbergeld's myths compared to a matched sample of non-dysfunctional men (Baker and De Silva, 1988). Whilst this finding is in keeping with the suggestion that adherence to maladaptive beliefs may result in sexual difficulties, it is equally possible that such beliefs are the result of the experience of sexual difficulties rather than their cause.

Sanders and Cairns (1987) also propose a range of beliefs that may interfere with sexual functioning. In particular, they stress the effect of beliefs about spontaneity in sex and the role of passion and romance. Whilst spontaneity, passion and lust tend to decline in the course of most relationships, Sanders and Cairns suggest that many couples continue to hold certain beliefs such as:

- Good sex requires spontaneity.
- Good sex requires passion/lust.
- Good sex requires romance.
- Spontaneity will increase with an increase in sexual contact and experience.

Given that these requirements are often not met as a relationship progresses, couples are left with a series of unmet expectations which may trigger or exacerbate sexual difficulties.

There are a variety of other beliefs that may interfere with sexual functioning, which should be mentioned here, such as:

- All other couples have sexual intercourse several times per week.
- Sex for all other couples includes orgasm on every occasion.
- All other couples are able to attain orgasm simultaneously.
- If sex is not good then there must be something wrong with the relationship generally.
- Partners should instinctively know what type of stimulation their partner needs.
- If a partner does not respond sexually to his/her partner then he/she does not find the partner sexually attractive.

Furthermore, there are a range of traditionally held beliefs or 'female sexual myths' which apply more to women than men and which were not a focus of Zilbergeld's work:

- A woman should always take part in sex if her partner makes approaches.
- A woman should not make the first sexual moves towards her partner.
- It doesn't matter if a woman doesn't have an orgasm as it doesn't serve any reproductive purpose and/or most women don't have orgasms anyway.
- A woman should always be capable of intercourse, even as a passive recipient.
- A woman should not expect her partner to wait until she is sufficiently aroused before penetration begins.
- A woman should be capable of orgasm without requiring manual stimulation of the clitoris – intercourse should be sufficient.

- 'Respectable' women should not demonstrate high levels of enjoyment and excitement.
- 'Respectable' women do not communicate their sexual needs and preferences to their partners.
- 'Respectable' women should not masturbate.
- 'Respectable' women should not use fantasies during sexual activity with their partner.
- 'Respectable' women should never have sexual fantasies.

Fortunately, the power of the 'women's movement' over the past decade has led to a shift away from such attitudes, but they are still strongly held by many older women and even the most forceful feminist may find adverse beliefs, such as those outlined above, hard to dispel. The recent emphasis in women's magazines and the media towards the 'liberated' woman has generated a new set of sexual myths which may result in sexual problems, such as:

- In order to be a 'modern woman' I must be able to achieve orgasm. Being able to experience orgasm is one of the most important things in life.
- In order to be a 'modern woman' I must initiate sex with my partner.
- In order to be a 'modern woman' I must have premarital sexual relationships.
- In order to be a 'modern woman' I must give my partner plenty of feedback about my sexual likes and dislikes.

It is perhaps not surprising that such recent attitudes may create their own set of difficulties for both male and female members of the partnership.

The role of beliefs and attitudes in deciding our emotional and behavioural response to situations has been beautifully illustrated by Ellis (1958). This model remains one of the most influential in psychotherapy today. Ellis proposed that our emotional and behavioural consequences (C) to any activating event (A) depends on our beliefs (B) about that situation. He suggested that 'people do not directly react emotionally or behaviourally to the events they encounter in their lives; rather, people cause their own reactions by the way they interpret or evaluate the events they experience' (Ellis, 1977, pp. 3–34). Many instances of severe negative emotions and maladaptive behaviours are suggested to result from irrational beliefs which influence the interpretation of events. These irrational beliefs are characterized by fixed rules concerning: (1) what should, ought, must occur; (2) how awful and terrible things are when they are not the way they should be; (3) how intolerable situations are when they are not the way they should be; and (4) damnation of oneself or others when things do not work out the way they should. Other authors have subsequently outlined alternative models which also emphasize the central role of maladaptive thoughts or beliefs in psychopathology. For example, Beck *et al.* (1979) summarize six forms of systematic errors in the thinking of depressed persons, which maintain the person's belief in the validity of negative concepts despite contradictory evidence, involving:

1. Arbitrary inference – in which a response set exists, leading to a specific conclusion in the absence of support;
2. Selective abstraction – a stimulus set in which the person focuses on a specific detail taken out of context, ignoring other more salient features of the situation;
3. Overgeneralization – a pattern of drawing conclusions on the basis of one or more isolated incidents and applying the concept generally (e.g. always/never);
4. Magnification and minimization – distortions which involve exaggerations or reductions in the significance or magnitude of an event (e.g. catastrophizing);
5. Personalization – the tendency to relate events to oneself when there is no basis for this;
6. Absolute, dichotomous thinking – the tendency to place all experiences in one of two opposite categories, such as saint/sinner, clean/dirty, safe/dangerous.

Maladaptive thoughts and beliefs can be suggested to influence sexual functioning, in the same way as any other form of human behaviour. Inspection of Zilbergeld's male sexual myths and others shown above reveals a high level of errors of thinking in line with those outlined by both Ellis (1977) and Beck *et al.* (1979). Many examples can be found of 'shoulds', 'oughts', 'musts', 'always' and 'nevers'. If failure to meet these demands is perceived as being of great importance (catastrophizing – it is terrible/awful/a disaster), then the individual is likely to experience a great deal of subjective distress when things do not go according to the rule. He or she is also likely to behave in a way that attempts to fulfil the requirements. For example, a variety of problems may occur if either partner strongly holds the belief that 'Men *must* always be capable of responding sexually'. The male in this partnership will feel under considerable pressure to take part in sexual activity whenever the opportunity arises. Inevitably there will be occasions on which the man does not desire sex and would prefer not to take part. It would not be surprising if the fear of not being able to perform and the specific thoughts that accompany this may inhibit sexual responsiveness.

Maladaptive attitudes, beliefs and thoughts may also play an important role in maintaining the sexual problem once it has occurred. Masters and Johnson (1970) placed considerable emphasis on thoughts of fear of failure, 'spectatoring' or focusing on one's performance rather than on pleasure, and anticipation of pain or hurt. Thoughts such as 'what's my penis doing now? . . . I must get an erection . . . is it going erect? . . . oh no . . . it isn't . . . this is awful, terrible . . . I know that I'm not going to be able to get one. I'll never be able to get one now. What's the point of trying? I'm always going to be like this', illustrates the type of maladaptive thinking that can accompany a sexual problem and exacerbate the difficulty. This series of thoughts contains many examples of the type of faulty thinking outlined by authors such as Ellis (1958) and Beck *et al.* (1979). Quadland (1980) outlined three forms of negative cognitions that may act to maintain secondary psychogenic erectile dysfunction: (1) focusing attention on oneself in a critically evaluative way; (2) attributing the responsibility for erectile failure to one's own inadequacies; and (3) believing that one should always perform perfectly in every situation. In the same way that thoughts may act to enhance or create sexual arousal and orgasm, it is suggested that certain thoughts may have an inhibitory influence on sexual arousal and orgasm. The exact mechanism by which this is proposed to occur is outlined above within the context of psychopathology.

When considering this area during assessment, it is important to explore the specific thoughts which the client experiences during different stages of sexual encounters and the beliefs and attitudes which tend to govern his/her behaviour. This may pinpoint maladaptive cognitions and beliefs which are impairing sexual responsiveness. It is also relevant to consider how and why such attitudes, beliefs and cognitions become established. A great deal of emphasis has been placed on the contribution of family attitudes during childhood towards the development of subsequent beliefs and thoughts relating to sexuality. The suggestion that parental attitudes regarding sex and sex roles, child-rearing strategies and general family relationships will subsequently affect a person's belief systems in adulthood has a great deal of face validity. However, there is little empirical evidence to enable us to evaluate the proposition. Hawton (1985) reviewed the limited evidence available to date and suggests that there is tentative support for the contribution of poor parental and parent–child relationships to the development of sexual disorders for some clients. Hawton pointed out, however, that studies have typically used retrospective reports, which leaves open the possibility that recall of information about family relationships may be biased as the result of current problems. In addition, the mechanisms of causality are unclear. It is possible that poor sexual functioning is the result of other factors, such as poor self-esteem or poor communication skills, which result from adverse family experiences, rather than being a direct result of maladaptive family relationships or attitudes. Although clear-cut evidence is lacking, it does seem sensible to suggest that certain types of parental attitudes or family relationships may lead to the development of maladaptive attitudes and beliefs in adulthood. For example, a person who is brought up within a family in which discussion about sex is discouraged, and where sex is regarded as something dirty or taboo, may incorporate this type of attitude within their belief system in adulthood. Such attitudes are then likely to have a significant impact upon sexual behaviour and responsiveness.

Whilst understanding these influences may be helpful in identifying specific maladaptive thoughts and attitudes, the past cannot be changed and the emphasis of treatment must be upon restructuring of current, negative cognitive influences.

Emotional reactions

Models such as that of Ellis (1958), outlined above, suggest that the emotions we feel will be dependent upon our thoughts about particular events. If events are interpreted in certain ways, then negative emotions will be experienced such as anger, guilt, disgust, fear or shame. All such emotions may interfere with sexual functioning if they are experienced during sexual interactions. In the same way that attitudes, beliefs and thoughts should be considered during assessment and treatment, so too should emotional reactions before, during and after sexual activities. In particular it is important to explore the client's emotions and thoughts with regard to their partner during sex: do they feel physical attraction for each other, do they like/dislike each other, would they prefer to be with someone else? It may also be possible to identify fear, anxiety, guilt or anger reactions, either in relation to sexual activity or more generally within the clients' lives, which have an impact on sexual functioning.

Sexual preference

Sexual preferences can be seen as another form of cognitive organization which determines our thoughts and behaviour. The client's sexual preferences in terms of degree of arousal to heterosexual or homosexual stimuli may influence their response to their partner's stimulation. The type of self-statements and sexual responsiveness will be strongly influenced by sexual preferences. For some individuals, erotic preferences may not be for either usual hetero- or homosexual activities but may be for some type of anomalous stimuli such as voyeuristic, sado-masochistic or transvestite situations (Freund and Blanchard, 1981).

Fantasy ability and use of erotic material

Fantasy, in the form of visual imagery or verbal rehearsal, has been suggested to be an important means of achieving and enhancing sexual arousal (Heiman *et al.*, 1976). Ability to fantasize varies across individuals and this skill may be lacking for some individuals. The use of fantasy should therefore be considered during assessment, being explored from two perspectives. First, it should be determined whether the individual has the ability to use fantasy, given that individuals tend to differ in their ability to generate fantasies that are sufficiently clear, intense and durable to create sexual arousal. Second, it must be established whether the client chooses to make use of fantasy given that such a skill exists. This brings us back to the role of attitudes and beliefs which may be held in relation to the use of fantasy. Some individuals hold the belief that sexual arousal and orgasm should be achieved solely through partner stimulation and that additional methods of producing arousal, such as fantasy, erotic material or self-pleasuring, are not acceptable.

The use of erotic material to trigger or enhance sexual arousal also requires a mention here. Couples vary considerably in their attitudes towards and use of erotic material such as pictures, literature and videotapes. Many couples find the use of erotic material helpful in generating sexual interest or arousal and in enhancing their responsiveness during their sexual activities. For others, the use of sexual aids or additional sources of sexual stimulation is taboo, or perhaps the couple may just not have thought of incorporating erotic material into their sexual relationship. There is considerable empirical evidence to demonstrate the effectiveness of erotic stimuli in creating sexual arousal and as such it may be a useful adjunct to partner or self-stimulation for cases of low sexual desire or arousal (Gillan, 1977). Traditionally it has been held that women tend to respond more to written text and orally presented stimuli, whereas males tend to show most arousal to visually presented stimuli (Julien and Over, 1988). Recent studies, however, suggest that women show similar increases in sexual arousal to erotic film presentation as men (Rubinsky *et al.*, 1987).

Attention to sexual stimuli and misinterpretation of stimulation and response

It is possible that for some people the processes of attention, reception, perception and interpretation relating to incoming sexual stimuli may be faulty. For example, a person may fail to attend to the cues available and be unaware of their signs of arousal. Distractibility and problems of concentration may occur if a person is preoccupied with other thoughts. Clients may report examples such as 'I can be quite enjoying my partner stroking me and I am beginning to become aroused when I suddenly lose my concentration and start thinking of something totally different, such as what to put on the shopping list or things I have to do the next day.' Anxious, worrisome thoughts may also interfere with the ability to concentrate on sexual sensations, by entering conscious awareness at inappropriate times.

In some instances, the person may be able to focus on arousal cues but these may be misinterpreted as an aversive feeling rather than pleasurable, or may be interpreted as a sign of anxiety rather than sexual arousal. In such instances, arousal is unlikely to continue.

A MODEL SHOWING THE ROLE OF COGNITIVE EVENTS IN THE DETERMINATION OF PSYCHOSEXUAL DYSFUNCTION

Psychosocial factors have a marked influence over our sexual functioning and in some circumstances may impair sexual responding. It is important to ask the question: how do psychosocial factors operate to affect the biological processes involved in sexual behaviour? The

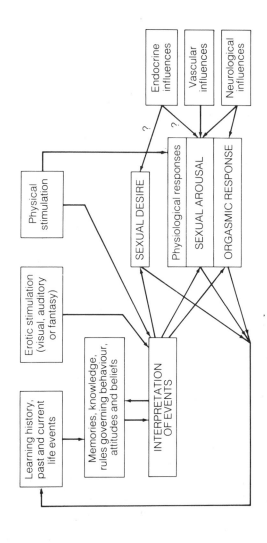

Figure 2.3 A model showing the role of cognitive events in the determination of human sexual responding.

model in Figure 2.3 attempts to summarize the way in which psychogenic and biogenic factors act upon the responses of sexual desire, arousal and orgasm. In particular, an emphasis is placed on the role of cognitive events in the interpretation of stimuli and events, and which influence sexual responsiveness at various points of the sexual response cycle.

The model assumes that past life experiences act through the processes of learning (classical and operant conditioning, plus observational learning) to determine our current memories, rules to govern behaviour, knowledge, attitudes and beliefs. These constructs can be suggested to influence our interpretation of incoming stimuli, which occur in the form of erotic physical, auditory or visual stimulation or fantasy. Current life events such as one's marital relationship also impinge upon our knowledge, attitudes and beliefs. The way in which incoming stimuli are interpreted will determine whether the physiological responses of sexual arousal and ultimately orgasm will occur. Sexual desire is seen as being dependent upon cognitive interpretation of external stimuli and low level of physiological, sexual arousal.

The physiological responses of sexual arousal and orgasm are suggested to be closely monitored and are also subject to the process of interpretation. The physiological responses of sexual arousal are not therefore automatically perceived as such and may be subject to biased interpretation. It is also suggested that our memories, knowledge, attitudes and beliefs are constantly being updated as the result of new information. Hence information about physiological reactions in specific situations may, in turn, influence the cognitive structures of memories, knowledge, attitudes and beliefs. Finally, the importance of biological factors in the determination of sexual desire, arousal and orgasm are recognized. It is also accepted that the processes of sexual desire, arousal and orgasm may occur independently, although they are frequently found to occur in a sequential manner.

In summary, the model aims to demonstrate the important mediational role of cognitive processes, which interact with the numerous biological influences over human sexual functioning. Cognitive processes influence the desire, arousal and orgasm components of the sexual response cycle and are, in turn, influenced by our sexual behaviour and its consequences.

3

Types of sexual difficulties

Given the enormous number of factors that may influence sexual functioning, it is not surprising to find that the process frequently breaks down, resulting in problems in the areas of sexual desire, excitement or orgasm. It is difficult to find a reliable estimate of the extent of sexual problems amongst the general population, with estimates suggesting that between 10% and 50% of adults report some type of sexual difficulty at a given time (Stuntz, 1988). Unfortunately, there is a paucity of data regarding the incidence of psychosexual dysfunctions, in comparison with other human disorders. Nathan suggested that the lack of information about the incidence of sexual problems reflects the facts that sexual dysfunctions are neither disabling, a cause of death, congenital, communicable, heridatary, hospitalizable or work related and hence are not included in routine health statistics. We must therefore rely upon the results of specific surveys in which the samples are typically skewed or restricted in some way, with many studies being limited to students, university staff, attendees at contraceptive clinics or general hospital patients. Nathan (1986) reanalysed the data from 22 studies published over a fifty-year period in order to estimate the incidence of psychosexual dysfunctions. Bearing in mind the methodological limitations of existing studies, her findings confirmed the high incidence of sexual dysfunctions in the general population.

DEFINITION OF TERMS

Various systems have been used to classify sexual disorders and numerous terms have been used to describe them. Given the complex nature of human sexual behaviour, it is not surprising to find a variety of sexual dysfunctions each of which may be associated with a complex range of determinants. Generally, sexual problems can be viewed as a failure of the desire, arousal and/or orgasm components of the sexual response. The most commonly used classification system for psychosexual disorders is probably the American Psychiatric Association's Diagnostic and Statistical Manual of Mental Disorders (DSM-III-R). The DSM-III-R criteria for diagnosis of a psychosexual dysfunction require that the problem cannot be attributed entirely to organic factors, an Axis I mental disorder such as a major depression, or due to inadequate sexual stimulation. The various types of sexual dysfunctions are categorized into disorders of sexual desire, arousal, orgasm and sexual pain.

The DSM-III-R system also requires specification of the following:

1. Whether the dysfunction is psychogenic only, or psychogenic and biogenic;
2. Whether the dysfunction is lifelong or has been acquired after a period of adequate sexual functioning;
3. Whether the dysfunction is generalized (i.e. occurs in all sexual situations) or situational (i.e. occurs only in certain sexual situations).

This system therefore accepts that all forms of sexual difficulty may vary in the degree to which they can be categorized as psychogenic/biogenic, lifelong or acquired and generalized or situational.

Hypoactive sexual desire disorder

Hypoactive sexual desire disorder is defined by DSM-III-R as 'persistently or recurrently deficient or absent sexual fantasies and desire for sexual activity. The judgement of deficiency or absence is made by the clinician, taking into account factors that affect sexual functioning, such as age, sex and the context of the person's life' (APA, DSM-III-R, 1987, p. 293). Various other terms have been used in the literature, such as inhibited, low or impaired sexual desire. In practice, the characteristics of this problem may vary considerably, with responses ranging from active avoidance of sex, to participation in sexual activities upon partner initiation despite a lack of desire. The lack of desire may or may not be accompanied by negative feelings about sexual activity, such as disgust, anxiety or guilt. If negative emotional reactions are sufficiently severe and result in extreme aversion or avoidance of sexual contacts then a diagnosis of sexual aversion disorder would be given (see below). For some individuals the lack of desire may be specific to certain partners or types of sexual activity, whereas for others it may be a more global problem. If the lack of desire is situational, then normal levels of sexual desire occur in preferred sexual situations. The consistency of the problem may also vary, with fluctuations in desire occurring over time for some clients. For others the problem may be consistent or may even be a lifelong problem. Interestingly, few authors have discussed the difficulty in establishing a criterion by which it can be determined whether or not a person's level of sexual desire is adequate. Furthermore, it must be questioned whether the term hypoactive sexual desire disorder should be used if both members of the partnership are content with a low level of sexual desire and activity. It is unlikely that a couple will seek help if both partners experience low levels of sexual desire and find this situation satisfactory, whereas a referral is more likely to occur if disparate levels of desire occur between the partners. In some instances, this disparity may reflect excessive desires on the part of one partner, rather than a low level of desire on the part of the other partner. These factors need to be taken into account during the assessment process.

Individuals also tend to vary in the impact that low sexual desire has upon subsequent stages of sexual response. Intense sexual stimulation will generally trigger sexual arousal and subsequent orgasm if the individual takes part in sexual activities despite an initial lack of desire. In many cases, however, the lack of desire leads to a low frequency of sexual interaction, with the result that arousal and orgasm are rarely experienced. For some clients, of course, dysfunctions of arousal and orgasm may also be present and arousal and orgasm would be impaired even in the presence of adequate desire and stimulation. A careful behavioural analysis will clarify the nature of the presenting problem, as the label 'hypoactive sexual desire' actually tells us very little about the nature of the presenting problem. It is essential to identify the exact cognitive, overt behaviours and physiological responses of the person's current sexual activity in order to design an appropriate intervention. In particular, it is important to distinguish low sexual desire that is associated with intense anxiety about sexual activities (see below) from a lack of desire in the absence of any negative affect or cognitions.

Nathan (1986) suggested that low sexual desire is a relatively common problem, with prevalence rates varying according to the question being asked. Only a small proportion of men and married women report never having any desire for sex at all (1–3%), whereas the figure is much higher for unmarried heterosexual women (15–20%). If subjects are asked to indicate whether 'disinterest' in sex constitutes a problem for them, the rates are much much higher for men and women, being 16% and 25% respectively (Nathan, 1986). It seems likely that many couples experience a stage at which either or both partner(s) have little desire for sex and this phenomenon is far more common than previously thought.

Lack of sexual interest seems to be the most common presenting sexual problem. Schover and LoPiccolo (1982) reported that around 50% of their referrals reported inhibited sexual desire, and Friedman *et al*. (1982) reported that 69% of completed cases at the Sex Therapy Center at Stony Brook included a complaint of low sexual desire. Hawton (1985) reported that 52% of female and 6% of male referrals presented with impaired sexual interest in a large sample of couples in the UK. The low incidence of requests for therapy for low sexual desire by males may reflect the reluctance of many men to admit to lack of sexual desire, given the stereotype of the competent male as always desiring sexual activity. Alternatively, it is possible that the high frequency of lack of sexual desire amongst women means that many women do not pressure their partners into seeking help, being grateful for the lack of sexual demands placed upon them. It is clear, however, that inhibited sexual desire is a frequent problem for both males and females and men are now seeking help more often for such difficulties (Lief, 1985).

Research into problems of sexual desire is in its infancy. It was not really until the work of Kaplan (1974) that a clear distinction was made between disorder of sexual desire and arousal, and until recently many studies failed to make a distinction between these types of dysfunction. Hence, there was a tendency to explore the characteristics of samples which were labelled 'sexually unresponsive' or 'frigid' and which contained a hotchpotch of different types of sexual dysfunction. Such studies cannot be interpreted with any degree of validity and provide minimal insight into the aetiology of hypoactive sexual desire disorder. Fortunately, recent studies have been more careful in using specific diagnostic criteria and in limiting their samples to those who meet the criteria for specific sexual dysfunctions. Several studies have explored possible causal factors in inhibited sexual desire. Attempts to identify specific personality characteristics associated with the disorder have not produced significant

56

findings (Schreiner-Engel and Schiavi, 1986; Stuart *et al.*, 1987). Stuart *et al.* (1987) did, however, find evidence to suggest that the inhibited sexual group reported significantly lower levels of marital satisfaction and lower feelings of romantic love towards their partner, compared to women whose sexual desire levels were normal but had been referred for some other sexual problem within the partnership. It is possible therefore that inhibited sexual desire is associated with a general deterioration in the couple's relationship, although the cause and effect relationship between these factors is unclear. This study also investigated whether inhibited sexual desire was associated with abnormalities in circulating sex hormone levels. No differences in circulating testosterone or prolactin levels were found between the two samples of women, suggesting that levels of these hormones are not implicated in low sexual desire in women. It should be pointed out that the definition of inhibited sexual desire used by Stuart *et al.* (1987) did not exclude phobic avoidance of sex as would now be the case in recent DSM-III-R definitions of hypoactive sexual desire disorder.

Depression has been suggested to be associated with low sexual desire. Schreiner-Engel and Schiavi (1986) compared 46 women with inhibited sexual desire with a matched sample of 36 women who experienced normal levels of desire. Again, no differences in personality characteristics emerged and current levels of psychopathology were equivalent. When lifetime prevalence of depressive disorder was considered, the clinical group were found to report a much greater incidence, with the depressive disorder generally preceding the onset of the lack of sexual desire. The authors suggested that some common biological aetiology is involved in both affective psychopathology and low sexual desire. Interestingly, the inhibited sexual desire group also reported significantly higher levels of severe symptoms of pre-menstrual syndrome. Whilst it seems feasible to suggest that some biological pathway may be involved in the determination of sexual desire, the exact mechanisms involved are yet to be identified. This is also true for psychogenic factors which are suggested to influence desire. So far, the quality of the general relationship appears to be the only psychosocial variable that has been demonstrated empirically to be associated with inhibited sexual desire in women. Factors such as fatigue, general anxiety and attitudes towards sexual activities or genital contact have all been suggested by various therapists to lead to inhibited sexual desire, but as yet there is a lack of data to support these proposals.

As the incidence of referrals for problems of hypoactive sexual desire in males has increased, researchers have started to examine factors which may cause the disorder in men. A recent study by Schiavi *et al.* (1988) examined levels of circulating sex hormones amongst a sample of 17 healthy men with hypoactive sexual desire compared to an age-matched sample of 17 non-dysfunctional men. Unfortunately, 11 of the dysfunctional sample also experienced problems of secondary erectile dysfunction, leaving only six men whose sole problem was hypoactive sexual desire. The results indicated that men who reported low sexual desire had significantly lower levels of plasma testosterone, based on hourly overnight measurements. No differences were found between prolactin, oestrodiol and luteinizing hormone levels between the low and normal desire groups. Comparison between the subtypes of men with hypoactive sexual desire (i.e. with and without erectile difficulties) revealed testosterone levels to be reduced in both these groups, with no difference between them. Of even greater interest was the finding that an association was found between the severity of hypoactive sexual desire, as measured by combined monthly frequency of intercourse attempts and masturbatory experiences, and the level of overnight plasma testosterone. Whilst this result is in keeping with the view that sexual desire levels may be influenced by levels of testosterone, it is equally possible that the low level of sexual activity that results from lack of desire may cause a reduction in testosterone levels. The nature of the cause–effect relationship remains unclear. Hopefully, the increased recognition of problems of sexual desire amongst men will lead to greater research into causal mechanisms.

Sexual aversion disorder

This term is defined by DSM-III-R as 'persistent or recurrent extreme aversion to, and avoidance of, all or almost all, genital sexual contact with a sexual partner' (APA, DSM-III-R, 1987, p. 293). Although the DSM-III-R manual does not provide details regarding the presenting feature of this disorder, it appears that this category includes those cases of low sexual desire which are accompanied by extreme negative affective and cognitive reactions, with marked avoidance behaviours. It is unclear how this disorder would differ from a specific phobia of sexual situations, although in some instances the 'extreme aversion' to genital sexual contact may take the form of disgust or guilt, rather than fear.

An aversion to and avoidance of some forms of sexual activity, such as oral–genital contact, is relatively common and would not be labelled as dysfunctional. A sexual aversion disorder is only said to exist when the aversion and avoidance responses are sufficiently generalized so as to include all forms of genital sexual contact with a sexual partner. If the problem is triggered by a sexual phobia, the nature of the feared stimulus may vary considerably. In some instances the phobic stimuli may be specific, such as the touching of a penis or contact with ejaculate. In others, fear responses may be triggered by a wide range of sexual stimuli, including the sight of a partner's naked body, the sight of one's own sexual parts or physical contact that is perceived as a preliminary to sexual activity (e.g. hugging or kissing).

Given the high level of avoidance behaviour, it is often difficult to establish whether the components of sexual arousal and orgasm would be satisfactory if sexual behaviour was to occur. The association between anxiety and the inhibition of sexual arousal makes it likely that the excitement phase would be impaired for many individuals.

The relatively recent recognition of sexual aversion disorder as a category of sexual dysfunction means that minimal information is yet available concerning its incidence and aetiology.

Male erectile disorder

According to DSM-III-R this term is applied to either '(1) persistent or recurrent partial or complete failure in a male to attain or maintain erection until completion of the sexual activity or (2) persistent or recurrent lack of a subjective sense of sexual excitement and pleasure in a male during sexual activity' (APA, DSM-III-R, 1987, p. 294). Elsewhere in the literature terms such as erectile failure, erectile difficulty and impotence have been used.

The incidence of erectile difficulties in the general population is hard to estimate. The figures produced tend to vary according to the definition used, in terms of frequency of erectile failure and the degree of turgidity or lack of turgidity required. Almost all the literature available on the topic of male disorders of sexual arousal focuses on erectile functioning, with minimal attention being paid to the subjective aspect of lack of arousal. Nathan (1986) in a review paper suggests that estimates of the incidence of diagnosable erectile disorder

59

vary between 10% and 20% of the population, with higher rates being reported for men over the age of 60 years. A study reported by Spector and Boyle (1986) found that 6% of men within a non-clinical sample reported current erectile difficulties and 25% reported difficulties at some point in their sexual lives to date. If occasional erectile failures are taken as the criteria, almost 70% of men report problems, suggesting that it is extremely normal to experience occasional difficulties in attaining an erection (Hite, 1976). Erectile disorder certainly appears to be the most common reason that men seek therapy for a sexual problem. Hawton (1985), for example, reported that 60% of male sexual problem referrals involved a problem of erectile dysfunction. This report is in keeping with the figure of 55% found by Masters and Johnson (1970) amongst their clinical referrals.

Psychogenic factors may be primary or secondary to organic causes of erectile failure. It is becoming increasingly clear that a high proportion of cases of erectile difficulty involve organic causes for which medical assessment and intervention are necessary. The percentage of cases in which organic factors are found tends to vary greatly across different studies. Segraves *et al*. (1981) suggested that this is due to the different samples studied. Samples taken from self-referrals for psychological therapy for a sexual problem tend to include a much lower proportion of organic cases than those obtained through medical clinics, such as urology departments. These authors found that only 5% of cases in the self-referred sexual dysfunction clinic sample had identifiable organic causes, compared to 31% of cases of erectile failure whose initial contact was with the urology clinic. It is also important to note that 17% of the urology referrals could not be classified definitely as organic or psychogenic, indicating that it is frequently difficult to make clear-cut distinctions between organic and psychogenic aetiology. Segraves *et al*. (1987) subsequently concluded from a review of the literature that at least 30% of men who experience clinically significant erectile difficulties are found to have organic aetiologies. The organic causes included a wide range of endocrine, neurological and vascular disorders which may influence erectile functioning, as outlined in Chapter 2. The results of the Segraves *et al*. (1987) study contrast markedly with the frequently held belief that erectile dysfunction is rarely of organic origin. This erroneous view probably resulted from Masters and Johnson's (1970) finding that only 3.3% of their cases of secondary erectile failure and apparently none of the primary cases could be attributed to organic pathology. Segraves *et al*. (1987) suggested that the low rate of organic aetiology at the Masters and Johnson Institute was probably due to a self-referral, selection process.

In order to exclude organic causes, a wide range of vascular, neurological and endocrinological factors must be considered. These are summarized in Chapter 4, but the point must be reiterated that it is extremely difficult to draw firm conclusions as to the relative contribution of organic and psychogenic causes in many cases. For example, the use of a certain drug which is known to cause erectile problems for some men does not automatically indicate that the drug is responsible for the erectile difficulties of a given case. It is possible that the drug is not producing an adverse effect on erectile functioning and psychogenic causes are present. Similarly, whereas lack of night-time and early waking erections is suggestive of organic cause, this pattern may also be found amongst some men for whom the aetiology is psychogenic. Generally, the judgment regarding organic versus psychogenic aetiology must take into account the combined response to different indicators of organic pathology. Hence a pattern of lack of night-time erections, in conjunction with the use of a specific drug, would provide a better indication of organic pathology than either measure alone.

Although organic problems are found to occur in many instances of erectile failure, the evidence still suggests that the majority of cases result from psychogenic cause. It must be remembered, however, that the judgment of psychogenic cause is frequently a diagnosis by exclusion, in that organic factors have not been found. It is feasible that biological causes may exist that medical science has not yet been able to detect. In the meantime the assumption of psychogenic cause is typically made for these cases, even though evidence to confirm psychogenic aetiology may be lacking.

Various psychosocial factors have been implicated in the aetiology of psychogenic erectile failure. As described in Chapter 2, evidence supports the suggestion of therapists, such as Masters and Johnson (1970), that negative cognitions concerning sexual performance play an important role in the development and maintenance of erectile disorder. Hence, the focusing of thoughts or attention on one's lack of ability to perform or on the consequences of failure is suggested to limit the level of sexual arousal. Whether the focusing of attention on negative thoughts is a cause or effect of the sexual dysfunction, however, remains to be demonstrated. Barlow (1986) suggests that the tendency towards negative evaluation and expectancies reflects a personality characteristic which predates the development of the erectile difficulty. Studies which have attempted to identify particular personality characteristics of individuals with erectile failure, and which would support Barlow's proposition, have produced conflicting findings. Generally, attempts to identify a personality profile which is characteristic of psychogenic erectile failure have not been successful in making this determination (Kinder and Curtiss, 1988).

It is possible that the tendency towards negative evaluation and focus on potential negative consequences of sexual activity is related to depression and general tendency towards negative interpretation of events. Evidence is emerging to support an association between depression and erectile dysfunction (Thase *et al.*, 1988; see Chapter 2), although it is unclear whether depression impairs erectile functioning or erectile difficulties cause depression. It seems possible, however, that the negative cognitive style that accompanies depression may predispose to the development of erectile dysfunction as a result of negative expectancies and negative self-evaluation.

Masters and Johnson (1970) suggested a variety of causal factors to be responsible for the erectile problems of their large sample. They made a distinction between primary and secondary impotence, in which primary was defined as an inability to achieve and/or maintain an erection quality sufficient to accomplish intromission at the point of first attempted coitus and thereafter. Secondary erectile dysfunction was taken to refer to all cases in which at least one successful intromission had been achieved. This classification differs from that used by DSM-III-R, which distinguishes lifelong from acquired, and generalized from specific erectile problems. Masters and Johnson (1970) emphasized a multitude of factors in the development of *primary* erectile problems, such as religious orthodoxy, lack of sexual knowledge of both the male and his partner, an excessively sexual relationship with the mother, early homosexual experiences, or a traumatic experience with a prostitute. Similarly, it was not possible to identify any fixed set of factors that were associated with *secondary* erectile problems, with a wide range of determinants being found. In some instances erectile failure was triggered by an acute alcoholic episode, with subsequent reactions of the man and his partner serving to maintain the problem. Patterns of excessive maternal or paternal dominance were found for some cases, with religious orthodoxy and homosexual influences also being reported. In addition to these personal characteristics, a major emphasis was placed on the role of spectatoring and performance orientation.

The nature of erectile difficulties may vary considerably depending on whether the problem has been lifelong or acquired, generalized or specific. The ability to maintain an erection may vary according to the location, the partner, the time of day/night and the type of stimulation being received (e.g. self, manual-partner, oral-partner or intercourse). In extreme cases the problem may always have been evident and erections may not occur at any time, including during rapid eye movement (REM) sleep or upon wakening or during attempted self-stimulation. Such case are generally found to be of organic origin. Other cases may present with a pattern of erections during masturbation, fantasy, during erotic visual stimulation or with another partner, but not during attempts at intercourse with their present partner. Yet another pattern may exist in which erections are not attained during any form of stimulation, after a previous history of normal sexual functioning. Some men within this category will be found to have organic causes but this pattern of erectile dysfunction may also be found amongst men with no detectable organic pathology (Wincze *et al.*, 1988).

Female sexual arousal disorder

Female sexual arousal disorder has also been termed low/impaired/ inhibited sexual arousal/excitement and can be defined as 'persistent or recurrent partial or complete failure to attain or maintain the lubrication–swelling response of sexual excitement until completion of the sexual activity or persistent or recurrent lack of a subjective sense of sexual excitement and pleasure in a female during sexual activity' (APA, DSM-III-R, 1987, p. 294). A distinction is made therefore between the physiological and subjective components of arousal, given that these aspects are not always concordant. It is interesting that this definition does not require that the woman engages in sexual activity that is of adequate focus, intensity and duration, as was the case for the DSM-III criteria for inhibited sexual excitement. It is unclear why this requirement was dropped, given that many cases of lack of sexual arousal response are associated with inadequate stimulation.

In cases where inhibited arousal is the sole presenting problem, the desire phase and orgasm may remain intact. Many of these women are able to attain orgasm through the use of a vibrator without the experience of sexual arousal. For many women, however, problems of desire accompany lack of sexual arousal and it becomes difficult to determine whether the problem is one of low sexual arousal or lack of desire, given that the lack of desire is likely to limit the amount of sexual arousal that is experienced during stimulation. Hawton (1985) and Kaplan (1983) suggested that lack of sexual arousal in the presence of adequate sexual interest is relatively uncommon, but these authors do not provide empirical support for this claim.

Data concerning the incidence of sexual arousal disorders in women are lacking and the few studies available have typically failed to make a distinction between a lack of desire and lack of arousal. Hopefully, future studies will investigate the extent of sexual arousal disorders in women and determine the degree to which these are associated with lack of appropriate foreplay. It is also difficult to estimate the incidence of referrals for therapy which involve problems of sexual arousal in women. Many investigators have not distinguished between disorders of desire and arousal in the classification of female referrals (e.g. Hawton, 1985; Masters and Johnson, 1970), which probably reflects the traditional view that the desire and arousal in women are closely linked.

This failure to distinguish desire from arousal disorders in women has meant little research has been conducted into the causes of female sexual arousal disorders. For example, Masters and Johnson (1970) limited their female samples to orgasmic dysfunction and vaginismus and made no mention of disorders of arousal or desire in women, although erectile dysfunction was distinguished from orgasm/ejaculation problems in males. This neglect of female sexual arousal disorders has continued until recently. Such a lack of attention to female arousal disorders is rather amazing, given that it is basically equivalent to erectile difficulty in males and an enormous number of studies have been conducted into the nature and aetiology of erectile problems. Perhaps if coitus was not possible in cases of low female sexual arousal (as is the case for erectile failure) then greater attention would be paid to the disorder. Lack of sexual arousal in women may often have been dismissed in the past as a problem that can easily be overcome by the use of a lubricating jelly, which permits intercourse to proceed, but is hardly an effective treatment if satisfactory arousal levels are taken as the criterion for success. It is possible that women who lack sexual arousal, but who are able to take part in intercourse with the assistance of lubricating gels, may fail to seek treatment, whereas a man with an erectile problem would be more likely to request therapy. Unfortunately, the lack of attention paid to female sexual arousal disorders means that we know very little about the characteristics and aetiology of the problem.

Although we know very little about causes of low sexual arousal in women generally, we do know that physiological arousal problems in the form of poor lubrication tend to occur for some women during menopause, in association with certain spinal injuries and following use of certain drugs, as outlined in Chapter 2.

Inhibited female orgasm

Inhibited female orgasm or female orgasmic dysfunction/anorgasmia may be defined as 'persistent or recurrent delay in, or absence of, orgasm in a female following a normal sexual excitement phase during sexual activity that the clinician judges to be adequate in focus, intensity and duration' (APA, DSM-III-R, 1987, p. 294). As with other psychosexual disorders, anorgasmia may be situational or global and may also be lifelong or have developed after a period of orgasmic ability in the situation(s) of concern. Hence, the lack of orgasm may be limited to specific situations, with orgasm being possible in other situations. The most common situation in which orgasm does not occur is intercourse, so much so that Kaplan (1983) estimated that only 20–30% of women are able to experience orgasm during coitus if they rely purely on vaginal stimulation by the penis. If this estimate is correct, then it is more normal to have difficulty in attaining orgasm during intercourse (if no additional forms of stimulation are used) than it is unusual. This brings into question whether coital anorgasmia, in the absence of additional stimulation, should be classified as a sexual dysfunction. It is clear that the vast majority of women require some form of direct clitoral stimulation in order to achieve orgasm. Evidence also suggests that many more women are able to experience orgasm through self-stimulation than they are by partner stimulation. This is probably because self-stimulation provides immediate and direct feedback about the most appropriate form of stimulation. Estimates concerning the percentage of women who have never been able to achieve orgasm in any situation range from 5% to 15% (Nathan, 1986).

Female orgasmic dysfunction is a frequent case for referral for therapy. Hawton (1985) reported that 19% of his female referrals concerned orgasmic dysfunction. Masters and Johnson (1970) found that 56% of female dysfunction referrals concerned primary orgasmic dysfunction (lifelong, in all situations) with another 44% reporting problems of situational anorgasmia. It must be remembered that Masters and Johnson did not use a category of disorders of desire and arousal for women, hence it is not feasible to compare their classifications with more recent studies. Nevertheless, it is clear that some form of orgasmic dysfunction was experienced by all of their female clients. One would be unlikely to find such a high incidence of primary orgasmic dysfunction today. Fortunately, women are now better educated about methods of achieving orgasm and fewer negative attitudes exist concerning the use of self-stimulation techniques by women. Vibrators are easily purchased and are found to be the form of stimulation most likely to trigger orgasm in women. As a result, it is suggested here that it is now much less common for women never to have experienced orgasm than was the case back in 1970 when Masters and Johnson reported their pioneering work.

It is important to examine the aetiology of female orgasmic dysfunction separately for the different types of difficulty. If we first look at total inorgasmia, various suggestions have been proposed, including the existence of a normal distribution of thresholds for orgasm, with some women requiring much higher levels of stimulation than others in order for the orgasmic response to be triggered. This hypothesis is difficult to test out, but it seems that orgasm may be triggered for some previously inorgasmic women purely through the use of a vibrator which provides strong levels of clitoral stimulation. Various other contributory factors can be found throughout the literature, including religious influences, lack or absence of appropriate stimulation by self or partner and negative family influences during childhood. Generally, it is accepted that numerous factors may inhibit orgasm in women and these may differ widely across different clients. One of the few studies to investigate the characteristics of anorgasmic women was reported by Derogatis *et al.* (1986). This study identified two main subtypes of women who had never experienced orgasm. The first type involved a minority of the sample, who were characterized by good sexual knowledge, adequate body image, liberal sexual interest, higher sex drive, an adventurous approach to sexual activities and frequent use of sexual fantasies. The majority of the sample fell into the second group, which was characterized by higher levels of psychological distress, negative self concept and body image, reduced interest in sex, limited sexual experiences and minimal use of fantasy, in comparison to a matched sample of non-dysfunctional women. Derogatis *et al.* (1986) suggested that lack of orgasm in the first type may reflect inherent constitutional factors, rather than psychogenic influences. The second type, on the other hand, manifest a range of psychosexual influences that would be likely to inhibit orgasm. Most importantly, this study demonstrates that anorgasmic women are not a homogeneous group. Indeed, Derogatis *et al.* suggest that it is likely that other subtypes would be identified if other marker variables were used in the procedure for identifying subtypes.

A rather different approach needs to be taken in relation to the aetiology of situational orgasmic dysfunction. Given that we know that many women, perhaps even the majority, have difficulty in reaching orgasm by partner stimulation alone (without a vibrator) and particularly during coitus if no additional stimulation is used, then perhaps we should really be asking what factors enable some women to reach orgasm in these difficult situations, rather than asking what factors prevent orgasm for others. Unfortunately, there is minimal information about women who are able to attain orgasm easily in situations such as intercourse. It seems likely that women differ markedly in terms of sexual desire, arousability and ease of attaining orgasm. Some women, albeit a small minority, are able to produce orgasm just through fantasy alone. Others require only small amounts of physical stimulation in order to produce high levels of sexual arousal and orgasm. If a normal distribution of ease of sexual arousal and/or orgasm exists, then some women will fall at the lower end of this distribution. This suggestion is not an answer in itself, as it does not explain *why* women vary in orgasmic responsiveness. It is possible that the distribution is biologically determined, perhaps as the result of variations in circulating sex hormone levels. Alternatively, individual differences in some other characteristics could explain the variation in orgasmic ability, such as differences in ability to attend to sexual cues.

Even if a distribution of ease of attaining orgasm exists, there is undoubtedly a wide range of variables which may interfere with the process. Numerous factors such as marital disharmony, lack of partner skill, lack of sexual knowledge, negative sexual attitudes and negative body image, to mention just a few, are likely to inhibit orgasm for women. There may be some women for whom there are no negative psychosexual influences, but unfortunately they may lie at the low end of the distribution of ease of attaining orgasm. For these women, the aim of intervention would be to provide maximum stimulation through a wide range of channels in the situation in which orgasm does not occur (e.g. through use of fantasy, erotic materials, increased attention focus on sexual cues, increased communication skills for providing guidance and feedback to partner and maximizing appropriate physical stimulation). Given that orgasm during coitus is relatively unusual in the absence of direct clitoral stimulation, it may be necessary for some women to accept that orgasm by penile thrusting alone is an unrealistic goal.

Inhibited male orgasm

A variety of terms have been used to refer to inhibited male orgasm, such as delayed or retarded ejaculation or ejaculatory incompetence. The disorder refers to 'persistent or recurrent delay in, or absence of, orgasm in the male following a normal sexual excitement phase during sexual activity that the clinician, taking into account the person's age, judges to be adequate in focus, intensity, and duration. This failure to achieve orgasm is usually restricted to an inability to reach orgasm in the vagina, with orgasm possible with other types of stimulation such as masturbation' (APA, DSM-III-R, 1987, p. 295).

A total absence of orgasm is extremely rare, with studies suggesting an incidence of less that 0.2% of the adult male population (Nathan, 1986). Less severe difficulties in attaining orgasm are somewhat more common, with studies suggesting an incidence of 3–4% of men below the age of 65 (Nathan, 1986). Such problems most frequently occur in relation to intercourse and are less likely to occur during partner-hand, oral or self-stimulation. Hence the majority of cases present with difficulties in reaching orgasm during vaginal penetration and yet are able to do so during masturbation. Erectile functioning is usually satisfactory. The relative rarity of inhibited male orgasm is reflected in the low proportion of referrals for treatment of sexual dysfunctions, with studies suggesting a figure between 3% and 6% of male referrals (Hawton, 1985; Schull and Sprenkle, 1980). Derogatis (1983) suggested that the low referral rate for inhibited male orgasm results in part from the unwillingness of many cases to seek help.

Schull and Sprenkle (1980) emphasized the variation in presentation of the characteristics of the disorder in terms of the situations in which ejaculation is impaired (location, sexual activity, specific partner), the frequency with which ejaculation is inhibited in the problem situation(s) and the degree of delay of orgasm. These authors also stressed the arbitrary nature of the criteria used in determining what is normal, what is satisfactory to the couple and what duration of stimulation before orgasm should be regarded as a problem. Is the judgment of inhibited male orgasm made after 40 minutes, 30 minutes or 20 minutes of stimulation before orgasm occurs?

Numerous theories have been proposed to account for inhibited male orgasm. Any compound or action which interrupts or disturbs the neurophysiological basis of ejaculation may inhibit ejaculation. Hence a variety of drugs, surgical procedures and injuries are found to inhibit the male orgasm. Psychogenic models of aetiology have also been proposed. For example, anxiety and negative thoughts about performance (such as 'I really must try . . . am I going to be able to make it?') have frequently been suggested to inhibit orgasm in males. Although the suggestion that anxiety will inhibit orgasm appears to have face validity, Schull and Sprenkle (1980) pointed out that there is very little evidence to support the proposition, and indeed it does not make sense from a neurological perspective. Anxiety, which is associated with sympathetic nervous system activation, would be predicted to increase the probability of ejaculation, which is also mediated by the sympathetic nervous system, rather than have an inhibitory effect.

Other aetiological models have emphasized a range of factors in the inhibition of male orgasm, such as hostility towards women, negative feelings towards the genitals, relationship conflicts, fear of pregnancy and lack of physical attraction towards the partner. There is a marked lack of evidence to permit us to evaluate these proposals, partly as the result of the rarity of the disorder, which makes it hard to obtain adequate sample sizes for research. Schull and Sprenkle (1980) suggested that a lack of psychological and/or physical stimulation (stimulation deprivation), related to factors such as inadequate technique or lack of attention to sexual cues, may account for difficulties in attaining orgasm. These authors also proposed that individual differences exist in ejaculatory threshold and for some men the basic genital contact of intercourse is not sufficient to trigger orgasm. These authors suggest that their model is supported to some degree by the increase in ejaculatory competence that occurs with additional physical stimulation (e.g. from vibrators) or psychological stimulation (e.g. use of erotic materials or fantasy).

One of the few studies to investigate the characteristics of men with inhibited orgasm was reported by Derogatis (1983). Data were presented for 13 men who were attending a sexual dysfunction clinic. The sample tended to be somewhat younger and better educated than other sexual problem referrals and typically did not view the difficulty as a serious problem. Help was usually requested under pressure from their partner and half of the sample did not accept the offer of treatment. The men tended to have less sexual knowledge, to engage in less foreplay prior to intercourse, to have less satisfactory communication with their partner and to use fewer sexual positions compared to normative data. The limited sexual repertoire was not found when it came to anal intercourse, in which the inhibited orgasm group tended to have more experience. Derogatis (1983) did not find any evidence of reduced sexual drive (fantasy or activity) and the level of depression, anxiety and hostility was found to be lower than for other types of sexual disorder, albeit somewhat elevated compared to normal levels. These findings bring into question the validity of models which emphasize the role of hostility in retarded ejaculation. The results of the study did, however, suggest that the men with inhibited orgasm were more likely to experience sado-masochistic fantasies and reported more dissatisfaction with their partner compared to men with other forms of sexual dysfunction. Generally, orgasm was not reported to be fulfilling and foreplay was not found to be sufficiently arousing. Derogatis (1983) pointed out that our knowledge of the characteristics and aetiology of psychogenic inhibition of male orgasm is very limited. Since that date, little progress seems to have been made towards our understanding of the disorder.

When ejaculation is disrupted, this usually involves an inhibition of both emission and expulsion phases. In rare cases, the process of expulsion may occur (including the rhythmic contractions) but in the absence of emission, resulting what may be termed 'dry' ejaculation. Kaplan (1983) also reports rare cases in which the physical process of ejaculation occurs but without any pleasurable sensations. Yet another disorder of ejaculation is termed retrograde ejaculation, in which semen is propelled backwards into the bladder rather than forwards into the urethra. Such a phenomenon is associated with the subjective feeling of orgasm, but no ejaculation is propelled from the penis. These disorders are generally associated with physical causes, such as bladder neck problems or prostatectomy and some forms of medication (e.g. certain types of antipsychotic drugs), rather than psychogenic aetiology.

Premature ejaculation

It is extremely difficult to find a satisfactory definition of premature ejaculation. DSM-III-R defines premature ejaculation as 'persistent or recurrent ejaculation with minimal sexual stimulation or before, upon, or shortly after penetration and before the person wishes it. The clinician must take into account factors that affect duration of the excitement phase, such as age, novelty of the sexual partner or situation, and frequency of sexual activity' (APA, DSM-III-R, 1987, p. 295). This definition places emphasis on the subjective opinion of the individual as to whether ejaculation occurs when desired, a criterion which is somewhat different from those used in many research studies which have tended to set some criterion regarding duration of stimulation before ejaculation occurs. Masters and Johnson (1970) proposed yet another approach to the definition of premature ejaculation, making the judgment dependent upon the extent to which a man could delay ejaculation during intercourse in order that the partner could reach orgasm. This definition was obviously inadequate as some partners may take a long time to reach orgasm. Such variations in definition make it rather difficult to compare the results of studies which use different criteria for the disorder.

Nathan (1986) took up this point when attempting to establish the incidence of premature ejaculation. She pointed out that the majority of individuals who are dissatisfied with their ejaculatory performance would also tend to meet the criteria for premature ejaculation based on duration of stimulation before ejaculation, hence it is generally feasible to compare the results of different studies. Nathan (1986) emphasized the remarkable consistency of results across different studies, which typically report an incidence of around 35% despite current differences in the phrasing of the questions, populations surveyed and the dates of the studies conducted. Spector and Boyle (1986), however, reported a somewhat lower incidence of 18% for current problems of premature ejaculation amongst a non-clinical sample of 109 men. Although estimates vary across different studies, it is clear that premature ejaculation is extremely common and is probably the most common form of sexual problem in males.

Estimates regarding the proportion of male sex therapy referrals that present with problems of premature ejaculation have varied considerably. For example, 42% of male sexual dysfunctions in the Masters and Johnson (1970) sample experienced premature ejaculation whereas only 16% of Hawton's (1985) referrals did so.

Various factors have been suggested to be important in the aetiology of premature ejaculation, given the involvement of the sympathetic nervous system in both processes. Attempts to reduce anxiety through the use of anxiety-reducing drugs, such as propranolol, have not been

71

found to be effective in increasing ejaculatory control, bringing into question the role of anxiety in premature ejaculation (Kinder and Curtiss, 1988).

Spiess *et al*. (1984) investigated the contribution of five potential causes of premature ejaculation to determine whether premature ejaculators (a) showed faster sexual arousal, (b) showed greater arousal in the same sexual situation, (c) showed arousal to a wider range of situations, (d) required less arousal to ejaculate and (e) had longer intervals between ejaculations or attempts at intercourse, when compared to non-dysfunctional males. The results showed that the arousal patterns of the premature ejaculators did not differ from the comparison group, but the dysfunctional males tended to have longer intervals between ejaculations and subsequent intercourse. This led Spiess *et al*. (1984) to suggest that premature ejaculation is characterized by, and may even be caused by, low frequency of ejaculation and intercourse.

Strassberg *et al*. (1987) examined a hypothesis originally proposed by Kaplan (1974) that premature ejaculators may be poor at assessing accurately their level of sexual arousal during intercourse, in particular during those moments just prior to orgasm. This hypothesis suggests that inaccurate assessment of arousal makes the individual less able to institute the necessary control mechanisms required to maintain a high, but not critical, level of sexual arousal. Comparison of a group of 13 premature ejaculators with a group of 13 non-dysfunctional males indicated no difference in accuracy of estimation of sexual arousal. Patterns of sexual arousal were also similar for the two groups. The hypothesis that premature ejaculators have difficulty in estimating accurately their arousal levels was not therefore supported. Interestingly, Strassberg *et al*. (1987) found rates of intercourse and masturbation to be equivalent to those of control subjects, which brings into question Spiess *et al*.'s (1984) suggestion that premature ejaculation may be the result of infrequent sexual activity. Kinder and Curtiss (1988) pointed out that the Strassberg *et al*. (1987) study required subjects to be involved in a regular sexual relationship, and the low frequency of intercourse and ejaculation in the Spiess *et al*. (1984) study may have reflected a consequence of premature ejaculation, rather than a cause. In other words, the negative experience of premature ejaculation may have led to an avoidance of sexual activity. Kinder and Curtiss (1988) suggested that it would be interesting to evaluate whether an increase in sexual intercourse and ejaculation would, on its own, result in an increase in ejaculatory control.

The model behind this approach suggests that ejaculation occurs faster as the length of time since the last ejaculation increases. Further investigation of this premise and the possible contribution to premature ejaculation seems warranted. Certainly the possibility should be considered with individual clients.

Dyspareunia

Psychogenic dyspareunia can be defined as 'recurrent and persistent genital pain in either a male or female before, during and after sexual intercourse'. The condition must not be caused exclusively by a physical disorder nor be due to lack of lubrication or vaginismus (APA,DSM-III-R, 1987, p. 295). Obviously, many cases of dyspareunia are caused by physical disorders and these must be excluded before the problem is suggested to be psychogenic. A wide range of physical causes exist for dyspareunia, such as rigid hymen, painful hymen tags, endometriosis, pelvic inflammatory diseases, senile atrophy of the vagina, pelvic tumours, childbirth pathologies, stenosis of the vagina, urethral carbuncle, haemorrhoids, episiotomy scars, inflammations, adhesions, infections, allergic reactions, constipation, ectopic pregnancy, cysts and excessively vigorous or prolonged coitus (Sandberg and Quevillon, 1987) to mention just a few. Lack of lubrication is one of the most common reasons for pain during intercourse and again this must be excluded as a cause if the criteria for psychogenic dyspareunia are to be met. The wide range of physical problems that may cause painful intercourse makes a thorough medical examination essential. Generally, the physical cause can then be dealt with.

A psychogenic diagnosis tends to be given in the absence of detectable physical pathology, without requiring any specific evidence of psychogenic causes. Psychogenic dyspareunia is typically therefore a diagnosis by exclusion of organicity, rather than demonstrable evidence of psychological causal factors. Psychogenic causes are therefore more likely to be assumed amongst longstanding cases of dyspareunia in which no physical causes have been found and physical treatments, if used, have failed. For example, Fordney (1978) reported that no organic factors could be found for 60–70% of longstanding cases of dyspareunia. In practice, such cases would be labelled psychogenic, despite the possibility that some physical pathology exists but has not been identified. This possibility should always be borne in mind when working with clients whose pain has been attributed to psychogenic causes.

There are various types of pain that may be experienced during or immediately after intercourse. The pain may occur at the point of entry, during deep thrusting or during more shallow thrusting and may be experienced as a deep/internal pain or nearer to the vaginal entrance. As with other psychosexual disorders, the condition may be lifelong or acquired and generalized or situational.

Dyspareunia has been reported to be linked to vaginismus in that one may cause the other. Whereas a diagnosis of vaginismus may be given even if the problem occurs in conjunction with dyspareunia, a diagnosis of dyspareunia cannot be given if vaginismus is present according to the criteria used by DSM-III-R. This requirement is included given that forced intercourse in cases of vaginismus would obviously cause pain. If vaginismus is the cause of pain, then a primary diagnosis of vaginismus should be given (Sandberg and Quevillon, 1987). Dyspareunia can be distinguished from vaginismus in that women who experience dyspareunia are generally able to achieve penetration even though it may be very painful, whereas in vaginismus the muscles at the base of the vagina contract involuntarily, thereby preventing penetration from occurring. Unfortunately, repeated attempts at painful intercourse may result in vaginismus, as the anticipation of pain begins to trigger involuntary muscle contraction. As a result of the pain produced, most clients with dyspareunia will attempt to avoid intercourse and this may generalize to other aspects of sexual interaction for fear that they may lead on to demands or pressures to take part in intercourse. A high proportion of women with dyspareunia also exhibit inhibition of arousal and/or orgasm, probably as the result of anticipatory fear of intercourse and pain.

Dyspareunia of psychogenic origin is a relatively rare disorder. Nathan (1986) reported that virtually no survey data about the prevalence of the disorder in the general population exist. In terms of referrals for therapy, Hawton (1985) reported dyspareunia to be an infrequent cause for referral, occurring in only 4% of female cases and none of the male cases in his sample. This report contrasts with the suggestion by Sandberg and Quevillon (1987) that dyspareunia is a relatively common cause for referral because of its disabling effects, which are more severe than those of other sexual disorders. The discrepancy may reflect differences in the samples considered, according to whether purely psychogenic or organic cases are included. Organic dyspareunia seems to be more common than psychogenic dyspareunia and it is likely that Sandberg and Quevillon included organic dyspareunia in their sample, whereas Hawton did not. It also appears that sufferers are more likely to be women than men (Sandberg and Quevillon, 1987). Those cases of painful intercourse in males that have been reported in the literature have typically been associated with physical pathology, such as excessively tight foreskin, infections or injury to the frenulum. In rare instances, males may also report the experience of pain at the point of ejaculation, which is again typically associated with organic causes, such as infections.

Several models have been proposed to account for dyspareunia, but little evidence exists to permit their evaluation. Factors such as guilt, fear, lack of sexual knowledge, anger and conflict with the partner have all been implicated in the aetiology of dyspareunia. Any model must explain how, in the absence of physical pathology, the individual can experience sensations that are labelled as painful and which result in the occurrence of a variety of pain behaviours. It is unclear how the affective responses outlined above could become converted to the experience of pain. To date, there is a marked lack of empirical data to permit evaluation of any of these models and we remain ignorant as to the causal mechanisms involved in psychogenic dyspareunia.

Vaginismus

The term vaginismus refers to the 'recurrent and persistent involuntary spasm of the musculature of the outer third of the vagina that interferes with coitus' (APA, DSM-III-R, 1987, p. 295). The degree of interference with coitus varies from vaginal tightness that makes penetration difficult, to a point at which penetration becomes impossible. In severe cases, this may also involve the rectal and gluteus leg muscles (Kaplan, 1974). The response may be triggered by real, imagined or anticipated attempts at penetration of the vagina. In many cases of vaginismus there is a marked phobia concerning vaginal penetration. In addition to the muscular contraction response of the vaginal and associated muscles, various physiological, cognitive and overt behavioural responses typical of phobias can be identified. The physiological responses may include sweating, shaking or hyperventilation, whereas the cognitive responses may involve a range of fearful thoughts concerning possible negative consequences of penetration. The overt behavioural components typically include avoidance responses, so that attempts are made to ensure that intercourse or even vaginal examination do not occur.

A variety of faulty beliefs have been suggested to underlie the development of vaginismus. In some instances it may develop following the experience of painful intercourse and the anticipation of further pain triggers the vaginismus response. Other women may believe that their partner's penis is too big or their vagina is too small to permit painless intercourse to occur. Unfortunately, even mild vaginismus may result in pain when intercourse is attempted, hence a self-fulfilling prophecy occurs in which pain is feared and pain occurs, reinforcing the faulty belief. This in turn creates a further vaginismus- muscle contraction reponse, making painful intercourse even more likely in the future. A vicious cycle may therefore become established.

The degree to which vaginismus generalizes from sexual penetration with a partner to other types of vaginal contact tends to vary across individual cases. In some instances, the problem generalizes to such an extent that a vaginal medical examination is not possible, tampon insertion is not feasible and even simple touch of the external genitals is avoided. On occasion, generalization extends to a wide range of sexual interactions or stimuli, to the degree that an extensive sexual phobia develops. Many different beliefs and thoughts have been suggested to underlie such responses, such as fears of pregnancy, strict religious adherence, dislike or disgust about genitalia and dislike or disgust concerning the partner. In rare instances, sexual abuse as a child has been linked with vaginismus in adulthood (Jehu, 1989), reflecting one component of a post-traumatic stress response.

Vaginismus may be a lifelong problem or have developed after a period of normal sexual functioning, usually after some trigger event such as childbirth, a medical disorder associated with painful intercourse, an abortion, miscarriage or significant trauma. In lifelong cases the couple may present with a problem of an unconsumated marriage. For example, one couple referred to the author's clinic had been married fifteen years without consummating their marriage and had finally decided to seek help because they wanted to have children before the woman reached the age of forty. Assessment revealed a severe case of vaginismus but a reasonable degree of sexual activity in which the woman was able to manually stimulate her partner to orgasm but avoided any form of physical contact with her own genitals.

The level of sexual responsiveness and sexual activity in non-coital activities tends to vary from case to case. In some instances vaginismus may form part of a multi-component sexual dysfunction in which desire, arousal and orgasm are also inhibited. Some women, however, will show normal patterns of sexual desire, arousal and orgasm whilst avoiding all attempts at sexual intercourse. It was interesting to find that 14 out of 20 women with vaginismus studied by Scholl (1988) were able to attain orgasm by partner stimulation, indicating the specific nature of the vaginismus reponse for many cases.

Although transient episodes of vaginismus are quite common amongst women, persistent occurrence of the disorder is thought to be relatively infrequent. There is a marked absence of epidemiological data (Nathan, 1986) and estimates concerning the incidence amongst referrals for sex therapy vary according to the centre studied. For example, Hawton (1985) reported that 18% of female sexual problem referrals involved a problem of vaginismus. This compares with a figure of 8.5% for the sample of 342 female sexual problems reported by Masters and Johnson (1970).

Studies which have attempted to identify the characteristics and likely aetiological factors associated with vaginismus have also produced conflicting results. Masters and Johnson (1970) found 12 women in their sample of 29 were strongly influenced by religious orthodoxy, whereas a recent study reported by Scholl (1988) with 23 women found that only five of their sample held strong religious beliefs. Other factors found by Masters and Johnson (1970) to be linked with the development of vaginismus were sexual abuse/trauma, sexual dysfunction of the male, a history of dyspareunia and homosexual orientation. Each of these factors was found in only two or three cases and hence should not be viewed as general causal variables.

The Scholl (1988) study produced some fascinating findings. This paper reported the characteristics of 23 women who were involved in unconsummated marriages, secondary to vaginismus. Of the 20 women who successfully completed therapy, 13 reported their husbands to be unassertive, 15 believed their anatomy to be defective, 12 were lacking in sexual knowledge, seven held negative attitudes towards their genitals, four reported a fear of sexually transmitted diseases, 17 had not received any sex education from their parents and seven reported that their parents held negative attitudes to sex. Only one woman reported a history of sexual trauma. This pattern of results suggests that different characteristics are associated with the development of vaginismus for different women. Scholl (1988) discussed the role of the unassertive husband, suggesting that some women may actively select partners who are passive and unassertive and who are unlikely to put pressure on them to engage in intercourse. He suggested that more assertive partners would be more persuasive in encouraging the women to take part in intercourse and hence make it less likely that vaginismus would continue.

The data from Scholl's study also support the importance of irrational beliefs, such as that the sexual anatomy is inadequate in some way, or that the genitals are disgusting. The importance of family influences such as attitude to sex and communication about sex are also illustrated. Scholl (1988) also investigated the incidence of sexual dysfunctions amongst the partners. In five out of the 20 couples, the male was found to exhibit a sexual problem, but Scholl points out that this may be a consequence of the woman's vaginismus and is not necessarily a causal factor. This figure was in keeping with the finding of O'Sullivan (1979) that 26% of husbands exhibited a sexual dysfunction. One final point to emerge from Scholl's study was the use of surgery for some cases of non-consummated marriages. Eight of the original 23 women had received previous surgery designed to facilitate intercourse, but without success. Scholl suggested that attempts at surgery only served to reinforce beliefs in physical abnormalities with these cases. It is interesting to find that surgery continues to be used, given the warnings of Masters and Johnson back in 1970 that medical practitioners frequently mistake the vaginismus response for a pressure-resistant hymen, leading to surgical excision. Unfortunately penetration remains impossible after surgery as the vaginismus reaction tends to remain.

Although a range of precursor factors can be identified for vaginismus, the mechanisms involved in the development of vaginismus remain to be determined conclusively. Various theories have been proposed, including a range of psychoanalytic models, some of which revolve around castration desires. The behavioural model proposes that vaginismus is a conditioned, learned response to actual or anticipated pain, which results in a muscle spasm response and avoidance behaviours. The anticipation of pain may be associated with a history of actual painful intercourse or a range of irrational beliefs concerning the probability of pain. It seems likely that for some women, however, it is not the fear of pain that underlies vaginismus but a more generalized fear of sexual interactions.

4

Assessment of sexual problems

The assessment of sexual problems is a complex process which reflects the multiplicity of variables involved in the human sexual response. Given the wide range of psychosocial and physical factors which may lead to sexual difficulties, the assessment process must be wide ranging and integrate the findings of the physical and psychosocial investigations. Ultimately, the assessment process must provide an indication of those aetiological factors which are operating for a given individual or couple. This information provides the basis for designing an individually tailored intervention programme.

Even if organic causes for a sexual dysfunction are found, it is likely that the person will also experience secondary psychological reactions which confound the problem. There is therefore just as great a need for behavioural assessment of sexual problems which are of organic origin as is required for those problems that are of primary psychogenic cause. In order to understand the assessment process, the cognitive-behaviour therapist requires an extensive knowledge of both physical and psychological influences on sexual behaviour. By understanding the outcome of medical/physical assessment, in addition to the results of the cognitive-behavioural assessment, the practitioner is in a better position to ensure that all appropriate aspects of the problem are tackled.

GENERAL POINTS REGARDING THE ASSESSMENT PROCESS

The majority of clients presenting with sexual difficulties will be involved in a regular relationship with a partner, hence it is important that both persons are involved in the assessment. Given that a sexual relationship involves two people, the difficulty should generally be viewed as one concerning the couple, rather than being any one person's problem. Furthermore, the presence of both members of the partnership has the advantage of maximizing the amount of information provided. Inconsistency between the partners' reports may provide useful information in itself. The assessor is also able to ask each person how they feel their partner would answer each question. This may highlight distortions of perception and misunderstandings, if discrepancies are found.

It is important that the assessor remains flexible about the way in which the assessment is conducted, in order to adapt to the characteristics of each case. Some clients may be single or their partners may not be willing to participate in assessment or therapy. Obviously, the assessor must then rely on information from the client alone. More often, it is possible for both partners to attend and assessment may include an interview with the couple together followed by an interview with each member of the partnership separately.

Some clients may feel anxious or threatened by either the couple or the individual interview format and discretion will be needed in deciding which procedure to use. Throughout the assessment process, it is important that the assessor attempts to make the clients feel relaxed and comfortable. An atmosphere must be created in which the clients feel able to reveal extremely sensitive, personal information in an honest and accurate fashion. This may be facilitated by assuring the clients that such problems are not uncommon and that it is necessary to ask personal information in order to plan an effective treatment strategy. The clients also need to be assured as to the confidentiality of any information revealed. Therapist skills in achieving these goals are likely to be greater if a degree of empathy for the clients' feelings can be obtained. Imagine for a moment that you are attending a clinic for the first time to request help with a very personal, sexual problem. You are shown into a room where you meet a total stranger who begins to ask questions about a topic that is generally not mentioned. For many clients the presenting problem may be associated with a wide range of negative emotions and this may be the first time that the topic has been discussed with anyone other than their partner. If you spend a few moments to create an empathic response as to the likely thoughts and emotions experienced by the client, this may provide indications as to the most appropriate ways of creating a constructive therapist–client relationship.

If members of the partnership are to be interviewed separately, it is debatable whether the interviewer should encourage clients to divulge information that they do not wish their partner to know. On the one hand, it is possible to state at the outset of client contact that all information must be freely shared by the couple. On the other hand, some therapists prefer to elicit such sensitive information, respecting each partner's right to confidentialty. There are advantages and disadvantages to both approaches. Allowing confidential information to be held between the therapist and one member of the partnership may produce dilemmas. For example, the interviewer may discover that one member of the partnerhsip is involved in a satisfactory sexual relationship with someone else, unknown to their partner. This may make therapy a questionable goal, particularly if one member does not really wish to engage in therapy, or does not desire to achieve a satisfactory relationship with the regular partner. The assessor may then need to convey to the couple that therapy is not possible, without divulging the exact reason why. Allowing confidential information to be held between the therapist and one member of the partnership does, however, have the advantage that clients may be more willing to reveal confidential information that is crucial to the understanding of the problem. A further disadvantage of this approach is that some clients may feel very threatened by what their partner may be revealing to the therapist. The decision as to which format to use will depend on the preferred style of the practitioner and the characteristics of the presenting clients.

The style of interviewing used during assessment is also important. In particular, the terminology used must be easily understood by the clients. It is important to avoid the use of technical or medical terms with which the layperson may not be familiar. Frequently, it is useful for the assessor to elicit the jargon or preferred terms used by the clients to refer to various sexual activities or body parts. This can generally be achieved without resorting to excessively slang or impolite terms!

Various interview techniques may be useful in encouraging clients to overcome their reluctance to reveal very personal information. For example, highly personal questions may be inserted amongst other, less threatening questions. Alternatively, questions about sexual behaviours that the client may be reluctant to admit to may be phrased so as to create the assumption that everybody engages in such behaviours, hence normalizing the behaviour (e.g. 'How often do you masturbate?' or 'Are you able to have an orgasm during oral sex?')

81

Throughout the interview, it is important that questions are not presented in a way that leads clients to expect orgasm on every occasion or to see orgasm as an over-valued goal. Where possible, the terms 'achieve', 'attain, and 'reach' should be avoided in relation to orgasm/erections/arousal.

Finally, it is suggested that clients seeking psychological treatment for sexual disorders are asked to undergo an examination by a medical practitioner. It is important that any organically caused sexual disorders receive the appropriate medical intervention necessary for a successful outcome. However, even if organic causes are found, the cognitive-behavioural assessment should still progress, as there may be secondary psychosocial factors which are exacerbating or maintaining the problem and which would benefit from a psychologically based intervention, in conjunction with a medical approach.

THE COGNITIVE-BEHAVIOURAL INTERVIEW

The cognitive-behavioural interview is one of the primary sources of information regarding the nature and aetiology of the sexual disorder. Generally, the information produced is combined with questionnaire assessment data and that revealed from medical and physiological evaluations. The interview can be divided into two main sections:

1. Identification and specification of the presenting problem;
2. Identification of determinants of the problem.

The following plan for the cognitive-behavioural interview is that used in the author's clinical practice and is used in the training of postgraduate trainees in clinical psychology. It is adapted from an assessment guide reported by Wilson *et al.* (1989). Although several other formats for sexual interviewing have been outlined (e.g. Lobitz and Lobitz, 1978; LoPiccolo and Heiman, 1978), the present interview plan is organized according to a framework of cognitive-behavioural assessment. In addition to specific questions, general suggestions for topic areas of questioning are outlined, in order that the practitioner may adapt the interview to the needs of individual cases.

Identification and specification of the problem

The first step in the assessment interview is to determine the exact nature of the problem and why the client is seeking help. In specifying the presenting problem, the assessor needs to identify exactly what the client does overtly, how he or she responds physiologically and what thoughts and emotions are experienced in the cognitive domain. This enables the assessor to determine whether the sexual response of the client(s) differs in any way from normal and whether a problem can be said to exist. The information provided allows the assessor to determine whether a sexual dysfunction is present that requires intervention, or whether the referral is a reflection of unrealistic expectations on the part of the client(s) which would be best dealt with by giving them appropriate information and reassurance. If a genuine dysfunction is evident, this first phase of the assessment permits identification of the exact stage of the sexual response at which the problem occurs, whether it be before sexual interaction begins (e.g. avoidance of sex, or desire to enage in sexual activity), in the arousal stages or the orgasm phase. It also demonstrates the *overt/motoric* (i.e. the actual observable behaviours or responses of the individual), *physiological and cognitive* aspects of sexual behaviour which can be viewed as components of the sexual problem.

The approach taken to the cognitive-behavioural assessment is that sexual behaviour should be assessed in the same way as any other human behaviour, with the recognition that we are dealing with an interaction between two people. Hence, the assessor should consider the *assets, deficits and excesses* of the client(s) in sexual behaviour. This information provides an indication of:

1. The strengths (assets) within the couple's or individual's sexual relationship which intervention should aim to maintain;
2. The deficits in their sexual responding (i.e. behaviours or skills that are lacking) and which need to be enhanced during intervention;
3. Excesses in behaviour, which refer to responses which occur too frequently or intensely and which require reduction during intervention. Examples of excessive sexual behaviours in the sexual context could be ejaculation in an excessively brief period or excessive fearful thoughts concerning sexual interactions.

The assets, deficits and excesses of sexual behaviour may be overt behaviours, cognitions or physiological responses and are identified through careful questioning as to the occurrence, frequency and intensity of each of these aspects at different stages of sexual responding. This process commences with evaluation of sexual urges or desire, progressing to assessment of arousal and orgasm stages of sexual interactions.

Some of the following suggested questions may help the assessor to specify the nature of the problem.

What do you see as being the problem?

What triggered you to seek therapy?

For whom is it a problem? What effect does the problem have on each of you?

Under what circumstances does the problem occur? (When, who with, in what locations?)

When did the problem begin? (Try to establish whether the onset was gradual or sudden.)

Is it always a problem, or is it only problematic in certain circumstances?

When is the problem *not* present? Are things better at some times rather than others (The aim is here to establish whether the problem is situation specific or generalized and whether it is primary, i.e. always having been a problem.)

Can you describe to me what typically happens in your sexual relationship at the moment? (Ask the client(s) to describe their sexual relationship over the past month. Try to obtain some indication of the severity or intensity of the problem.)

How often do you feel the urge or desire to take part in sexual activity with your partner?

Do you try to avoid sex? If so . . . **What methods do you use to try to get out of it?**

How often do you and your partner begin some form of sexual activity? Where would you usually be (location) and when would you try? (time of day, etc.)

Who would make the first move? How is this done?

What do you/he/she say/do? What methods of foreplay do you use? For how long? What kind of foreplay do you enjoy? How often do you give/receive this?

Do you orgasm during intercourse, during petting, during self-pleasuring? (If yes . . . **What type of stimulation is needed? What methods do you use to help you have an orgasm?) Are there any things your partner could do to help which he/she doesn't do now?**

How do you feel emotionally before . . . and during sex? What thoughts are going through your head at different stages? Do you become aroused physically (e.g. erection in the male/lubrication in the female)? Is this ever a problem to you? Do you ever try to vary what you do before and during sex? In what way?
Can you tell me how you would like your sexual relationship to be? How often would you like to have sex? How often would you expect to have an orgasm? What sexual activities would you like to engage in? Can you describe what you think good sex should be like?
How long would you like intercourse to last?

Having determined the nature of the presenting problem, the assessor is then in a position to compare the client's current sexual functioning with what could be considered 'normal' sexual behaviour. This allows the practitioner to decide whether the problem is one of inadequate sexual functioning or unrealistic expectations. Later on in the interview, the role of each member of the partnership in contributing to the problem can be determined. For example, the inadequate response of one member may be the result of inadequate stimulation from the other.

Identification of determinants

During this part of the interview, the assessor needs to separate out the historical and current determinants of the problem. It is likely that the current sources of influence will be those that can be manipulated during therapy to produce behaviour change. The approach taken here assumes that sexual behaviour is influenced by the same principles as other forms of human behaviour. A detailed explanation of cognitive-behavioural models of behaviour is beyond the scope of the present text. It is therefore assumed that the reader has a clear understanding of cognitive-behavioural assessment and the principles underlying it. If this is not the case, a useful summary is provided in a chapter by Barrios (1988). According to this approach, current influences can be classified into the *antecedents* (external and internal in nature) and *consequences* of behaviour. External antecedents refer to events within the environment, such as the partner's touch or the sight of a naked body, which may contribute to successful or problematic sexual responding. Internal antecedents, on the other hand, refer to physiological or cognitive events within the client. Physiological antecedents could be factors such as a state of tiredness, the use of a specific drug, an illness or menstruation. Cognitive antecedents, on the other hand, refer to specific thoughts experienced by the client which influence the sexual response, for example 'I know I am not going to be able to do this.' The assessment of antecedent conditions therefore covers the numerous psychological and physiological factors which influence sexual functioning, as outlined in Chapter 2.

The consequences of the problem behaviour involve internal or external events which happen after the sexual problem occurs. Internal consequences may be specific thoughts or feelings such as 'I will never be able to do this. I'm a real failure' or physiological reactions. External consequences are events coming from outside of the individual such as the response of the partner. A detailed evaluation of possible antecedents and consequences of the behaviour is necessary in order to understand why the problem continues. It also identifies those factors that need to be changed during intervention, whether they be of a cognitive, physiological or external nature.

The following interview guidelines are designed to elicit information regarding current and historical determinants of the sexual problem. The major emphasis should be on current influences, but the role of historic factors should not be ignored, as these may be important in enabling the assessor to fully understand why the problem developed and the type of intervention required. Having obtained the necessary information, the practitioner must then organize it within a comprehensive framework as suggested above in order to develop a treatment strategy.

Relevant background factors

The following outline pinpoints some of the most likely life events which may have occurred and which may have bearing on the clients' current difficulties. The assessor may find other relevant areas that should be covered with particular clients.

Age. (To consider influence of age on sexual behaviour)
Religious and moral influences. **Do you currently belong to a religious group? Is this a serious commitment? Does this influence your views about sex? How about as a child or teenager? What are your strong moral beliefs about sex or any sexual activities?**

Cultural/ethnic influences. **Are there important beliefs in your culture about sex which might be relevant here?** Explore sex roles, in particular, sexual taboos, etc.

Parental influences. **What kind of attitudes did your parents have towards sex? Was sex discussed in the home? Did your parents give you any education about sex?**

Educational level. Age upon leaving school/college, attainments if relevant.

Puberty/menstruation.

Male: **How old were you when you first became aware of having erections? When did you first ejaculate? Did you have any problems related to going through puberty? What were your parents' attitudes towards you at this time?**

Female: **How old were you when you had your first period? Had you been warned in advance about this? Did you have any problems with your periods? How about now?**

Work history. **Have you been in regular employment? What type? How about now? Do you find your work very demanding or tiring? What kind of hours do you work? Do you have any stresses or worries related to your job? How secure is your current position?**

Leisure and social activities (current and historical). **Do you have any hobbies, interests or activities? Do you go out much socially? Who with? What type of social events? Do you have many friends. How much contact do you have with them? Did you make friends easily as a child?**

Previous relationships. **How old were you when you first started dating? How serious were these relationships? How long did they last? How did you feel when they ended? Have you been married before? Can you tell me about that?**

Children and pregnancies. **Do you have any children? How old are they? Are they currently living with you? How do you get on as a family? Are there any problems related to children that concern you?**

Female: **Have you experienced any difficulties related to pregnancy? Have you suffered any miscarriages?**

Non-sexual stress event. **Have you experienced any events in your life which caused you upset or worry? How about any illnesses or financial problems? Have there been any deaths in the family? When did this happen? How did it affect you? Have you ever experienced any psychiatric problems?** Explore details. The possible role of anxiety and depression also needs to be explored.

Health and medication. **Are you currently taking any medication? What type is it? What is it for? How about in the past, have you had any major illnesses? Do you suffer from any diseases or health problems? When did you last have a medical check-up? Do you find that you feel particularly tired and that this may interfere with your sex life?**
Female: **Do you currently have any problems with your periods? If so, does this affect your sex life at all?** For middle-aged females the assessor should explore details regarding menopause and whether problems have been experienced.
Have you recently taken any non-prescription drugs, such as LSD, heroin or amphetamines? How about previously? How much alcohol do you drink each week? Do you drink most days?

Sexual history

It is important to explore the clients' previous sexual experiences and sexual development in order to identify the exact nature of the problem and any factors which may account for the current difficulties. Further information may be revealed regarding where and when the sexual dysfunction occurs or does not occur. Depending on the couple, the interviewer must decide whether to cover this section with the partners together or apart. Some clients may feel very reluctant to discuss sexual details in front of their partner and it is advisable to ask each member of the partnership which format they would prefer. The following areas should be considered when taking a sexual history.

Early sexual experiences. **Can you remember playing sexual games as a child? How about as an adolescent? Can you recall any sexual foreplay or petting before you first had intercourse with someone? Did you find this arousing? What happened, did you have an orgasm? Can you tell me about the first time you experienced orgasm? . . . and about the first time you had intercourse? Do you know much about sex and how best to stimulate your partner? What books have you read about sex?**
It is important for the assessor to confirm the accuracy of sexual knowledge at a later stage to ensure that the information held by the client with regard to anatomy and sexual techniques is correct.

Masturbation and self-pleasuring. **How old were you when you first started to masturbate? How often do you do this currently? How about in the past? Do you need any particular type of stimulation for orgasm when you masturbate? How would you describe your attitude towards masturbation?** (In cases of erectile failure, questions should be asked concerning whether the erection would be adequate to allow penetration.)

Nocturnal penile tumescence and emissions (males). **Do you wake up in the night with an erect penis? What about in the mornings? About how many times per month? If you haven't noticed, has your partner ever commented on this? Have you ever actually ejaculated in your sleep or during a dream? When was this? . . . how often? . . . does this still happen now?**

Use of erotic materials and fantasy. **Do you get turned on by any particular things, like sexy pictures, stories or films? Which do you find most arousing? Are there any other things, like perfumes or music? Anything else? Do you or your partner use any of these things now to turn you on during sex? How about previously? Do you use any kinds of fantasies during sex? Can you tell me about these? How about when you masturbate?**

Adult sexual relationships. **Can you tell me about your sexual experiences as an adult? Have you been involved in sexual relationships before this one? Did you become aroused during previous sexual relationships? Did you orgasm during these?**

Previous sexual problems and treatments. **Have you experienced any sexual problems in any of your previous sexual relationships? Can you describe these? How long ago was this? Did you seek any treatment? Can you recall what action the therapist suggested? How successful was this? Have you had any other sexual difficulties in your current relationship?**

Sexual stress events. **Have you experienced any events in your life that caused distress or worry that were related to sex or pregnancy?**
It is important here to consider events such as being raped, an incestuous relationship, an unwanted pregnancy or abortion. Bear in mind that the client may be reluctant to divulge this information initially and it may be several sessions before sufficient trust is established to enable the client to disclose details relevant to such sensitive incidents.

Current relationship

Nature of current relationship. Details of the current relationship need collecting from both a sexual and non-sexual perspective, as both may influence each partner's responsiveness during sex. Much information can be obtained from interview, but self report inventories, as outlined later in this chapter, may provide a useful adjunct.
Can you tell me about the relationship you are involved in now? Are you married? If not, ask about the frequency of contact, type of relationship, etc. **How long have you been together? How long did you go out together before you got married? Did you go away on a honeymoon? How did you get on sexually in the early stages of your relationship? What attracted you to each other sexually in the early days?**

Sexual experiences early in the relationship. **When did you first have sex together? Did you both orgasm when you first started having sex together? What kind of things have changed in your sexual relationship from then to now?**

Common activities and interests. **What kind of things do you do together besides sex? Do you spend much time chatting together? How often do you go out together as a couple? Would you like to spend more time together? Do you have many interests in common? What do you do together on a typical weekend?**

Feelings of physical attraction, arousal and emotion. **Do you find your partner physically attractive? Does it turn you on to see him/her in the nude? Do you feel aroused when he/she touches you sexually? How would you best describe your feelings for you partner? Does this change during sex . . . and if so, can you describe these feelings? Do you really want to have a good sexual relationship with your partner? How much do want to have sex with him/her?**

General satisfaction with the relationship. **How satisfactory is your relationship generally? Do you get on well together? Are there any aspects of your relationship, other than sex, that you would like to change? Does your partner have any habits that you feel are contributing to the difficulties the two of you are having sexually?**

Communication between the couple. **How well do you communicate with each other? Do either of you find it hard to** express your feelings? How about during sex, do you talk much then? Can you both say what things you would like the other to do? Do you actually ask? Do you say when you like something? What kinds of things would you say? How do you go about refusing sex when you don't feel like it? How about when you do feel like it, do you let your partner know?

Issues regarding contraception. Are you or your partner using any form of contraception? If so . . . What type? Have you had any problems with this form of contraception? Do you have any worries about contraception? Do either of you have any worries about becoming pregnant?

Attitude regarding sex roles, self and treatment

Various aspects of the clients' cognitions can be explored at this stage. These may have important implications for maintenance of the problem and may need to be modified where maladaptive.

Ideals about sex. How do you think a man should ideally behave sexually? How about a woman? How do you think you differ from this ideal? How about your partner? Can you describe to me how you would really like your sexual relationship to be? What kinds of activities would you both do . . . How often?

Self-image. Do you think that your partner finds you sexually attractive? Do you feel attractive to the opposite sex? Do you feel that you are sufficiently masculine/feminine?

Sexual attitudes generally. How would you describe your attitude to nudity . . . to masturbation . . . to sexual cleanliness? What are your feelings about sex during menstruation? Is this a problem at all in your sexual relationship? Do either of you find semen unpleasant? What about female lubrication, and its taste and smell?

Interview content for specific sexual problems

The above outline summarizes the areas of questioning that would be relevant for the majority of cases presenting with sexual difficulties. Obviously there are also a range of questions that are specific to certain types of presenting problems which warrant a mention.

Hypoactive sexual desire disorder

The following questions aim to determine whether the lack of sexual desire is global or specific to particular types of sexual activity. The assessor also needs to distinguish between lack of desire and active avoidance of or aversion to sexual situations. Similarly, it is important to establish whether the problem is limited to sexual desire, with arousal and orgasm being unaffected if/when the individual does engage in sexual activity, or whether the problem includes all three aspects of the sexual response cycle.

- How often does sex occur? What activities are involved? When does it occur?
- Are there any particular times when sexual desires or urges are felt? These situations should be described.
- Ask the client to imagine that the partner makes a sexual approach. What thoughts would be going through his/her mind? How would he/she be feeling?
- How often does the client masturbate? What are his/her views about masturbation?
- What type of sexual activities does the client think about during fantasies? How often does he/she fantasize?
- If sexual desire occurs and sexual activity begins, does the client become sexually aroused? . . . Does orgasm occur?
- Ask both partners to describe their non-sexual relationship. How do they get on with each other generally?

Sexual aversion disorder

If the assessment indicates that the problem may be one of sexual aversion or sexual phobia, the assessor needs to establish the exact nature of the aversion response. These include the cognitive components of the problem (e.g. the actual thoughts and emotions that occur), the physiological reactions that are experienced and the behavioural responses. The questions need to determine the situations which trigger the aversion responses and the consequences of the behaviour. Many of the questions included in the general interview will provide some answers to these questions, but additional information may be obtained through the following line of questioning.

- Ask the client to describe his/her feelings about sexual situations (it is important to get the client to identify the exact emotional reactions, such as guilt, anxiety, fear or disgust).
- What would he/she be saying to him/herself during different sexual activities? What about at the start of intercourse?
- What bodily reactions occur in the problem situations? (e.g. sweating, muscle tension, shaking, nausea.)
- Does the client try to avoid having sexual contact with the partner? What behaviours occur in order to avoid sex? What types of sexual activity are avoided most?
- What sexual situations make the client feel worst of all? Are there any types of sexual contact that are found to be pleasant?
- How does the partner react to refusals to have sex?
- How does the client feel about physical contact with the partner that does not involve sex, such as kissing or cuddling?
- The assessor will typically need to develop a hierarchy of trigger situations as described in Chapter 6.

Erectile disorder

The interview information should provide an indication of whether the disorder is organic or psychogenic in origin, and provide pointers to likely causal factors. Although a medical assessment is essential in cases of erectile failure, the behavioural assessment should also cover topics relating to likely physical causes for the disorder, as this information can be used for cross validation with the medical evaluation. Questions should cover the following.

- The presence/absence/frequency of morning erections and whether these are sufficient to allow penetration.
- The presence/absence/frequency of erections during sleep and whether these are sufficient to allow penetration.
- The presence/absence/frequency of erections during self-stimulation and whether these are sufficient to allow penetration.
- The presence/absence/frequency of erections during fantasy or while watching/reading/listening to erotic material and whether these are sufficient to allow penetration.
- The presence/absence/frequency of erections with other partners and whether these are sufficient to allow penetration.

- The course of development of the problem, whether of rapid or gradual onset.
- Detailed coverage of alcohol use and health-related items as outlined above.
- Detailed assessment of cognitions before, during and after situations in which erections are desired, in order to establish cognitive events which may be maintaining the problem.
- Investigation of likely trigger events which are known to be associated with erectile failure, both organic and psychogenic.
- Does erection occur and then fade at a particular point (e.g. just before or immediately upon vaginal entry)?

Female sexual arousal disorder

As with male arousal disorders, it is important to determine whether the inhibition of sexual arousal is related to organic factors. Assessment also needs to determine whether the lack of sexual arousal is secondary to lack of desire and whether orgasmic difficulty is also present. The distinction between cognitive feelings of desire and the physiological components of the arousal response should be investigated. Similarly, it needs to be established whether the problem is global or specific to certain situations.

- How often does the client feel the desire for sexual activity?
- What type of sexual activities are likely to produce sexual arousal?
- What happens when the client has sexual fantasies? . . . Does she become sexually aroused?
- How often does she have sexual fantasies?
- Are any types of sexual activity found to be pleasant? What are these? Does vaginal lubrication occur?
- Does the client ever reach orgasm? What methods are used to produce this?
- Does the client become sexually aroused during self-stimulation?
- What would be some examples of the client's thoughts during sexual activity with her partner?

Inhibited female orgasm

It is important to check whether the problem has developed after the client has previously been orgasmic in the situation of concern, as this may suggest organicity (see Chapter 2 for discussion of organic factors which may impair orgasm).

- Are there any situations in which orgasm occurs now . . . or occurred previously?
- Has the client tried to use a vibrator? If so, with what result? What is her attitude to the use of a vibrator?
- What is her attitude to self-stimulation? And to use of erotic materials? The response to these questions obviously has important implications for the use of these approaches in therapy.
- Exactly what methods does the client/partner use when attempting to reach orgasm? Is clitoral stimulation by self/partner perceived as pleasurable or uncomfortable?
- Does the client become sexually aroused and then fail to progress to orgasm or is there a lack of arousal too?
- Is the client able to relax and focus her attention on sensations during stimulation?
- What are the client's sexual attitudes regarding the female role during sex?
- If the problem is specific to sexual situations involving the partner, detailed questioning should be conducted regarding feelings about the partner, the ability of the couple to communicate sexually and the partner's sexual skills and knowledge.

Inhibited male orgasm

In addition to the general interview questions, Kaplan (1983) suggests that the following questions are relevant for couples presenting with a problem of delayed ejaculation.

- Does ejaculation occur during self-stimulation and if so, after how long? . . . And during partner manual stimulation?
- If not, has ejaculation ever occurred? If so, in what situations?
- Does ejaculation ever occur during sleep?
- What thoughts occur during sexual stimulation in situations in which ejaculation is delayed? In particular, thoughts relating to spectatoring need to be identified.
- Does the client use fantasy to assist ejaculation? Does this occur during self-stimulation? And during intercourse?
- What does he see as being different between situations in which ejaculation is delayed versus not delayed (if situational)?

- Is he able to focus his attention on sexual feelings and relax?
- Does he feel sexually aroused during the stimulation? Is stimulation perceived as pleasurable?
- Does the male find his partner sexually attractive? Ask him to describe his ideal sexual partner.
- What methods has he tried in order to speed up ejaculation? Have any of these helped?
- Has the problem always been present? Was onset rapid or gradual?

Premature ejaculation

- The frequency of masturbation and intercourse is relevant here, given that time taken for ejaculation tends to decline with more frequent ejaculation patterns. Hence, infrequent intercourse may be associated with faster ejaculation when intercourse does occur (Kaplan, 1983).
- Is control over ejaculation easier during masturbation? How long can self-stimulation last before ejaculation occurs?
- At what point does ejaculation occur? (e.g. before vaginal entry or immediately after penetration?)
- What is the partner's response when ejaculation occurs quickly?
- What methods are currently used to delay ejaculation? What methods work best?
- What thoughts occur before and during penetration?
- Do any factors make the problem worse?

Dyspareunia

Obviously the medical assessment is of crucial importance for referrals involving dyspareunia. The cognitive-behavioural assessment may add to the medical evaluation through a detailed exploration of the problem and its determinants.

- It is important to establish the exact location of the pain, whether it occurs with the anticipation of sex, during foreplay/arousal, at the onset of penetration, during deep thrusting, at the point of orgasm or during the refractory period. The information obtained should be shared with the medical practitioner in order that a detailed picture of the problem emerges.

- It is also important to establish whether orgasm occurs after prolonged periods of arousal, in order to establish whether pain may be associated with prolonged vasocongestion.
- Does the pain always occur in the identified trigger situation? Has it always been the case, or when did the problem begin?
- If the pain is associated with penetration, does it also occur during medical examination or tampon insertion?
- Does lubrication occur during foreplay? Is the foreplay period adequate? How skilled is the partner in arousing the woman?

Vaginismus

In addition to the basic sexual interview questions the assessor needs to establish a hierarchy of situations that can be used in a desensitization approach to treatment. It is important to establish the point at which the muscle contraction response commences and whether this is preceded by thoughts relating to fear, anxiety, disgust or anticipation of pain which could be suggested to trigger the behaviour. Given that the vaginismus response may be triggered by imagined as well as real sexual stimuli, the questioning needs to cover a range of imaginal situations. By taking recent examples, and by exploring a wide range of situations, a hierarchy of vaginismus trigger situations can be developed. For example:

- Reading material with sexual content;
- Shaking hands with the opposite sex;
- Partner undressing in the bathroom before he gets into bed;
- Kissing partner when he gets into bed;
- Oral sex with partner.

It is important to distinguish generalized sexual anxiety from vaginismus. For most cases of vaginismus, the vaginismus response only occurs when penetration is anticipated. It is not the situation per se which triggers the muscle contraction, but the client's cognitions about likely penetration. It is important that the assessor determines the exact cognitions that are associated with each trigger situation, as the emphasis of treatment may vary. The focus of cognitive restructuring and exposure treatments will differ according to the stimuli that generate anxiety and the specific thoughts that occur in the feared situations.

- Hence, it is important to establish exactly what the client's thoughts are in those situations which trigger a vaginismus response. In particular, thoughts regarding pain, that sex is dirty or disgusting, that the vagina is not large enough or the penis too big, should be elicited.
- The possibility of sexual trauma events should be explored.
- Is the problem associated with a lack of desire or arousal?
- What avoidance behaviours does the client engage in?

INFORMATION FROM OTHER SOURCES

Although it may seem that the content for the interview is enormously detailed, this is necessary given the great complexity of the human sexual response. The collection of data during assessment will generally involve two to three sessions prior to the onset of therapy. In addition to interview data, valuable information may also be obtained from a wide range of self-report instruments and self-monitoring. These methods have the advantage of being less embarrassing to some clients and may be completed at home, saving professional time.

Self-report assessment measures

Extensive batteries or those that assess satisfaction with the sexual relationship

Many self-report questionnaires are available from which the client's sexual behaviour, attitudes and responsiveness can be assessed. These range from extremely extensive instruments which cover various aspects of sexual functioning, to those that have a more specific focus. One of the most extensive instruments is the Derogatis Sexual Functioning Inventory (DSFI, 1975, revised 1978), which assesses the individual's level of current sexual functioning. There are ten primary content areas, namely sexual information, sexual experience, desire/drive, sexual attitudes, affect/emotions, symptoms of psychopathology, gender–role definition, fantasy, body image and sexual satisfaction. Each scale produces a standardized T score and a global Sexual Functioning Index may be obtained. The internal consistency and test–retest reliability of the scales are reported to be good (Derogatis *et al.*, 1988) and the instrument has been shown to discriminate between sexually dysfunctional and non-dysfunctional individuals (Derogatis and Meyer, 1979). The greatest advantage of the DSFI is its wide-ranging coverage of different aspects of sexuality and its inclusion of a general psychopathology measure, which permits identification of relevant psychological problems such as depression or anxiety. As such, it provides an excellent self-report method for use in clinical and research situations.

Other available self-report measures tend to have a more specific focus. In terms of the assessment of satisfaction with the sexual relationship, the most well-known measure is probably the Sexual Interaction Inventory (SII; LoPiccolo and Steger, 1974). The SII has been reported to have acceptable reliability and to discriminate between sexually dysfunctional and non-dysfunctional couples (LoPiccolo and Steger, 1974). It consists of a list of 17 heterosexual behaviours to which the male and female are separately asked to respond to six questions. For example, question 16 states 'The male and the female having intercourse'. Each partner is asked to rate this activity on six 6-point scales concerning the frequency of occurrence, preferred frequency of occurrence, how pleasant they find it, how pleasant they feel their partner finds it, how pleasant they would like it to be ideally and how pleasant they would like their partner to find it, ideally. This procedure is rather complicated and time consuming for the couple and the scoring is equally complex. Responses from each partner are summed across all 17 behaviours in order to derive an 11-scale profile. These scales reflect the difference between actual and desired frequency of activities and between preferred activities of each member of the partnership. An overall difference score is also produced for the couple. If clients and assessors can be encouraged to persevere with the SII, despite its complexity, it reveals extremely valuable information about the satisfaction of the couple with their sexual relationship.

A recent addition to the assessment of sexual satisfaction and functioning is the Golombok–Rust Inventory of Sexual Satisfaction (GRISS: Rust and Golombok, 1986). This is a short, 28-item self-report instrument, with separate versions for males and females. Scales concerning dissatisfaction, avoidance, non-sensuality, infrequency, vaginismus, anorgasmia, impotence and premature ejaculation are produced and these have been confirmed through factor analysis. The subscales are reported to be of acceptable test–retest reliability and internal consistency, with questionnaire responses being sensitive to treatment effects (Rust and Golombok, 1986). Clinical groups were also reported by these authors to differ significantly from non-dysfunctional controls on relevant subscales. Rust and Golombok suggest that the main use of this questionnaire is in the evaluation of treatment outcome in sex therapy programmes. The number of questions concerning each dysfunction are, however, few and many questions may be irrelevant to some clients. There is a danger, therefore, that important treatment benefits may be missed for some clients whose progress is not evaluated by the questionnaire. It is suggested that additional outcome data should also be collected, such as specific target data for each couple, rather than relying solely on a multi-problem questionnaire. Nevertheless, the GRISS is certainly much shorter to administer and easier to score than the SII and has the added advantage of screening for the presence of specific sexual dysfunctions, whereas the SII is limited to the assessment of sexual satisfaction. Ideally, the assessment of treatment outcome should consider both satisfaction with the sexual relationship and changes in the exact target behaviours which were the focus of treatment, as it is possible for marked change to occur in sexual satisfaction without concomitant changes in the targeted responses (e.g. ability to attain an erection during intercourse).

A valuable alternative to the GRISS is a 28-item multiple-choice sexual history questionnaire described by Schover *et al.* (1980, 1982). The questions cover actual and desired frequency of sexual activities, initiations for sex, satisfaction, specific sexual problems and duration of important sexual activities. The responses are integrated within a multi-axial classification system to produce a description of the presenting problem(s). Another method which may be useful in screening couples in order to identify problems of sexual adjustment that may warrant intervention is the Self-Evaluation of Sexual Behaviour and Gratification questionnaire (SSBG; Lief, 1981), which assesses sexual activities, duration of sex play, frequency of sexual intercourse and satisfaction with frequency.

Sexual activities, experience and knowledge

The most widely used questionnaire to assess what sexual activities people actually take part in is the Bentler Scale (Bentler, 1967, 1968), which may be used to assess the frequency of occurrence of 21 heterosexual behaviours. Separate forms are available for males and females, and its psychometric properties are acceptable. The major problem with the Bentler Scale concerns its outdated terminology, which needs to be adapted for use in current clinical practice. Bentler (1968) initially suggested that the questionnaire could be used to assess response to systematic desensitization in the treatment of sexual phobias, but it is also valuable as an indication of sexual activity levels in clients whose difficulties include a low frequency of occurrence of heterosexual activities. It does not, however, assess whether the activities were satisfactory for those involved nor whether any sexual problems occurred. Alternative methods of assessing sexual activity include the Experience Scale of the DSFI as outlined above and the Heterosexual Behaviour Inventory (Robinson and Annon, 1975).

A useful measure of sexual knowledge is the Sexual Knowledge and Attitude Test (SKAT; Lief and Reed, 1972), which assesses a wide range of sexual activities and also explores the client's attitudes and knowledge in relation to various aspects of sex. This measure has been widely researched and standardized, albeit with a student population.

Sexual arousal, interest and anxiety

The Sexual Arousal Inventory (SAI; Hoon *et al.*, 1976) is a frequently used means of assessing arousal in women. This involves a list of 28 sexual activities for which clients must rate, on a 7-point Likert scale, the degree to which arousal is affected adversely or positively. Its psychometric properties have been investigated with a population of North American women. A similar scale is available for men (Annon, 1975). Although the female scale has been widely used, it is only recently that data concerning its reliability and validity have become available. Andersen *et al.* (1989) investigated the psychometric properties of the SAI with a group of 57 normal, sexually active women and a comparison sample of 66 women who were about to undergo surgical gynaecological treatment that was predicted to result in sexual difficulties. The scale was found to have excellent test–retest reliability and internal consistency. Factor analysis revealed a five-factor solution accounting for 85% of the variance, with this factor structure remaining constant across the two groups of women and over time. The factors assessed erotica and masturbation, body caressing, seductive activities, oral–genital and genital stimulation and intercourse situations, thus supporting the construct validity of the questionnaire. The SAI was not able, however, to predict the occurrence of sexual dysfunction in the clinical sample, either concurrently or at the time of follow-up.

101

Harbison *et al.* (1974) developed an interesting method for assessing interest in sexual activities. The technique asks clients to evaluate five sexual activities (kissing the partner, being kissed by the partner, touching sexually, being touched sexually and sexual intercourse) in terms of four bipolar scales (seductive–repulsive, sexy–sexless, exciting–dull, erotic–frigid). Each scale has five positions upon which the activity can be judged. Test–retest reliability and internal consistency are reported to be good and normative data are provided (Harbison *et al.*, 1974). These authors demonstrated that male and female sexually dysfunctional clients reported significantly lower sexual interest scores than non-dysfunctional controls, with the female clinical sample reporting particularly low scores.

Patterson and O'Gorman (1986) report an adaptation of this method for assessing sexual anxiety which they named the Sexual Orientation Method and Anxiety (SOMA). Using a similar questionnaire structure, a self-report method was developed which includes 112 items. The authors report good psychometric properties, ability of the questionnaire to discriminate between a client group and non-clinical controls and the ability to assess sexual anxiety as distinct from general anxiety. The SOMA is suggested to allow greater evaluation of the degree of sexual anxiety than other methods such as that reported by Janda and O'Grady (1980), which simply involves 25 items in forced choice response format, in which one choice reflects sexual anxiety. An alternative method of assessing sexual anxiety was reported by Spence (1985), which asks clients to rate their degree of anxiety during 21 sexual situations on a 5-point scale ranging from 1 (extremely anxious) to 5 (not at all anxious). The situations were taken from the Bentler (1968) questionnaire of sexual activities, although the terminology was updated to suit current usage.

Sexual attitudes

Although a considerable amount of information concerning attitudes towards various aspects of sex may be revealed during the interview, there are several questionnaires that can be used to assess such attitudes and beliefs in more depth. The attitude scale of the DSFI (see above) contains 30 statements relating to liberal versus conservative beliefs concerning sexual behaviour. The SKAT (see above) provides a measure of attitudes to heterosexual relations, sexual myths, abortion and masturbation. Although the SKAT is probably most useful in a research context, the attitude scales are of considerable value in a clinical situation. A recent study reported by Baker and DeSilva (1988) outlines an alternative attitudinal scale for use with males, which evaluates acceptance of Zilbergeld's myths of sexual functioning (see Chapter 2).

Questionnaires can therefore be used to assess attitudes and beliefs regarding issues such as:

- What sexual behaviours are normal?
- Sex roles: who should do what to whom . . . and when?
- The role of orgasm in sex.
- Self-image regarding sex.

In addition to attitudes and beliefs, the assessment should also identify specific thoughts (self-statements) which are relevant to the presenting problem. This may be achieved through interview or self-monitoring (see below). In the cognitive arena, the person's ability to use fantasy and to focus attention on bodily sensations during sex should also be explored, generally during the interview.

Marital questionnaires

Given that the quality of the couple's relationship has important implications for the decision to proceed with intervention and in the design of therapy programmes, it is essential that the assessment process evaluates this area. Various self-report measures exist for the assessment of marital satisfaction. The Locke–Wallace (1959) Marital Adjustment Scale was widely used for many years but is now frequently replaced by the Dyadic Adjustment Scale (DAS; Spanier, 1976). This 32-item scale incorporates the 15 items of the Locke–Wallace and has been factor analysed to yield scales of consensus, satisfaction, cohesion and affectional expression. Alternatively, a total score may be used. The scale has been shown to discriminate well between distressed and non-distressed couples and has good psychometric properties (Spanier, 1976). It also has the advantage of being phrased in terms suitable for de facto relationships, rather than assuming formal marital status. A wide range of alternative methods are available for assessing the quality of the relationship in more depth. Whilst the DAS is a useful screen for

103

relationship difficulties it does not provide a detailed analysis of the couple's interactions and difficulties. It is important to establish the general communication skills of the couple, their ability to express affection and feelings, whether each partner actually 'likes' the other, whether the couple engages in positive activities together and whether they have time alone together. This information can generally be obtained during the assessment interviews, but numerous marital evaluation methods are available if a more extensive investigation is required. A detailed summary of marital assessment methods can be found in Margolin *et al.* (1988).

Sexual communication skills

The majority of self-report instruments that have been developed for the assessment of sexual communication skills were designed for use by college students, hence they may not always be appropriate for use with clinical populations. Furthermore, measures such as the Survey of Heterosexual Interactions (Twentyman and McFall, 1975) tend to be limited to the early stages of dating and do not cover communication during the more advanced stages of sexual interactions. Spence (1983) outlined an approach to the assessment of sexual communication skills which incorporates data from self-report with information from the partner and direct behavioural observation during role play. Assessment should focus both on micro-skills (such as use of appropriate eye contact, facial expression, tone of voice) and macro-skills which refer to strategies of responding to particular sexual situations. There is also a need to assess the client's ability to correctly interpret their partner's non-verbal cues. The assessor needs to consider communication skills in a wide range of sexual situations, including:

- Initiating sexual activity with a partner;
- Requesting a particular activity;
- Providing feedback to the partner about what activities or types of stimulation are pleasurable/not pleasurable;
- Expressing affection and other emotions;
- Refusing a partner's sexual advances.

In each situation the assessor needs to establish each client's ability to communicate effectively, in a way that leads to a successful outcome. Given the lack of suitable self-report questionnaires for evaluation of these areas, the assessor may find it useful to create role-play situations in the clinic in which the clients are asked to respond *verbally* to each of the above situations in a way that reflects the couple's usual communication strategies at home. Self-monitoring methods (see below) may also provide a useful source of information concerning communication skills during sexual interactions.

Self-monitoring tasks

Valuable information may be obtained by having clients complete various self-monitoring tasks. If clients can be trained to record observations from the natural setting, then this overcomes the ethical and practical constraints of direct behavioural observation. There are many aspects of sexual responding that couples can be asked to observe and record, such as frequency of certain events or activities, antecedents and consequences of target behaviours and emotions or specific thoughts before, during and after specified events. This information facilitates the behavioural assessment process and may provide details of which the couple were previously unaware, or which may not have emerged from interview and questionnaire evaluations. The type of information that the couple are asked to record will vary according to the presenting problem, hence a fixed format for self-monitoring is not appropriate. The example given below is taken from a case in which the couple presented with a problem of difficulty attaining an erection during intercourse. The man had great difficulty in describing his thoughts during sexual activity, hence the self-monitoring task shown in Table 4.1 was assigned. (Note: during the assessment phase, the couple were asked to continue to engage in sexual activities as usual, which in this case included attempts at intercourse. Given that this period was considered an essential part of the assessment, no ban on attempted sexual activities was given at this stage.)

Table 4.1 Self-monitoring example

Date	What type of sexual activity?	What were your thoughts before the activity began?	What were your thoughts during the activity?	What were your thoughts after the activity?
15 Oct.	Stroking my penis. She wants to make love	What am I going to do if she wants to make love tonight? What excuse can I use to get out of it?	Oh, no. Not again. Nothing's happening. I knew this would happen	Thank goodness that's over. I feel awful – such a failure, humiliated. I'll have to make sure we don't try again – it's bound to fail

As with self-monitoring of any aspect of behaviour, the assessor should be aware of the possibility of reactive effects which lead to a change in behaviour from that which would ordinarily occur. Reactive effects may lead to an improvement or deterioration in behaviour, hence it is important to use self-monitoring tasks cautiously. For example, it is possible that certain clients may react adversely to being asked to monitor the strength of their erections or duration of penetration prior to ejaculation. Recent evidence suggests that self-monitoring of erection quality and concern about erection by men with erectile difficulty does *not* generally lead to a negative effect on sexual functioning (Fichten *et al.*, 1988). This finding is interesting in view of the results of a study by Abrahamson *et al.* (1989), who report that males with erectile difficulties showed reduced penile response to erotic stimuli in high-demand conditions. The apparent difference in results may perhaps be explained if the self-monitoring task is not perceived as a high-demand situation. If self-monitoring is conducted in a way that does not create high-demand perceptions for the client, then this may reduce possible adverse effects on sexual performance.

Psychophysiological recordings

Although psychophysiological recordings may provide valuable information to supplement the assessment process, the majority of cognitive-behaviour therapists do not possess the necessary equipment to conduct such evaluations. Furthermore, many non-medical practitioners feel uncomfortable using this type of equipment with their clients. The decision as to whether to make use of psychophysiological recordings therefore depends on the availability of equipment and the desire of the practitioner to use it. Conte (1986) points out that psychophysiological data provide information about arousability in particular situations for both males and females which may have important implications for the type of intervention to be used. Details concerning psychophysiological assessment are provided below, under the topic of medical and physiological assessment, although it is recognized that some assessors may wish to conduct their own psychophysiological evaluations, rather than relying on information from medical practitioners.

UNDERSTANDING THE MEDICAL AND PHYSIOLOGICAL ASSESSMENT PROCESS

Although the majority of readers of this book will not be medically qualified and will therefore not conduct the medical aspects of the assessment, it is important that all persons who are involved in the assessment and treatment of sexual problems are able to understand the nature of the medical and physiological assessments that are likely to be carried out. Non-medical personnel may indeed be involved in the assessment of sexual functioning using physiological measurement methods, such as penile plethysmography, which have not been limited to use by the medical profession.

Traditionally it has been held that certain characteristics of sexual responding can be identified that suggest organic rather than psychosocial causes for sexual dysfunction. With male clients, for example, the selective occurrence of erection or orgasm, rather than total absence, has frequently been proposed to imply a psychosocial aetiology, whereas total absence of these responses may be more indicative of an organic aetiology. Similarly, an organic cause for ejaculatory failure is often assumed to be unlikely if the male can masturbate to orgasm but cannot achieve ejaculation during coitus. Freund and Blanchard (1981), however, caution as to drawing conclusions concerning organic versus psychosocial aetiology on the basis of such simplistic criteria. These authors point out that an organic basis should not be excluded when intermittent sexual functioning is present. Hence the presence of nocturnal penile tumescence should not necessarily be taken as definite evidence against the involvement of organic factors in erectile failure. Similarly, the ability to masturbate to orgasm or achieve an erection during masturbation should not be taken as conclusive evidence against organic involvement in orgasmic dysfunction or erectile failure. Given the enormous complexity of the biological systems involved in sexual behaviour, it is suggested strongly here that the task of excluding organic variables is left to suitably qualified medical practitioners. Nevertheless, the assessor should acquire an adequate knowledge of the numerous organic determinants of sexual dysfunction.

In the medical evaluation, the practitioner is likely to commence with a detailed interview concerning the description and history of the presenting problem, with particular emphasis on indicators of organicity. The content normally covers the general health of the client(s), specific illnesses known to be associated with the sexual problem being presented and drug usage. The development of the problem is explored, in order to determine whether onset was gradual or sudden, whether it coincided with any specific health issues and whether the severity of the problem is increasing. The assessment then typically progresses to a physical examination, the nature of which varies according to the presenting problem. Basically, the physician explores any possible physical malformations or injury to the sexual body parts or related structures which could explain the sexual dysfunction. Evaluation of vascular, endocrine and neurological factors associated with sexual dysfunction would also be considered during the medical assessment.

Physiological and medical assessment of erectile failure

Erectile difficulty is probably the area of sexual dysfunction that has been found to be most frequently linked with organic aetiology. Estimates vary across different studies but it is becoming increasingly clear that a sizeable proportion, suggested to be in excess of 30%, of erectile problems are the result of organic causes (Segraves *et al.* 1987; Virag *et al.*, 1985). As erectile problems may result from a variety of neurological, endocrine and vascular influences, various assessments have been developed in order to evaluate these areas. These include a detailed sexual interview, endocrine assessments, evaluation of nocturnal penile tumescence (NPT), penile blood pressure, penile brachial index (PBI), bulbar cavernosal latency responding, penile perfusion, cavernosography, arteriography and response to pharmacological agents (Williams, 1987). A brief summary of these methods will be outlined here.

The sexual history: in search of organic factors of erectile dysfunction

Various indicators which can be elicited from careful questioning of the client have been suggested to be indicative of organic cause of erectile dysfunction. Segraves *et al.* (1987) reported that the single best predictor of organic versus psychogenic aetiology was the presence or absence of early morning erections as reported by the patient. The response to this question alone correctly classified 100% of their sample of organic erectile failure and 86% of psychogenic cases. This question asked: 'During the last month did you experience erections upon wakening greater than or equal to two per week? [yes/no] and if you experienced two per week erections upon wakening was the erection sufficient for vaginal penetration? [yes/no]' (p. 135). Two other questions were found to discriminate between these two groups to a statistically significant degree, namely (1) presence/absence of adequate masturbatory erections (during masturbation are your erections sufficient for vaginal penetration? [yes/no]) and (2) presence/absence of adequate non-coital erections (do you have frequent and lasting erections during non-coital activity or fantasy, for example during foreplay? [yes/no]). Men with an assumed organic aetiology tended to report the absence of turgid erections in these situations.

Nocturnal penile tumescence

This test is based on the finding that most men experience penile tumescence during REM sleep. The frequency, strength and size of such erections tends to decline with age and varies across individuals. Underlying the use of this test is the assumption that psychogenic influences over erectile functioning do not operate during sleep, whereas organic causes continue their influence even during sleep. The occurrence of erections during REM sleep, but not in specific sexual situations, is therefore considered suggestive of psychogenic causes, whereas the absence of erectile responses during REM sleep is thought to indicate organic aetiology. The NPT procedure usually requires individuals to sleep overnight in a sleep laboratory, whilst linked up to a penile plethysmograph and EEG monitoring equipment. Various measurements of penile tumescence may be obtained during NPT recordings, such as the percentage of full erection reached or changes in circumference or volume of the penis (Earls *et al.*, 1987; Wheeler and Rubin, 1987).

Unfortunately, 100% accurate discriminations between psychogenic and organic pathology cannot be made on the basis of NPT assessments (Williams, 1987). Individuals do not always respond in unfamiliar sleep environments as they normally would, hence a significant proportion of men whose erectile problems should be categorized as primarily psychogenic in origin fail to show positive NPT responses and may be mistakenly classified as organic. Also, as the test is measuring tumescence rather than rigidity, it is possible that some men who produce positive NPT erections would not be able to achieve penetration during intercourse. Such cases could be considered to be of psychogenic aetiology when in fact an organic explanation exists for the insufficient rigidity. Frequently, it is not possible to make a clear-cut distinction between organic and psychogenic cause, as many cases of organic pathology develop secondary psychological factors which serve to influence the condition. As a result of inadequacies in the NPT method, it seems essential that additional sources of information are used in distinguishing between psychogenic and organic aetiology, rather than relying solely on NPT results to make this distinction. Other authors, such as Williams (1987), stress the need for a minimum of three nights of recording in the sleep laboratory in the hope that clients will adapt to the new surroundings.

Penile response to erotic stimulation

Wincze *et al.* (1988) suggested that NPT measures should be used in combination with erectile response to 'daytime' erotic stimulation. In comparing non-dysfunctional males with vascular and psychogenic erectile dysfunctional males, these authors found that two types of psychogenic problems could be identified, which were not distinguished by pattern of NPT responding. As expected, males with vascular problems showed little erectile response to erotica. Whereas psychogenic subjects who reported erections during masturbation did respond with erectile tumescence to erotica, those men who reported no erections during masturbation (primary psychogenics) did not exhibit erections to presentation of erotic material. Wincze *et al.* (1988) suggested that NPT evaluations do not distinguish between these two forms of psychogenic erectile failure, in that both forms demonstrate NPT responses. Given that treatment requirements are likely to be different for primary versus situational psychogenic erectile difficulties, the authors suggest the need to use NPT measures in association with daytime response to erotic stimulation.

Assessment of penile vascular responses

Given that any disease or impairment of functioning of the penile vascular system may result in inadequate erections, it is essential that vascular causes are checked out. Various medical procedures may be used for this purpose and detailed coverage is beyond the aims and scope of this book. Such methods include assessment of penile blood pressure, penile brachial index (PBI), bulbar cavernosal latency responding, penile perfusion, cavernosography and arteriography

(Williams, 1987). Penile systolic blood pressure can be measured using a Doppler stethoscope, and the ratio of penile systolic pressure to the brachial systolic pressure can be determined in order to produce the brachial penile index (PBI). A PBI ratio of less than 0.6 is typically considered to be abnormal and suggestive of vascular causes. Although the PBI measure is useful in identifying vascular causes of erectile problems, it is not always highly accurate and is generally used in conjunction with other sources of information, rather than being used in isolation as a diagnostic measure.

Pharmacological induction of erections in the assessment process

Drugs which are known to induce erections may also be used during assessment in order to explore possible vascular abnormalities. For example, intercavernosal injections of a combination of the drugs papaverine and phentolamine have been found to lead to erection in cases of psychogenic and neurological erectile failure. If the cause of the problem is one of abnormal venous outflow, which means that insufficient blood can build up in the penis in order to make it erect, then injection of these drugs will still not produce an erection. This test may therefore be used as a way of identifying venous leakage. Typically, this method would be used in conjunction with other methods of assessing vascular functioning. Furthermore, because considerable knowledge and experience is required in order to establish the appropriate dosage for such injections, and because of the danger of side effects (e.g. prolonged erection) if administered incorrectly, the use of intercavernosal injection of erection-producing drugs should be limited to those medical practitioners who possess the necessary skills.

Endocrine evaluations

Abnormal levels of a variety of sex hormones, including prolactin, follicle-stimulating hormone (FSH), luteinizing hormone (LH) and testosterone, may be responsible for some cases of erectile dysfunction (Kaplan, 1974). Generally, assessment of serum levels of these hormones should be conducted in order to exclude their role in the aetiology of the presenting problem.

Physiological and medical assessment with other sexual disorders

Much more attention has been paid to the physiological and medical

111

assessment of erectile difficulties, compared to disorders of ejaculation or female sexual problems. Our knowledge of the female sexual response and causes of sexual problems in women is particularly limited. It is interesting to ponder why this might be the case. One possible explanation could be that the arousal response in women is harder to evaluate, particularly in the absence of physiological methods of assessing arousal (e.g. measurement of vaginal vasocongestion), whereas the penile erection arousal response is much easier to observe. Alternatively, the lack of research into female sexual responding may reflect the general attitude of our society regarding the all-importance of male sexual prowess, whereas female sexual responsiveness is considered to be secondary. I prefer to think that the former explanation is the case.

Although our knowledge of female sexual responding is less complete, the medical assessment typically reflects that conducted for male sexual problems. Similar coverage of drug usage, illnesses, general fitness, physical examination and endocrine functioning would be included. In terms of primary female orgasmic dysfunction, Kaplan (1983) suggests that organic aetiology is rare and detailed medical evaluation is not usually justified, unless the woman does not respond to psychological intervention. In the case of secondary female orgasmic dysfunction, organic causes should be investigated more carefully, particularly if the woman has previously been orgasmic in specific situations in which orgasm no longer occurs and where no obvious environmental or interpersonal triggers can be identified.

Medical evaluation plays a crucial role in the assessment of dyspareunia, vaginismus and vaginal dryness. In the case of dyspareunia, detailed investigation of possible medical explanations for pain should be conducted before psychological interventions are considered. This investigation would include an examination to exclude physical abnormalities of the genitalia and evaluation of circulating sex hormone levels, in particular the level of oestrogen, which could explain problems of vaginal dryness.

Finally, the medical evaluation of ejaculatory disorders should be mentioned. Various drugs, illnesses or injuries may impair ejaculation and these should be explored in cases of inhibited male orgasm. Kaplan (1983) suggested that premature ejaculation is relatively rarely of organic aetiology, whereas inhibition of ejaculation is more commonly of organic origin. She suggested that, given the relatively high success rate of psychological treatments for premature ejaculation and the relative infrequency of organic pathology, psychological intervention may generally commence without the need for a detailed medical evaluation. Although this may be true, it is suggested here that a basic medical examination should always be conducted prior to psychological intervention.

INTEGRATING THE FINDINGS OF THE ASSESSMENT AND DECIDING WHETHER INTERVENTION IS APPROPRIATE

Assessment is an ongoing process which continues throughout treatment and follow-up. This permits evaluation of the effectiveness of treatment so that changes can be made to the content of intervention when required. New information tends to emerge in the course of treatment as the clients build up a more trusting relationship with their therapist. Details may be disclosed that the assessor initially omitted to cover, or aspects of the clients' situation may change that influence their sexual relationship (e.g. mother-in-law arrives for a visit). Furthermore, the process of therapy itself may create changes which need to be monitored and understood in order to ensure that they do not have a negative influence upon treatment outcome. Changes in the behaviour of one partner may have a marked impact upon the relationship. A classic and obvious example here is the female client who begins to be more assertive in her sexual approaches and behaviour. In some instances this may be highly threatening to her partner if he has difficulty accepting that his wife has an equal right to initiate sex. To make matters worse, any generalization of assertive behaviour to other aspects of their relationship could result in marital conflict, unless such change in their roles is accompanied by concurrent change in the husband's attitude about male–female roles in their relationship. Careful monitoring of such factors is therefore needed throughout treatment and follow-up in order that they can be dealt with as they emerge.

Assessment should be seen as an ongoing process, ultimately leading to evaluation of treatment outcome. Initially, it must be established whether a sexual problem exists, or whether the clients merely require education and reassurance that their sexual relationship is relatively normal. If a sexual dysfunction is identified, then the assessor would typically refer the couple/individual for a medical evaluation, in order to exclude organic causes which require medical intervention. Whether the problem is organic or psychogenic in

113

origin, the model of assessment presented here suggests that the cognitive-behavioural assessment should proceed, in order to identify psychosocial influences upon sexual functioning. Then, it must be decided whether psychologically based intervention is appropriate. Two important questions should be asked here: (1) is therapy likely to be effective, so that the investment of time required by the therapist and the couple can be justified? and (2) could attempts at therapy actually be detrimental to the couple? These issues will be discussed further in the following chapter. Such a decision can only be made, however, once the detailed assessment phase has been completed and a thorough analysis of psychosocial influence over sexual functioning has been conducted.

The assessor is now faced with the awesome task of integrating the enormous amount of information that has been produced into a coherent, meaningful explanation of the couple's sexual functioning. Such information provides an indication of the targets for intervention so that an individually tailored treatment programme can be designed according to the outcome of the assessment process. The following chapter describes this stage in more detail.

5

Integrating cognitive and marital therapies into the treatment of sexual dysfunctions

A COGNITIVE-BEHAVIOUR THERAPY APPROACH WITHIN THE CONTEXT OF THE COUPLE'S GENERAL RELATIONSHIP

This chapter provides practical information concerning the methods of tackling the various psychological causes for sexual difficulties. The approach taken is one in which a cognitive-behavioural perspective is applied within the context of the couple's general relationship. Such an approach emphasizes the need to consider cognitive factors during assessment and treatment, rather than focusing purely on overt aspects of sexual functioning. It also acknowledges that sexual behaviour is just one aspect of the couple's relationship, which should be viewed from the perspective of a system in which each individual constantly influences the other. Whereas the cognitive behavioural approach is seen to be important in understanding the behaviour of each member of the partnership, it is also recognized that all aspects of sexual behaviour occur within the context of the couple's relationship. Sexual behaviour is generally the result of two individuals interacting together. Furthermore, sexual activity also occurs within the context of the family (and all the complex factors that this brings with it) and is also subject to cultural and societal influences, as outlined in Figure 5.1. These sources of influence, and the way in which they interact with each other, are important considerations throughout the therapy process. Failure to consider the interactional aspects of sexual behaviour, the couple's general relationship and the influences of the family and sociocultural environment is likely to result in failure to tackle some important sources of influence over sexual functioning and hence less effective therapy. Indeed, Chapman (1982) suggested that one of the most significant predictors of failure

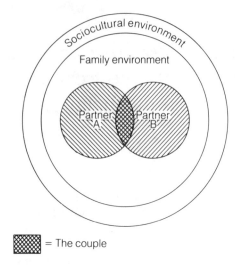

= The couple

Figure 5.1 The interaction between the individual, the couple, the family and the sociocultural environment.

in sex therapy is inadequate assessment and treatment of non-sexual issues which then interfere with the progress of therapy.

The following chapter therefore outlines various approaches which may be taken to the modification of cognitive and behavioural aspects of sexual functioning, with an emphasis on the integration of such techniques with methods designed to focus on the couple's general relationship and interaction with their family and sociocultural environment.

The suggestion that the treatment of sexual dysfunctions should be dealt with within the context of the couple's relationship and that a systemic approach to marital therapy should form part of the intervention is not new. Neither is the suggestion that cognitive components, such as self-statements, attitudes, beliefs or knowledge, should be considered during therapy. What is new is the detailed outline provided here, concerning ways in which specific sex therapy tasks may be integrated with techniques which are designed to tackle the cognitive aspects of sexual behaviour and to enhance the general relationship.

Various definitions of cognitive-behaviour therapy have been proposed and there is considerable dispute as to what composes a satisfactory definition. The term cognitive-behaviour therapy is used here to refer to an approach which accepts the need to tackle both overt and cognitive components of behaviour. Whilst traditional behaviour therapy techniques are important, it is suggested that intervention should also attempt to bring about change in cognitive aspects of behaviour, and that this may be achieved by tackling cognitive structures directly. Most programmes which have been developed for the treatment of sexual dysfunctions have involved a behavioural approach, which assumes that cognitive change will occur as a consequence of behaviour change. For example, changes in attitude and self-statements are assumed to occur following successful mastery during systematic desensitization of a previously feared situation. Cognitive therapy, however, attempts to enhance and speed up this process by focusing more directly on producing cognitive changes, rather than hoping that such changes will occur as a by-product of overt behaviour change. It is suggested here that failure to reduce maladaptive cognitions and cognitive skills deficits (e.g. fantasy ability) which are contributing to a sexual dysfunction will limit the long-term effectiveness of treatment. For example, if a client holds strong irrational beliefs about being physically unattractive, it may be necessary to tackle these beliefs directly, rather than hoping that they will dissipate during the process of behaviour therapy. Unless such maladaptive cognitions are dealt with, then it is unlikely that significant changes in overt sexual behaviour will occur.

Various behaviour therapy techniques may be used in the management of sexual and relationship difficulties, such as:

- Self-monitoring tasks;
- Skills training (instructions, discussion, modelling, role play/practice, feedback);
- Reinforcement of target behaviours, extinction of undesired behaviour;
- Graded task assignment;
- Relaxation training;
- Graded exposure to feared situations–systematic desensitization.

Cognitive therapy techniques, as applied to the treatment of sexual dysfunctions, consist of a range of methods which focus more directly on increasing cognitive skills or reducing maladaptive cognitive activities. Behavioural assignments may be used, but these are designed to provide empirical evidence in order to generate cognitive change.

Examples of cognitive therapy techniques that may be used in the treatment of sexual dysfunctions include:

- Increasing sexual knowledge (via information and education);
- Fantasy training;
- Attention-focusing skills (and sensory cue awareness);
- Behavioural tasks as experiments to provide evidence for cognitive challenging;
- Restructuring of maladaptive self-statements;
- Increasing positive self-statements;
- Restructuring of irrational attitudes and beliefs;
- Self-reinforcement;
- Problem-solving skills training.

These cognitive and behavioural methods form the basis of interventions which aim to bring about positive changes in sexual functioning and, indeed, within the relationship in general. Although a range of specific exercises are used, the methods outlined above represent the mechanisms which operate within these exercises and by which cognitive-behaviour change is produced. For example, the commonly used technique of sensate focus (see below) can be seen as providing the opportunity for a range of behavioural and cognitive techniques to operate. It may provide graded exposure to feared situations, communication skills training, graded task assignment, increased sexual knowledge, increased attention-focusing skills, and may even represent a behavioural assignment through which evidence is produced to reduce maladaptive cognitions.

The cognitive-behavioural approach outlined here also accepts the need to view each presenting case as different, bringing into treatment a unique set of causal factors. The treatment programme should be tailored according to the presenting characteristics of each couple. This requires a move away from a 'package' approach to the treatment of sexual dysfunctions in which a set of methods, usually those outlined by Masters and Johnson (1970), are applied according to the diagnosis received. A 'package' approach would typically commence with sensate focus 1, followed by sensate focus 2, leading on to a set pattern of exercises according to the diagnosis. Hence, if the presenting problem was given the label of premature ejaculation, the package approach to treatment would involve a progression to the squeeze or stop–start technique.

It is acknowledged that the exercises involved in sensate focus 1 and 2, and the graduated task assignments involved in the subsequent exercises for specific difficulties, are extremely important components of most intervention programmes. As mentioned above, the sensate focus exercises provide an ideal framework within which couples can learn to relax, to communicate, to increase their sexual knowledge and skills, to reduce performance fears and to focus attention on feelings of sexual pleasure within a non-threatening environment. In many ways, therefore, the basic components of the 'package' are designed to tackle aetiological factors which are commonly found to underlie sexual dysfunctions.

Whilst this approach is appropriate for straightforward cases whose causal factors are dealt with by the 'package' components, Halgin *et al.* (1988) suggested that an increasing number of couples are requesting help for sexual problems for whom other, more complex factors are involved in the development and maintenance of their difficulty. These components do not tend to be tackled by the traditional approach of Masters and Johnson (1970) and this has been suggested to account for the relatively poor results of many recent studies using the Masters and Johnson approach (Halgin *et al.*, 1988). As outlined in Chapter 1, it seems likely that the high success rate initially reported by Masters and Johnson partly reflected the population being treated, in which problems relating to lack of sexual knowledge and performance anxieties were dominant. The ready availability of self-help programmes and increased knowledge in the general population about sexual matters means fewer cases now present with problems relating to lack of sexual knowledge. Halgin *et al.* (1988) suggested that the couples requesting help for sexual difficulties today tend to be more complex, requiring a much more detailed assessment and individually tailored treatment approach.

A detailed assessment should provide a mass of information concerning the physiological and psychosocial factors which influence the couple's sexual functioning. Assessment should reveal the couple's assets, deficits and excesses in relation to a wide range of factors, such as:

- Sexual knowledge;
- Sexual skills;
- Anxiety in sexual situations;
- Cognitions and attitudes;
- Psychopathology;
- Quality of marital relationship;
- Communication skills;

- Opportunity for sexual contact;
- Sexual preferences;
- Fantasy skills;
- Use of erotic materials;
- Attention-focusing on sexual cues.

These factors must be considered within the context of life events, family and social situation, physiological influences, general health, age, and biological factors that may influence sexual functioning. The assessor is therefore faced with the awesome task of integrating the enormous amount of assessment information into a coherent, meaningful explanation of the couple's sexual functioning. This can be facilitated by identification of *assets*, *deficits* and *excesses* of the couple's behaviour and relationship, along with the *antecedents* and *consequences* of the sexual problem. Such information provides an indication of the targets for intervention, so that an individually tailored treatment programme can be designed according to the outcome of the assessment process. Intervention should aim to increase areas of deficit, to decrease areas of excessive behaviour and maintain aspects which can be considered as assets. An understanding of the antecedents and consequences of the presenting problem behaviours will provide an indication of causal factors, which may be changed in order to enhance sexual functioning. Although this approach is typical of a behaviour therapy perspective, it is also applicable to cognitive therapy methods. Just as assets, deficits and excesses may exist in relation to overt behaviours, the same is true in relation to cognitive skills and activities. Similarly, it may be feasible to identify the antecedents and consequences of cognitive activities and it may be amenable to change these in order to bring about reductions in maladaptive cognitions. From the perspective of the couple's relationship, it may also be possible to identify areas of asset, deficit and excess which will provide additional indications for intervention.

This chapter outlines a range of methods that may be used during the treatment of sexual dysfunctions in order to bring about relevant changes in sexual functioning and the general relationship. Once target areas have been identified during the assessment process, it will then be feasible to develop a personalized intervention programme, based upon the methods outlined.

GENERAL POINTS REGARDING THERAPY

There are no set rules regarding the way in which therapy should be conducted. There is little empirical evidence to enable us to make valid statements as to how therapy should be conducted. The limited evidence available is summarized in Chapter 7. What follows therefore is based primarily upon the author's own clinical experience, the suggestions of other practitioners in the literature on the treatment of sexual dysfunctions and empirical data, where available. Where recommendations regarding content or format are made, it should always be borne in mind that each case is likely to be different and what worked for one couple may not work for another. The therapist therefore needs to be flexible and to adjust the programme to fit in with the characteristics of different referrals.

When to accept clients for therapy

Once the assessment process is complete, a decision must be made as to whether psychologically based intervention is appropriate. Two important questions must be asked here: (1) is therapy likely to be effective, so that the investment of time required by the therapist and the couple can be justified? and (2) could attempts at therapy actually be detrimental to the couple?

Newcomb and Bentler (1988) suggested that couples with marked psychopathology should be screened out at this stage. Obviously, this decision is difficult and it is hard to make any fixed rules as to what type of psychopathology should warrant the decision not to proceed with therapy. There is a marked lack of information which would allow us to make such decisions with any degree of validity. In my own view, if psychological problems are identified, these should be dealt with before therapy for the sexual difficulty begins. There may be some cases, however, where the psychological problems are secondary to the sexual problem (e.g. depression) and may be reduced by successful resolution of the sexual problem. The same may be true with marital problems. Newcomb and Bentler (1988) cautioned against the use of sexual therapies with couples with severe marital difficulties. Indeed, it is possible that, for some couples, their marital difficulties are so severe as to make intervention for sexual problems ineffective and the tasks assigned to them may even exacerbate their marital problems. For other couples, however, the sexual problem may be the cause of marital disharmony and enhancement of sexual functioning may also enhance the general relationship.

121

Careful assessment is needed in order to work out the cause–effect relationship between sexual and marital problems. As a general guide, it is suggested that where a partner holds negative views about their spouse, with considerable feelings of hostility, therapy for the sexual problem should not begin unless the marital situation is improved first. For the majority of couples it is suggested that the marital and sexual aspects of their relationship are closely intertwined, with each of these aspects closely influencing the other. Ideally, intervention should tackle both aspects of the relationship. Couples with moderate levels of marital disharmony may therefore commence intervention for sexual difficulties within an integrated programme which is also designed to tackle general marital problems.

The level of motivation of the couple should also be considered when making the decision to commence intervention. Assessment of motivation relies upon the subjective reports of the couple as to their willingness to comply with assignments, their desire to change and to work towards meeting their goals. An adequate level of motivation is required from both partners and cases sometimes present in which the couple have sought help as the result of pressure from only one member. If either partner is unwilling to take part in therapy, or is lacking in motivation to participate fully in the therapy process, then a conjoint approach is likely to fail. The therapist does not have to give up altogether in such cases though, as it may be feasible to intervene through only one of the partners. Studies have found that intervention can be effective if only one individual attends for therapy, even when the other partner is unwilling to participate (Nelson, 1987). If both clients are lacking in motivation, then it may be decided that intervention is not appropriate. The situation is relatively rare, given that the decision to seek help demands a reasonably high level of motivation in the first instance.

Several authors have suggested that psychologically based treatments should not be commenced if there is evidence of organic involvement in a sexual dysfunction. Whilst it is acknowledged that medical assessment and intervention are crucial, it is also suggested that a combined psychological–medical intervention may be beneficial for many clients with organic aetiology. If the cognitive–behavioural assessment reveals psychogenic factors which may be exacerbating the organic problem, then psychologically based intervention may be a valuable adjunct to the medical treatment. Furthermore, some clients may find it difficult to adjust to the medical procedures used to rectify their difficulties and psychological interventions may be helpful here.

Various other situations may lead a therapist to decide not to commence intervention. For example, it may become apparent during assessment that one of the partners has no intention of developing a satisfactory sexual relationship with their partner. This may be the result of another relationship or may be purely a decision not to include a sexual component within the current relationship. In some instances, the referral may occur when one individual wishes to terminate the relationship and decides to hand their partner over to a 'therapist', in order to provide support during the time of separation. The knowledge that a therapist is there to 'pick up the pieces' then enables that individual to leave the relationship. For other couples, the pressure of one of the partners to seek therapy may have been so intense that the other partner has finally given in and agreed to attend, even though he or she has no desire to participate in treatment. Although such situations are relatively infrequent, it is important to explore such possibilities during the assessment process. For some couples, it may be feasible to generate the motivation required for conjoint therapy or individual sessions with an initially unmotivated partner. Unfortunately, in some instances, a partner may have made a firm decision to stop all sexual relations. If this state is recognized during assessment then therapy should not be commenced. Counselling towards acceptance of the situation or formation of other relationships may become alternative targets for the client. Generally, it is suggested that intervention with the aim of enhancing the sexual relationship should not begin if either of the partners are involved in a sexual relationship with someone else or if one of the partners is a firm preference for a non-sexual relationship.

The preparatory sessions

Several aims are involved in the preparatory stages of intervention. The first aim is to provide feedback to the couple regarding the outcome of the assessment process. The therapist provides a brief summary of the presenting difficulties and the major factors that are suggested to influence and maintain the problem. This serves to check that the information presented has been interpreted correctly and provides an opportunity for the clients to correct the therapist or provide important information that may have been missed. The way in which feedback is given should also facilitate the second aim, which is to create a perception within the couple that the difficulty is an interactional one, in which both partners contribute to its continuation. It is important at this point to build what is termed in the marital therapy literature 'a collaborative set'. This refers to the development of an acceptance by the couple that both members are responsible for the current situation and that effort will be required from both parties in order to bring about positive and long-lasting improvements. Examples may be used to illustrate the way in which the couple influence each other and how intervention is unlikely to be successful unless both parties work together on 'their' problem.

A third aim of the preliminary stages of therapy is to encourage the couple to focus in the positive aspects of their relationship. By the time that many couples seek help for a sexual problem they have developed a variety of negative thoughts about their relationship. Often the couple have developed views such as 'if we really loved each other, we wouldn't have this problem'. In some instances, the sexual difficulties may have resulted in a range of negative consequences, such as arguments, negative feelings and avoidance of close physical contact. It is important therefore that the therapist draws the couple's attention during the feedback process to the positive aspects of the relationship. For example, the couple may be asked to recall times when their sexual relationship was enjoyable and to identify characteristics that they found attractive about each other in the early stages of their relationship. Most importantly, the therapist should emphasize that their decision to seek help is an indication that they care enough about each other to want to enhance their relationship. This positive focus aims to divert attention away from some of the negative consequences that may have resulted from the sexual difficulties. It should also increase positive feelings between the couple, in order to enhance motivation and willingness to contribute to subsequent therapy tasks.

A fourth aim of the preliminary phase of therapy is the development of positive expectancies. Later in the preparatory session, the clients may be reassured as to the high frequency of sexual problems amongst couples and the high probability of positive results from therapy. This then leads onto the fifth aim, which is to provide an outline of the treatment programme. It is important for clients to understand the rationale for the therapy approach, namely that sexual behaviour is learned in the same way as any other behaviour and can be changed, given the appropriate learning experiences. As with any form of therapy for any type of problem, clients need to be able to understand the reason for a particular choice of treatment, to hold high expectations as to its effectiveness and be able to accept the explanation proposed for their difficulties. Some clients may find the focus on the relationship, the suggestion of the difficulty being a mutual one, or the focus on current events difficult to accept. They may have sought help with preconceived ideas about what therapy should involve. It is important that discrepancies between the approach being outlined and the clients' expectations and beliefs are identified and dealt with at this early stage. If such conflicts are not discussed and resolved then they are likely to interfere with and inhibit the progress of therapy.

A final aim of the preliminary phase of therapy is to encourage the couple to ensure that their social/family home is conducive to improving their sexual relationship. This requires that the couple are able to programme time together where they have privacy to carry out their home-based assignments. Unless this opportunity is available, therapy is unlikely to be successful. Similarly, it is important that couples are encouraged to reduce any external sources of stress which are likely to inhibit therapy gains. For example, if the couple are about to have a large number of visitors to stay and they find this very stressful, then it would not be sensible to commence therapy.

In summary, the aims of the preliminary phase are to:

- Provide feedback to the clients regarding the assessment summary, to check for correct interpretation, and allow additional information to be presented;
- Develop a collaborative set/concept of a 'mutual' problem;
- Develop a positive perception of the relationship;
- Develop positive expectancies with regard to outcome;
- Outline the treatment programme and generate acceptance of its rationale;
- Make necessary changes in their social/family/home circumstances conducive to programme participation.

The structure of sessions

Setting the agenda

Although the content of intervention varies according to the therapy plan for each couple, it is useful for each session to be structured in a way that permits the therapist to be maximally effective in producing the desired changes. Chapman (1982) reported that a significant predictor of treatment effectiveness with sexual dysfunctions is the ability of clients to stick to relevant issues during therapy, rather than diverting the topic away from the focus of treatment. One way in which the therapist may assist in the process of sticking to the topic is to use an agenda to control the content of the session. The agenda is developed and written down at the beginning of each session by the therapist, with input from the clients. This procedure is described in the preparatory session, where it is stressed that sessions must stick to the agenda in order for treatment to be effective. Clients are asked to make a note during the week of any items that they wish to place on the next agenda. The content of each session typically begins with a review of the home-based assignments. The agenda should also include a brief review of the previous session's content and discussion of the clients' reaction to it.

The therapist will have designed an individually tailored programme for each referral, based on the results of the assessment. This will involve an outline of specific intervention methods which previously have been demonstrated to be effective in producing change in the area of concern. Intervention generally includes a combination of 'within-session' therapy elements and home-based components. It is important therefore that the therapist ensures that the methods to be used within each session are included in the agenda and are dealt with. Once the agenda has been set, the therapist then plays an important role in ensuring that the session covers the agenda topics and does not wander off onto peripheral issues. Each session should introduce new material from the 'within-session' elements of therapy. It is also important, however, that the clients are able to bring their own items to place on the agenda which are relevant to the presenting problem. During the process of therapy, new situations will occur and important information will come to light which was not previously available, all of which will have an impact upon the direction of treatment. Furthermore, changes in the behaviour of either or both members of the partnership may have important repercussions upon the relationship. If the couple's relationship is viewed from a systems perspective, then it can be seen as being in a state of equilibrium in which changes in the behaviour of either partner may disturb this position. A systemic view suggests that individuals may attempt to restore the balance by behaving in a way that tries to limit the change in their partner. This process may impair the progress of treatment, hence it is important to monitor the effect that treatment is having upon the relationship and to be on the look out for attempts by either partner to sabotage treatment. Valuable information about each partner's reaction to treatment may be obtained through agenda issues. The clients should also be asked to provide agenda items for the cognitive restructuring components of intervention. Specific problem situations which have arisen in relation to the general relationship or sexual activities may be defined for discussion, in order to determine underlying negative thoughts or irrational beliefs which may then be subject to cognitive challenging.

Home-based assignments

The approach taken to intervention outlined in this text emphasizes both in-session therapy and home-based assignments. It is worth mentioning why the term 'home-based' has been used in preference to 'homework'. The term 'homework' tends to trigger negative memories for many people of school-days and compulsory homework. It has been suggested by several authors (e.g. Fennell, 1989) that some clients may respond negatively to being asked to complete homework tasks and that alternative phrases may lead to greater compliance. For this reason it is suggested that reference to 'homework' should be avoided and a 'neutral' term such as 'home-based' tasks should be used in preference.

Home-based tasks are typically set at the end of each therapy session and are designed to fulfil several purposes. First, they may provide an opportunity for clients to practise, at home, those skills which are important in order to enhance the sexual and general relationship, but for which practice in the clinic would be inappropriate or unethical. Second, practice within natural settings is an important means of producing behaviour change within everyday life. If skills training only takes place within a clinical setting, then lack of generalization of behaviour change to naturalistic situations could result. Third, home-based tasks may be used to collect information for therapy sessions. Finally, home-based tasks serve to place responsibility onto the clients, regarding the conduct of their therapy, which reduces problems of dependency and increases the likelihood that skills will be learned to enable the couple to solve subsequent problems within their relationship.

127

There are several points regarding the way in which home-based assignments should be organized. For example, Fennell (1989) emphasizes that the task should be clearly defined and specific so that it is clear to both therapist and clients exactly what is expected and whether or not the task has been completed. The assignment should be written down on a card or sheet for the clients to take home with them and to return to the next session. If a detailed exercise is set, it is preferable for written guidelines to be given to the client, so that they can refer to the instructions, rather than relying on memory. This also provides a prompt to the clients to remind them to complete their assignments. Ideally, clients should be asked to record when each task has been completed, so that the therapist has a record of compliance and the couple can obtain the reinforcing satisfaction of seeing their efforts on paper.

The great importance of home-based tasks should be emphasized right from the start of therapy and it should be made clear that the effectiveness of the programme is dependent upon task completion outside the sessions. Different therapists suggest different ways of dealing with non-compliance with home-based tasks. Some suggest that a gentle approach should be taken, with the following session focusing on reasons for non-compliance. Other therapists advise a tough stance, in which the practitioner terminates the session early and refuses to continue with therapy until the tasks have been completed. The present author tends to take a moderate position. Non-compliance results in a disapproving response from the therapist, who re-emphasizes that home-based tasks must be completed and that therapy is dependent upon their completion. To a large extent, non-compliance can be avoided if tasks are set within the couple's capabilities, if the steps between task difficulty are not made too great and if clients are asked to state their beliefs in their ability to complete the assignments set. If self-efficacy statements about being able to complete the task are low, then the therapist should design a home-based task that is more likely to be completed. Alternatively, therapy may focus on getting clients to a stage where they are able to complete the assignment. This is particularly important in relation to maladaptive cognitions or beliefs that may inhibit task completion. Considerable cognitive restructuring may be required before some clients are able to complete certain behavioural assignments. For some couples what appears to be the most simple task, such as sensate focus 1 (non-genital pleasuring), is extremely difficult to undertake. A range of negative thoughts may interfere with task completion, for example:

'I really shouldn't have to do this . . . this is stupid and degrading . . . it's like being back at school . . . an adult shouldn't have to do such basic stuff . . . surely everyone ought to be able to know what to do in sex'. Until such maladaptive thoughts and irrational beliefs are dealt with, progress with home-based assignments is unlikely to occur.

It may also be possible to pre-empt non-compliance by asking the couple to list the difficulties that they expect will prevent them from completing the assignment. It may then be possible to plan ways in which these difficulties can be overcome, thereby making compliance more likely. Once the home-based task has been outlined, it is also important to ensure that the couple understand the rationale for the task and the principle underlying it. These should be carefully explained and the therapist should check that the couple have not only understood fully but also find the approach acceptable. If the task is seen as sensible and appropriate, the clients are more likely to comply with the instructions than if they are philosophically opposed to the approach or do not perceive the value. Furthermore, if the basic principle underlying the task can be grasped, then it may be possible for the clients to apply the principle to subsequent difficulties, thereby increasing generalization of behaviour change.

Tasks should ideally be set at a level at which the clients are likely to succeed and be reinforced by the positive consequences of completion. The aim is to gradually increase the difficulty of tasks assigned, so as to generate successive approximations to the final goal in skill development. Each step should be mastered and well established within the person's repertoire before moving on to the next step in the chain of skills of behaviours. This approach requires that progress through the different stages of therapy occurs at the couple's own pace.

The beginning of each session usually focuses on the report of the outcome of the home-based assignment from the previous session. The therapist plays an important role in providing social reinforcement for efforts at task completion and for any gains in behaviour that may have been produced. It is important that praise focuses on effort and development of prerequisite skills, rather than on sexual performance, such as attainment of arousal or orgasm.

Programming for generalization

As with any form of psychological therapy, it is essential that treatment effects are maintained once therapy ends (generalization over time) and carry across from the therapy situation to the clients' normal situation at home (generalization over situation). In the case of sexual dysfunctions, generalization of therapy gains must also transfer across different situations (such as being alone to being with a partner), or across different types of sexual activities (such as from manual stimulation to vaginal intercourse). Various methods may be used to encourage generalization over time and across situations. Maintenance of therapy improvements is suggested to be enhanced by the gradual fading of therapist contact and the use of booster sessions during a follow-up period. This type of approach does not see a specific end to therapy, but rather a gradual shifting of the responsibility for therapy from the therapist to the client. Couples are encouraged to learn the basic principles which underlie their behaviour change so that they become able to apply these principles to new problems or the recurrence of old difficulties. The later stages of intervention should therefore focus on the teaching of underlying principles of behaviour change. Couples may be taught to identify the causal factors relevant to their problems and to learn the techniques necessary for behaviour change. The booster session phase also includes a general review of the major elements of the therapy programme, with exercises being set for regular practice for newly acquired skills until they are well established. The major risk at this stage is to terminate therapy when such skills, either behavioural or cognitive, are weakly developed and may be easily extinguished.

Several other methods may be used to programme for maintenance of therapy effects. In the later phases of therapy it is useful to encourage the couple to draw up a list of long-term goals that they want to work towards. Again it is important that these goals are not orientated towards sexual performance, but are focused instead upon relationship enhancement or skill development. For example, the couple may suggest that a long-term goal will be to organize a positive activity together at least once per month, such as going out to dinner or to a movie. Such goals may also focus on enhancement of the sexual relationship, perhaps by providing a non-genital massage to each other at least once per month. In addition, couples should be encouraged to set themselves rewards for attainment of their longer-term targets.

It may be possible to reduce relapse rates if the therapist and clients can anticipate events which are likely to trigger a recurrence of difficulties. These relapse triggers are likely to differ for different couples and may take many forms. Periods of high stress at work, fatigue, visiting relatives, conflict relating to non-sexual issues or child management problems are just some examples of the types of situations that may trigger relapse. If likely triggers can be identified in advance, the follow-up stages of therapy may focus on ways of preventing or dealing with such events. It may also be possible to set a criterion by which the couple immediately recontact the therapist if a specified set of events occur which are predicted to cause relapse. Alternatively, an early warning signal may be used. For example, the couple may be asked to recontact the clinic if erectile failure is experienced during attempts at intercourse on three occasions in a row. This provides the opportunity for early intervention, rather than waiting until the problem has again become well established.

General therapist skills

As was the case for the format of therapy, there are no hard and fast rules concerning the ideal set of therapist skills. Evidence is lacking to permit us to draw firm conclusions and we are required to rely on the subjective opinions of experienced practitioners. For the present purposes it is possible to list a range of therapist skills that various authors have suggested to be important when dealing with sexual difficulties:

- To be able to talk about sexual matters without experiencing anxiety;
- To be able to use sexual terminology without embarrassment;
- Adequate knowledge of sexual behaviour and its determinants;
- Good listening skills and empathic responding;
- Ability to provide social reinforcement where appropriate;
- Ability to generate positive expectancies about treatment outcome;
- To maintain a competent, knowledgeable and professional presentation;
- To focus the attention of the couple on the agenda content;
- To complete the agenda;
- To be able to make the couple feel relaxed; this may involve the occasional use of humour in a professional manner, where appropriate.

Many other therapist behaviours are also important and these are outlined with respect to the use of specific therapy techniques.

Certain therapist behaviours do, however, warrant a separate mention here. It is important that confidentiality is re-emphasized once therapy begins. Whilst this was essential during the assessment phase, it is important that the emphasis on confidentiality continues during therapy, in order that an atmosphere of trust remains. Similarly, it is important that the therapist maintains the professional presentation which was generated during the assessment phase. The terminology used should continue to be professional, yet understandable to the clients. This requires that excessively slang terminology is avoided. The use of excessive personal self-disclosure should also be avoided. This reflects the personal style of the author and differs from the writings of some authors (e.g. Barbach, 1980) in which the use of personal self-disclosure is recommended as a means of facilitating disclosure by clients. Unfortunately, it is difficult to draw the line between appropriate and inappropriate self-disclosure and some clients may find it embarrassing and may feel uncomfortable to hear about their therapist's sexual behaviour. There may be some cultural differences here between US populations (e.g. Barbach's) and the general clinic clientele in the UK and Australia, where the present author has practised. Whatever approach is selected, the aim is to create a therapy situation in which the couple feel confident with regard to their therapist's skills and feel able to disclose personal information.

The approach taken in the present text tends to be one in which one therapist works alone with a couple or individual client. This differs from the co-therapy approach outlined by Masters and Johnson (1970) and developed by many other therapists over the years. Co-therapy has the disadvantage of being very costly in terms of therapist time and there is little evidence to suggest that it is any more effective than a single-therapist format in the treatment of sexual difficulties (Crowe *et al.*, 1981; LoPiccolo *et al.*, 1985). Furthermore, many of us do not work in a context that provides the opportunity for co-therapy. Nevertheless, it is recognized that many therapists prefer to work in a co-therapy context. Where this is the case, there are several guidelines that may facilitate the smooth running of co-therapy work. It is important that the co-therapists have a clear idea of the content for each session. The major items for the agenda should be drawn up in advance between the therapists, providing room to include items that the couple may introduce. The co-therapists therefore need to meet before each session and ideally should hold discussions after each session is completed. Different co-therapists may prefer to work in different ways. My own experience has been in working in a supervisor–trainee context in which the two therapists develop clear roles in advance concerning who is going to conduct which aspect of the session. This avoids competition between therapists in the middle of a session, which may result in interruptions and diversion away from a particular direction that one of the therapists is working towards. Undoubtedly, good co-therapy requires a great deal of practice and gradually a preferred style of working will develop. Non-verbal communication plays an important role here, with cues being developed, such as to signal to the other therapist to take over control of the session at a particular point. A successful co-therapy team are able to work out an effective non-verbal communication system that facilitates efficient conduct of therapy.

Certainly, co-therapy can have its advantages. It has been suggested to provide a balance between sexes when working with couples, so that alliances do not develop between the single therapist and the same-sex client. It also provides an observer who may be able to detect valuable pieces of information that the single therapist misses. On occasions, the co-therapist may even intervene to prevent the other therapist from making a therapeutic error that would have been detrimental to the couple's progress.

Where to start in therapy

One would think that the issue as to where to begin therapy would not arise if an individualized approach is taken to treatment. The answer to the question of 'where to start therapy' should be . . . to begin at the beginning. The assessment process should provide an indication of the individual and couple's assets, in other words what the couple can already do. It should then be possible to organize the areas of deficit and excess in hierarchical order, in terms of degree of difficulty and steps towards sexual competence. Unfortunately, the process is not quite as simple as this. The presenting sexual problem may be influenced by a wide range of non-sexual factors, such as depression, anxiety and marital difficulties. It is suggested that, for many individuals, a reciprocal relationship exists in which non-sexual factors influence the sexual problem and are, in turn, adversely affected by the sexual disorder. A strong case can therefore be made for tackling sexual and non-sexual factors simultaneously. If, on the other hand, the non-sexual factor is a major cause of the sexual problem and the sexual problem is likely to dissipate if the non-sexual problem is removed, then it would make sense to deal with the non-sexual issue first.

Most authors appear to avoid the suggestion of simultaneous therapy with sexual dysfunctions and non-sexual, related problems, such as relationship difficulties or depression. The present approach suggests that intervention should commence with the integration of therapies. Hence, if a couple are found to have difficulties in marital problem-solving skills, communication skills or experience a low level of positive interactions within their relationship, therapy would commence with a view to enhancing these areas during the early attempts to improve sexual functioning. Similarly, if assessment reveals problems of maladaptive self-statements or irrational beliefs, attempts at cognitive challenging would begin early on in the therapy process. It is suggested that outcome of sexual skill assignments will be more positive if relationship problems and negative cognitions are also tackled. In turn, successful sexual skill development is likely to enhance positive, adaptive cognitions and have a constructive influence in the general relationship.

The exact skills in the sexual domain with which to start will also vary according to the couple. Some clients may be highly anxious about sexual activities and considerable preparation will be required before they reach the stage of being able to cope with tasks such as non-genital massage. Relaxation training and a process of graduated exposure through systematic desensitization may be required, with sexual skill exercises being a focus only in the later stages of intervention. Other couples may present with very few problems in non-sexual domains, with very good sexual knowledge and ability to communicate with their partner. Their sexual dysfunction may reflect a deficit in a specific sexual skill, such as difficulty in attending to sexual arousal cues. Intervention with this type of client would be very different from the former example.

A proscription on sexual intercourse?

A key element throughout the early phases of intervention with sexual dysfunctions has traditionally been the proscription or 'banning' of sexual intercourse. This component was emphasized in Masters and Johnson's (1970) programme and was included in order to reduce the performance demands which were suggested to contribute to sexual dysfunctions. Since 1970 the proscription on sexual intercourse appears to have been incorporated into most treatment programmes, even though the original Masters and Johnson approach has been transferred by many practitioners from what was designed as a two-week residential programme to a therapy approach which is usually carried out over several weeks in an out-patient context. Lipsius (1987) was highly critical of the automatic inclusion of a ban on intercourse if clients are required to abstain from intercourse for several weeks, or even months, compared to the two-week period which was initially intended by Masters and Johnson.

Lipsius (1987) suggested that a prolonged proscription on sexual intercourse may result in various negative consequences, including: (1) the loss of enjoyment and decline in erotic feelings from activities which should cause sexual arousal; (2) the loss of spontaneity concerning sexual activity; (3) unnecessary frustration; (4) loss of initiative; and (5) increased resistance to therapy in response to a perception of the therapist as 'omnipotent'. Lipsius proposed that there may be some couples for whom a total ban on intercourse may be counterproductive and for whom a more moderate alternative may be preferable. The moderate approach suggests that sensate focus exercises are to be practised in the spirit of 'not intentionally as a prelude to intercourse'. The couple are asked to practise the sensate focus exercises 'primarily for inherent pleasure, without letting themselves be distracted by goal orientation and performance, whether it be erection, lubrication, orgasm or intercourse'. It should be made clear to the couple that the therapist's preference is for them to complete the exercises without proceeding to intercourse, but that it is acceptable to have intercourse if desired by both partners.

This moderate proscription approach is suggested by Lipsius to have the advantages of reducing goal-orientated sexual performance and fears, whilst allowing the couple to retain their initiative, self-direction and spontaneity. It may also take advantage of the positive aspects of libido, passion and romance, which may enhance the sexual relationship. In addition, sexual problems are permitted to occur which may be used as material for the therapy process. For example, specific thoughts, beliefs, antecedent situations and consequences may be identified in relation to a sexual problem which may otherwise have remained undetected. Most importantly, Lipsius suggested that the moderate approach allows couples to integrate the principles acquired during therapy, such as the pleasuring activities from sensate focus exercises, into their evolving new patterns of sexual behaviour. Hence, it becomes more likely that the newly acquired skills will be retained within the couple's subsequent sexual relationship.

Lipsius (1987) acknowledged that there might be some couples for whom a total ban on intercourse is most appropriate. Cases involving vaginismus and premature ejaculation, in which an involuntary response is present, are suggested to require a total ban on intercourse in the initial stages of intervention. Lipsius also recommended abstention with cases where organic or physiological treatment is being carried out in order to correct an impairment. It is suggested by the present author that couples with extremely high levels of performance anxiety and maladaptive cognitions concerning intercourse would also benefit fom a total proscription on intercourse until such interfering factors are modified. Similarly, a total ban on intercourse is recommended for couples in which there is extreme pressure from one partner to proceed to intercourse without regard to the other partner's desires until this aspect of the relationship has been dealt with.

Only one study that I am aware of has investigated the contribution made by a ban on intercourse to the effectiveness of therapy. Takefman and Brender (1984) allocated couples who presented with erectile dysfunction to a sensate focus procedure with or without a ban on intercourse. These authors found no difference between conditions on any measure of erectile functioning, although the couples who were given the intercourse proscription reported more positive enjoyment. Further studies of this type are required before we can draw firm conclusions as to value of the ban on intercourse. Until such evidence is available to enable us to determine which couples are likely to benefit from the ban and which are not, it is suggested that the decision should be made according to the recommendations made by Lipsius (1987), in conjunction with the therapist's judgment based upon the outcome of assessment. As a general rule, it is suggested that an initial proscription is placed on intercourse during the sensate focus 1 exercises, which generally do not continue for more than two to three weeks. The proscription may then be modified towards the instructions outlined by Lipsius (1987), *in appropriate cases*, during the sensate focus 2 exercises, when genital pleasuring takes place and sexual arousal is more likely to occur.

ENHANCING THE GENERAL RELATIONSHIP

Sexual activity is just one example of the couple's reciprocal behaviour and it is clear that satisfaction with the sexual relationship is closely linked to the relationship in general. The mutual influences of sexual and general aspects of the couple's relationship were briefly mentioned in Chapters 1 and 2, but will be discussed in more detail here. The majority of couples seeking therapist help for sexual dysfunctions also report marital dissatisfaction and, similarly, the majority of couples presenting for marital therapy also report difficulties in their sexual relationship (Zimmer, 1987). It is not surprising therefore to find a high correlation between ratings of marital and sexual satisfaction (Halgin *et al.*, 1988; Zimmer, 1987). This association has led some therapists to emphasize the need to incorporate general relationship enhancement techniques with those methods designed to enhance the sexual relationship for the many couples who present with problems in both areas. Non-sexual aspects of the relationship have, in the past, been neglected. Enhancement of non-sexual aspects of the relationship was not a major focus of either assessment or therapy in the original Masters and Johnson (1970) approach and these aspects were subsequently neglected by their followers, including such authorities as Kaplan (1974, 1987) and LoPiccolo (1977).

It is perhaps not surprising to find that the long-term effectiveness of the treatment of sexual dysfunction is greater if intervention also incorporates marital therapy techniques. Zimmer (1987) compared the progress of three groups of women who were referred for secondary sexual problems of desire, arousal and/or orgasm. The women were randomly assigned to one of three conditions, namely a waiting-list control, nine sessions of attention placebo relaxation/education followed by 12 sessions of sex therapy, or nine sessions of marital therapy followed by 12 sessions of sex therapy. Significant improvements were found in measures of sexual functioning and marital satisfaction for both treatment conditions, but the benefits were significantly greater for the combined marital + sex therapy approach. These effects were maintained at the six-month follow-up. A good case therefore exists for a routine assessment of the non-sexual aspects of the relationship. If problems are evident, then a more detailed assessment of the general relationship is warranted followed by appropriate interventions.

Obviously the therapist will encounter some couples who seek help for sexual problems and yet are highly satisfied with other aspects of their relationship. These couples are likely to have good communication skills, to be competent at resolving conflicts and to experience high levels of positive interactions with their partner. If

137

deficits in these areas exist, however, then the couple is likely to have difficulty in maintaining a satisfactory general relationship. Just as adequate communication skills and positive partner behaviours are important in determining satisfaction with non-sexual areas of the relationship, they are also suggested to be important in enabling the couple to experience a pleasurable and satisfying sexual relationship. Communication discrepancies such as misreading of non-verbal cues, failure to express emotions or needs, and escalation of negative interactions are just as applicable to sexual situations as they are to non-sexual interactions. The same skills are suggested to underlie non-sexual and sexual aspects of the relationship and it is not therefore surprising to find that satisfaction with the two areas is closely linked. Furthermore, feelings of negative affect towards a partner stemming from earlier non-sexual conflicts are likely to be brought into sexual situations.

It is acknowledged that certain skills and behaviours are specific to sexual behaviour. Hence, problems in such areas may result in sexual dysfunction despite a satisfactory relationship in non-sexual areas. Unfortunately, the consequences of a sexual dysfunction often include a negative impact on the general relationship. Sexual difficulties may generate negative thoughts and emotions concerning the self, the partner and the relationship, which impinge on other aspects of living together. Relationship dissatisfaction may therefore result from the sexual problem and it is likely that a vicious cycle develops, in which sexual and non-sexual relationship problems act to exacerbate each other.

As a result of this reciprocal relationship, Hof (1987) stressed the need to continue assessment of the non-sexual aspects of the relationship and general marital satisfaction throughout therapy, given that these aspects will continue to influence and be influenced by the sexual relationship. Failure to make progress during intervention may reflect a negative change in the relationship, which needs to be dealt with in order for therapy to progress.

A variety of methods may be used to improve the couple's general relationship. In cases of marital or relationship distress, it is important that a detailed assessment is conducted in order to identify those factors that are contributing to the distress. These may include poor communication skills, poor problem-solving skills, and low levels of positive compared to negative interactions between the couple. A detailed outline of the assessment and treatment of marital satisfaction is beyond the scope of the present text and the reader is referred to classic texts such as Jacobson and Margolin (1979), Stuart (1980) or Gottman *et al.* (1976). A more recent review of developments in the area can be found in Schmaling *et al.* (1989). The methods described below are designed to enhance the general communication and conflict resolution skills of couples who present with mild or moderate relationship difficulties and where assessment reveals difficulties in communication and resolution of conflicts. An outline is also provided of methods for increasing the level of positive interactions (i.e. pleasant behaviours of one partner towards another) and couples are taught to focus on these events rather than negative spouse behaviours.

Increasing positive interactions

Satisfaction with the marital relationship has been shown to be highly influenced by positive interactions in non-distressed couples whereas distressed couples tend to be highly influenced by negative interactions (Jacobson *et al.*, 1980). It would therefore seem to be important to increase the level of positive interaction, decrease negative interaction and increase attention to positive partner behaviours when they occur. Increasing positive interactions typically results in an automatic decline in negative partner behaviours and aims to break the cycle of negative reciprocity which tends to occur for many distressed couples (Schmaling *et al.*, 1989). As the frequency of positive interactions increases, the couple typically perceive their relationship as more positive. This provides a positive base from which to commence the more difficult aspects of relationship therapy.

Several methods are available to increase the total level of positive interactions and to demonstrate the effect that this has upon the relationship. For example, the couple may each be asked to identify certain events or behaviours that they could engage in that would bring pleasure to their partner. Alternatively, the recipient may be asked to list various events or behaviours that they would like from the partner and which would create pleasure. The therapist may then instruct each partner to select and perform one of the suggestions each day. Perry and Weiss (1983) suggested an approach called Quality Time in which a menu of activities which both partners find pleasing is drawn up from a long list of suggestions. These are then carried out over the following days. A similar method involves the use of a 'lucky dip' in which each partner writes out a wide selection of events that they would find pleasurable if carried out by their partner. Each person then selects a card from the lucky dip and the aim is for the partner to carry out the assignment at some point during the day. Stuart (1980) makes use of Caring Days, where one person attempts to double the use of 'pleasers' that are given to the partner. Usually only one partner is the giver on a particular day and the couple take it in turns to be the giver and receiver. As with any positive partner behaviour, it is important that these events are high benefit and low cost. In other words, the events must be likely to bring considerable pleasure to the receiver and yet be relatively easy to carry out, without great cost to or effort from the giver.

Attempts at increasing positive interaction have been found to be effective in improving each partner's perception of the relationship and in the creation of a more positive atmosphere in which to commence the more difficult task of increasing communication and problem-solving skills (Jacobson and Margolin, 1979). These authors emphasized the need to commence relationship enhancement by increasing positive interactions, with a view to producing rapid, minor successes which are likely to reinforce the couple for their efforts at behaviour change and motivate them to continue their efforts in therapy. Other authors such as Perry and Weiss (1983) have recommended the teaching of communication skills first, to avoid possible disappointments during attempts to increase positive interactions if the couple have poor communication skills.

The task of increasing positive interactions may also provide some useful material for the cognitive restructuring components of therapy. Schmaling et al. (1989) point out that many couples hold the belief that a positive relationship should be automatic and should not require effort or work in order to make it satisfactory. The improvements in ratings of the quality of the relationship which result from the increase in positive interactions may be used to illustrate the point that the quality of the relationship depends upon the contribution of each partner. Discussions may be held about the frequently held belief that a great deal of effort is necessary in order to be successful at work. This view may then be contrasted with the irrational assumption that a successful relationship should not require effort from the couple and should somehow occur automatically.

Enhancing communication skills

General communication skills

One of the most useful descriptions of communication skills training for couples is provided by Gottman *et al.* (1976), who provided a self-help manual. The approach taken described a model in which the speaker sends a message to the listener. Effective communication occurs when the intent of the speaker equals the impact of the message upon the listener. The model points out that this process depends upon the skill of the speaker in sending the message accurately and the skill of the listener in picking up the message and interpreting it correctly. This model is extremely useful and easy for couples to understand when described diagrammatically, as shown by Gottman *et al.* (1976). The need for couples to become aware of the importance of non-verbal skills in transmission of a message and the value of listening skills can be clearly demonstrated.

The basic therapy techniques used to teach communication skills involve a combination of instructions, discussion, modelling, practice, feedback, role reversal and home-based assignments. Realistic role-played scenarios may be used in order to demonstrate the importance of various non-verbal and verbal skills. The non-verbal areas of eye contact, tone of voice, facial expression, gestures and posture should be explored initially. The ability to use these responses to communicate emotional content should be emphasized, along with the need to be able to interpret the non-verbal cues of the partner. The listening skills of eye contact, head movements, acknowledgements and use of empathic and reflective statements are important prerequisites of more complex skill development and these areas should also be a focus of intervention. The approach outlined by Gottman *et al.* (1976) asks the couple to attempt to discuss a relationship problem in the clinic and to indicate to each other the intent of each message and the impact produced. Whenever intent does not equal impact, the couple are taught to 'stop action' as a means of stopping cycles of miscommunication. The therapist plays an important role in demonstrating to the couple the reasons for the miscommunication and they may be asked to repeat the action while attempting to use their newly acquired communication skills.

Various skill areas have been emphasized by different authors in the literature relating to communication skills training. What follows is a summary of the important areas outlined by authors such as Perry and Weiss (1983), Jacobson and Margolin (1979), Gottman *et al.* (1976) and Stuart (1980). A major emphasis is placed on the elimination of a series of faulty, negative and often extremely impolite forms of communication which may occur between couples. These include selective listening, accusing/blaming statements, aggressive/abusive statements, emotional outbursts, defensiveness, justification by reference to past events, 'mind reading' (attributing motives or intent to the partner), overgeneralizing, changing the topic, justifying a negative behaviour by cross-blaming, use of negative trait labels, bringing in other negative issues to a discussion, interrupting, remaining silent and failing to express important emotions or feelings. Couples may be asked to give examples of these forms of negative communication as an illustration of the points involved. The session then progresses to a description of some of the important forms of communication that couples do need to be able to perform successfully. These include the expression of emotions, effective communication regarding intimate topics and resolution of the inevitable conflicts that arise whenever two people spend significant proportions of their lives together.

Teaching couples to communicate effectively in these areas requires that they are able to plan out appropriate responses, in addition to being able to make use of the necessary verbal and non-verbal skills that are involved in the performance of the response selected. The selection of a particular response to a given situation involves a series of cognitive decision-making steps. The decision-making process is highly influenced by the person's attitude and beliefs, hence the teaching of communication skills is closely tied to the cognitive therapy approaches of problem-solving skills training and cognitive restructuring. Generally, the cognitive and overt behavioural aspects of therapy may be conducted simultaneously, so that clients learn to choose appropriate strategies of responding in different situations and are then able to perform the chosen response in a skilled manner. There seems little point in teaching appropriate performance skills if maladaptive attitudes and thoughts lead the person to choose an inappropriate strategy for dealing with the situation. Take, for example, a situation in which one member of the partnership finds it difficult to initiate sexual activity with their partner. Although this behaviour may be rehearsed through role play in the clinic and the person may be able to perform the response appropriately under guidance from the therapist, this response is unlikely to occur successfully at home if a range of inhibitory thoughts and attitudes still exist, such as: 'I can't do this. I know that he'll feel offended if I suggest that we make love. He'll push me away and I'll feel terrible.' The underlying belief that it is the male prerogative to initiate sex prevails here and until this attitude is changed and until the inhibitory thoughts are eliminated, communication skills training of sexual initiations is unlikely to be of great benefit. An element of cognitive restructuring, within the context of communication skills training, is therefore necessary.

Communicating in sexual situations

The communication skills learned during sessions may be applied to the numerous non-sexual and sexual situations that couples encounter. Different situations may be selected as being relevant for training with different couples, according to the nature of their communication problems. In addition to non-sexual situations, it is important to ensure that the couple are able to communicate effectively about sexual or intimate topics. Sexual and intimate communication skills are closely linked and form a major focus for communication skills training for many couples. Training of these skills within clinic sessions and during home-based assignments also provides the opportunity for systematic desensitization as the result of exposure to many forms of communication that have previously caused anxiety and tend to be avoided. Various exercises may be used to serve this purpose. For example, the couple may be asked to take turns to discuss a particular sexual issue, which does not relate specifically to their sexual relationship, from a list of possible topics (such as a description of sexual anatomy, the functions of the different sexual body parts or common myths about sex). This task is very difficult for some individuals, who frequently resort to vague and inaccurate descriptions of various sexual parts or activities, rather than using specific and accurate terms. The therapist plays an important role in encouraging the couple to find acceptable and yet accurate terms relating to sexual activities or anatomy. These need not be excessively medical and yet should not be crude or degrading. Throughout the therapy process, the therapist models appropriate communication of sexual issues, and therapy itself provides a desensitizing experience.

Once the couple are able to communicate about sexual issues that do not relate to their own relationship, skills training should progress to focus upon the specific situations that the couple find difficult within their own relationship. Effective communication is important in a wide range of situations related to sex, as described in Chapter 4. For example, each partner must be able to successfully initiate sexual activity, refuse sexual approaches from their partner without causing offence, request particular types of preferred activities and provide feedback about unpleasant forms of stimulation. These areas may be rehearsed during clinic sessions, following discussion and therapist modelling (if required). Further practice may be conducted during home-based assignments. Additional tasks which are designed to facilitate communication about sexual issues may be given, such as:

- A brainstorming exercise in which each partner is asked to suggest as many ways as possible that could enhance their sexual relationship;
- Each partner is asked to describe what would constitute 'good sex' for them;
- Each partner is asked to describe what their aims and goals are from their sexual relationship;
- Each partner is asked to describe an ideal fantasy.

These exercises may be set as home-based tasks, or for therapist supervision within the clinic, depending upon the need for therapist guidance and feedback. Where the couple are unable to complete the assignment, their thoughts and attitudes related to the exercise should be explored, as these provide valuable material for cognitive restructuring.

Expression of emotions

The expression of emotions, particularly affection, is extremely difficult for many individuals. Treat (1987) suggested that many couples learn to communicate with each other about emotional matters at a very superficial level. Direct reference to specific emotions is avoided, with the result that each individual may have difficulty in determining the actual feelings of their partner. Treat suggested various techniques for the teaching of emotional communication with couples. Couples are asked to practise the use of 'I' statements in which expressions should include the term 'I' in relation to feelings, rather than the use of passive or third party references. For example, instead of saying 'you never cuddle me', the person would be asked to explain their emotions more clearly, such as 'I really feel happy when you give me a cuddle. Would you be able to do this more often?' Treat also asks couples to focus on the here and now rather than bringing up the past when discussing emotional issues. In addition clients are asked to build a hierarchy of statements which range from very superficial to deeper, specific expression in order to demonstrate the difference between superficial and accurate, clear communication of emotions. For example:

'You're never here'; (vague, superficial)
'I get fed up on my own all the time';
'I get lonely when you're away';
'I enjoy your company and would like to spend more time with you'. (accurate, specific)

Schmaling *et al.* (1989) suggested a useful exercise to encourage clients to focus upon specific emotions. Each partner is asked to generate a list of as many negative and positive emotions as possible, such as:

Postive: happy, ecstatic, joyful, relaxed, blissful, pleased, hopeful, loved, passionate, randy.
Negative: tense, angry, rejected, hurt, anxious, miserable, unhappy, afraid, disgusted, disappointed, guilty.

Each partner is asked to come up with a list of ten positive and ten negative emotions. These emotions may then be placed into context by asking each person to describe to their partner a situation related to their relationship in which each emotion would occur. The couple are asked to take turns in expression and to alternate a positive emotion and a negative emotion. For example:

Her:
I feel . . . loved . . . when you roll over and kiss me in the morning.
I feel . . . disappointed . . . when I have cooked a nice supper and you come home late from work.
Him:
I feel . . . passionate . . . when you nibble my shoulders.
I feel . . . angry . . . when you criticize the clothes I wear.

These expressions are made verbally and the partner may then be asked to paraphrase the statement. It is important that the couple are instructed not to attempt to problem-solve at this point nor to try to discuss the reason for the emotion, or conflicts and arguments may result!

Problem-solving skills training

It is extremely difficult for couples to communicate effectively if they do not have the skills necessary for solving problems. Conflict resolution involves a complex interaction between the communication skills outlined above and a series of decision-making steps that determine the response that a person chooses to engage in. An initial description of problem-solving was proposed by D'Zurilla and Goldfried (1971) and has since been adapted by numerous authors. The basic steps may be summarized as:

- Identification that a problem situation is present which requires solving;
- Generation of a range of potential solutions (irrespective of suitability);
- Prediction of likely consequences of possible solutions;
- Evaluation of the relative short-term and long-term costs and benefits;
- An estimate of the feasibility of possible solutions;
- Selection of the most appropriate solution.

Couples are taught to make use of these steps during attempts to solve the problems that occur within their relationship. At first, the steps are practised in the clinic under the guidance of the therapist. Real problems are selected for discussion and couples are asked to make use of appropriate communication skills. Certain rules may be set which facilitate the process. For example, the couple may be requested to set aside specified times at home during which problem-solving should be attempted and no attempts should be made outside of the set times (Jacobson and Margolin, 1979). In addition, the couple may be asked to hold an agenda-setting meeting in which a set topic is selected for discussion. The problem-solving session must then focus on this topic and neither partner may introduce other problems during this session. The description of the problem should commence with a positive expression about the partner, should include the use of 'I' statements and the expression of the emotions produced. For example:

> **'I really appreciate it when you pick up the children on the days that I have to work late. I know that my decision to go back to work has made picking up the children a problem but I am feeling really worried about having to leave work early each day to pick them up.'**

This example also illustrates another rule that suggests the individual should always acknowledge their own contribution to the problem rather than placing the blame on the partner. The partner is then asked to paraphrase the expression in order to facilitate accurate listening and to check that the impact of the message equals the intended message. For example, the partner may respond with:

'If I understand the problem correctly, having to take time off work is starting to bother you and we are going to have to find some other way of picking up the kids from school.'

This provides an opportunity for confirmation or correction about the problem being presented. The attempt at problem solution may then begin, following the steps of problem-solving outlined above. In the example given here the suggested solutions could include:

- She gives up her job.
- He gives up his job.
- They change schools to one that provides an after-school centre.
- They employ a person to collect the children.
- She works part-time.
- He works part-time.
- They continue without change.
- She can learn relaxation exercises to learn to cope.
- They can take it in turns to leave work early.

The problem-solving process then proceeds to predict the likely consequences of each, to work out the cost–benefit analysis and determine the feasibility of each alternative. The most suitable solution may then be selected. (In the actual case the couple advertised for a part-time person to collect the children.) This approach may also be useful in teaching the couple how to problem-solve issues related to their sexual relationship. The following example may illustrate this point. The husband in the situation expressed the following problem:

'I really enjoy making love with you. I know that I sometimes pick inappropriate times to want to make love but I am feeling pretty miserable that we never seem to find a time when we both feel like having sex.'

His partner responded with:

'You seem to be unhappy that we don't make love very often. I am usually too tired by the end of the day, or the children are around, or you are working late.'

A variety of potential solutions were proposed by this couple during a brainstorming session, initially without regard to their value or acceptability. These included . . . to give up sex; take a lover; put a lock on the bedroom door; go away together for a weekend and leave the children with grandma; go to bed earlier; he could force her; stop working so hard; give up work; try anyway despite tiredness; leave the kids with friends on Saturday afternoons. Each alternative was then evaluated in terms of a cost–benefit, likely outcome and feasibility. Eventually, the couple opted to ask a friend to take the children out occasionally for a few hours on a Saturday afternoon.

The aim of the problem-solving training is that the steps learned will eventually be used by the couple to solve current problems within their relationship and to deal with new conflict situations as they arise. Problem solution is important in order that areas of conflict do not remain unresolved, as these tend to make it difficult for the couple to enhance other areas of their relationship during the therapy process.

COGNITIVE THERAPIES

Cognitive therapies may be defined as those intervention methods that aim to produce change in overt and cognitive behaviour primarily through a direct focus upon changing cognitive skills, thoughts and attitudes. Two distinct types of cognitive therapy exist. The first type concerns those therapies that are designed to enhance cognitive skills such as sexual knowledge, ability to focus attention upon sexual cues and bodily sensations, ability to correctly interpret sexual arousal sensations and the ability to use imagery for sexual fantasies. The second type of cognitive therapy attempts to reduce specific thoughts or attitudes that interfere with or inhibit sexual functioning and to increase the occurrence of more adaptive, constructive thoughts or attitudes.

Enhancing cognitive skills

Increasing sexual knowledge

A significant component in the treatment of many cases of sexual dysfunction includes the enhancement of sexual knowledge. Obviously, the degree to which this is important will vary for different clients, according to the deficits in sexual knowledge identified during assessment. The major areas to be covered include sexual anatomy, the human sexual response and techniques for self and partner stimulation. The methods used to increase knowledge may include direct information from the therapist, discussion with the partner, reading material, films, guidance by the partner and observation of the partner. The education component of therapy may vary from sessions which specifically focus on provision of information, to an ongoing process which occurs where appropriate throughout therapy.

Accurate knowledge about sexual issues not only makes it more likely that practical skills will improve, but also serves to reduce adherence to the many myths regarding sexual functioning that abound in our society. For example, the provision of information concerning issues such as the normality of masturbation or use of sexual fantasy amongst women may result in marked shifts in inhibitory attitudes for some clients.

Fantasy training

Relaxation training is frequently conducted prior to fantasy training, since if the client is able to relax during fantasy training he/she will be less likely to be troubled by intrusive, negative thoughts. Some clients find imagery very difficult and it is important to begin by teaching control of the content of their thoughts, to prevent them wandering off the topic. During relaxation training, the instructions to focus the attention upon the sensations of the muscles and to describe these is a useful start in gaining control over thoughts.

Fantasy training usually begins with non-sexual images which are more acceptable to those clients who have negative attitudes towards the use of fantasy. Initially, imagery may focus on simple objects, with attention being drawn to colour, shape and size. For example, the client may be asked to image a series of shapes, perhaps beginning with a red triangle, then a blue square, which gradually move together until the square is positioned below the triangle. Interestingly, some clients find this type of basic imagery, which does not have any emotional content or personal involvement, very difficult to achieve. In some cases, it may be preferable to commence with more complex, emotionally involving scenes. Attention to bodily sensations is obviously important in sexual fantasies, hence it is important to train imagery which includes a focus on bodily sensations.

The following instructions may be helpful in increasing fantasy ability in clients who currently have poor fantasy skills or who have not previously used fantasy. These instructions were developed by the author for clinical psychology students to use with sexually dysfunctional clients:

> 'Now, I want you to continue relaxing and to imagine you are lying on the beach. Try to imagine that you are really there. There are very few people around and you are on your own. It is a hot, sunny day and you are lying on a towel. Concentrate for a moment upon the things you can hear. Really concentrate and block out any other thoughts that may intrude. What can you hear? Perhaps you can hear the sound of the waves breaking against the beach. Maybe you can hear some children playing. You continue to relax. Try to describe to yourself how you are feeling. You have no cares or worries, you can just lie there and enjoy the feelings. Now, concentrate upon other sensations in your body. Imagine the feeling of heat upon your skin. You can also feel the grains of sand between your fingers. Concentrate on those feelings until you can really imagine that you are there. You are still on the beach. You slowly sit up on your towel and look around you. Focus your attention on the things you can see. Look at the colours and the shapes. Describe them to yourself . . . and relax. Now, slowly open your eyes and describe to me what you could see, hear and feel.'

Other scenes may be used in order to shape up imagery ability. Clients may also be able to describe non-sexual images of their own. Common examples include water scenes and snow scenes, for example:

> 'You are on top of a mountain. It is winter and very cold, but you are dressed in warm clothing. Really concentrate on being there for a moment . . . feel the clean, fresh, chilled air as you breathe in. The air feels cold and sharp as it fills up your lungs. You feel the cold air against your cheeks. You listen, but there is silence. You are alone. The sun is shining and the sky is brilliant blue. See the colours around you. There is snow on the ground. Crisp and clean and sparkling. You take a coat and lie down in the snow. You can feel the chill through your body. You reach out and take a handful of snow in your bare hands. Concentrate on the sensations. Squeeze your hand and the snow compacts. It starts to melt and you feel the cold, icy water trickling through your fingers.'

In some cases it is useful to follow this image with the one related to lying in front of a large log fire!

A frequently used example in the training of imagery skills in pain management is the 'lemon scene':

'You are in the kitchen and go to the refrigerator and take out a large, fresh lemon. Concentrate upon the texture of its skin. Feel the waxy surface and the dimples in the skin. It is bright yellow. You lift it up and smell the skin. Then you place it on a board and take a sharp knife and cut it in half. Look down and see the pattern of the segments where you cut through the lemon. Now, you pick up one half of the lemon and you bite into it. You get a sudden surge of the bitter, lemon taste in your mouth. Really concentrate on that taste.'

Most clients find this scene extremely realistic and find their mouth watering by the end of the imagery practice.

Once the client is able to produce realistic, non-sexual images and is able to experience the emotions and sensations associated with the scene, then training progresses to include a non-sexual massage example. Subsequently, the image may progress to a sensual massage and feelings of mild sexual arousal may be described. In the therapy sessions, it is suggested that the therapist focuses on very mild sexual situations, given that these are initially spoken out aloud by the therapist. This avoids any ethical dilemmas concerning strong sexual fantasy talk by the therapist and the clients may practise these on their own at home.

During the clinic-based practice, the client is asked to describe a situation that would trigger mild levels of sexual arousal. Details about the scene are given to the therapist so that he or she may describe the scene realistically. The scene is therefore individualized to the client. Instructions are given to concentrate on the bodily sensations produced, to imagine really being present in the scene and to push out any intrusive thoughts. Each scene may then be practised at home, initially with audio-taped therapist guidance if the client is still having difficulties retaining the image under self-management. Again, it is not suggested that the therapist tape record strong sexual fantasy instructions, as this task may be left to the client.

For some clients, sexual fantasy is enhanced by the use of erotic materials. Short stories with sexual content are particularly useful for this purpose and clients may be instructed to imagine that they are one of the characters in the story, or that a similar situation is happening to them. Suggestions for this type of erotic literature are given in Chapter 6.

Attention-focusing skills

Several exercises may be used to teach individuals to improve their ability to discriminate and attend to their own physiological cues of sexual arousal. The following exercises were developed for use in the treatment of female orgasmic problems (Spence, 1985), with clients who reported having difficulty maintaining concentration upon sexual arousal cues, or did not seem able to identify physiological changes associated with sexual arousal when it was likely that such cues were present. The exercise may also be of value, however, in the treatment of premature ejaculation and retarded ejaculation for men who have difficulty attending to physiological sexual cues.

The first stage of training attention focusing skills involves the use of non-sexual situations. Clients are asked to relax and focus their attention on a particular object (in our clinic, we use a picture on the wall). The client is then asked to describe the object in fine detail, focusing upon colours, textures, shapes, interpretation of meaning, uses, etc. This is useful in demonstrating how we tend to ignore much of what goes on around us and how this also applies to bodily sensations. Practice in attention-focusing on non-bodily cues also demonstrates the need to inhibit interfering thoughts and to concentrate attention on a particular task if details are to be noticed.

The second stage of training in attention-focusing skills then teaches the client to attend to non-sexual bodily cues. After a brief period of relaxation, the client is asked to concentrate on the feeling in a particular part of their body, such as their left arm. They are then asked to describe the feelings that they are aware of. They are then asked to tense up that part of the body and are again asked to describe the bodily sensations in detail. Alternatively, clients may be asked when they last concentrated upon the feelings in their big toes. They are then asked to focus their attention on their big toes. This illustrates how bodily cues are always present and yet they may be ignored unless an effort is made to concentrate upon those sensations. A home-based assignment is then set, in which the above exercises are repeated and the client is asked to concentrate on the feelings of tension and relaxation in a sexual area. For women, it is usual to focus on the relaxation and contraction of the pubococcygeal muscles, as outlined in the Kegal exercises (see Chapter 6). These muscles should be tensed and then relaxed ten times, while focusing on the sensations and attempting to describe them to oneself.

In the later stages of training attention-focusing skills, the client commences with a home-based relaxation and self-pleasuring exercise in which the genital area is gently massaged, using a lotion if preferred. Again, the aim is to attend to sensations in the various genital areas and to attempt to describe (to oneself) the feelings experienced. Difficulties in maintaining attention may be discussed at the next clinic session. Finally, the same procedure may be repeated during genital pleasuring by the partner (during sensate focus 2 exercises, as outlined in Chapter 6) and later during intercourse situations.

Cognitive restructuring in relation to psychosexual dysfunctions

The underlying proposition of cognitive therapists such as Beck *et al.* (1979) is that an individual's thoughts (sub-vocal speech, self-statements) are important in determining emotions and ultimately in determining overt behaviour. In some instances an individual may develop a series of maladaptive thoughts which tend to be automatic in certain situations and which may result in negative emotions. Whilst this appears to be true in relation to depression and anxiety states, it is proposed here to be relevant in determining affective and overt behavioural responses to sexual situations. The treatment of psychosexual dysfunctions should therefore attempt to restructure maladaptive cognitions for clients whose thoughts and attitudes interfere with successful sexual functioning.

Two main cognitive restructuring approaches can be seen to be relevant in the treatment of psychosexual dysfunctions. The first is that outlined by Beck *et al.* (1979), which focuses on reducing the occurrence of maladaptive thoughts and self-statements. Although this approach was originally developed for use in the treatment of depression, the methods used can easily be applied to the reduction of maladaptive thoughts which contribute towards sexual problems. The second approach is adapted from the work of Ellis (1958), which attempts to alter irrational and illogical attitudes and beliefs and replace them with more rational and logical alternatives. The cognitive restructuring process therefore occurs at two levels: at a level of specific, currently occurring self-statements (i.e. the actual thoughts that we verbalize to ourselves), and also at the level of attitudes or beliefs which can be viewed as the rules that we hold about ourselves, others and the world. The importance of specific thoughts and attitudes/beliefs was outlined in Chapter 2. What follows here are suggestions for methods that may be used during therapy, to deal with negative cognitive influences.

The majority of programmes which have been developed to treat sexual dysfunctions have acknowledged the influence of thoughts and attitudes (e.g. Barbach, 1980; Kaplan, 1974; Masters and Johnson, 1970). These approaches have tended to assume that cognitive change will occur as a by-product of behavioural assignments and the general therapy process. It is only recently that it has been acknowledged that some couples presenting with sexual difficulties require a more direct approach to the restructuring of maladaptive self-statements and attitudes.

Although it is important to make a distinction between the actual thoughts that a person engages in and their attitudes and beliefs, it is difficult to separate out the two areas. In many respects a person's specific thoughts in a situation reflect their beliefs and attitudes about that situation. For example, a male client reported a series of thoughts relating to the expression of emotions which included: 'I can't do this. I can't tell her that I really care deeply about her. She'll think I've gone soft.' Such thoughts may be seen to reflect an underlying acceptance of the rule 'Real men do not expose their emotions. To do so would be to show weakness' (see Zilbergild's myths, Chapter 2). In other instances, however, it may be difficult to determine any general rules (attitudes/beliefs) that underlie the maladaptive thoughts. In practice, a two-tiered approach to cognitive restrucuring is required in which maladaptive thoughts and attitudes are tackled during therapy.

Maladaptive thoughts and attitudes play an important role in determining how information is interpreted in sexual situations and ultimately whether the individual experiences sexual desire, arousal and orgasm. If incoming stimuli are interpreted in a way which results in positive sexual thoughts, then this is likely to have a very different effect upon sexual responding than if the situation is interpreted in a way that triggers a range of negative thoughts. Weeks (1987) emphasize the need to explore maladaptive thoughts in relation to the self, the partner and the relationship and demonstrated how negative thoughts in these domains may have a marked impact upon sexual functioning. Consider the following situation for a couple who were referred to the clinic for treatment of female sexual orgasmic dysfunction in which the female partner was unable to experience orgasm during intercourse, whatever form of stimulation was tried. Her partner returned home one evening with a small bunch of flowers and a bottle of wine. He suggested that they practice the sensate focus, genital pleasuring exercises. The emotional and behavioural response of the woman could vary as dramatically, for example:

Maladaptive:
> 'There he goes again. I know what he's after. I don't see why I should do these exercises anyway. I'm never going to be able to have an orgasm with him around. I don't see why I should have sex with him. There's nothing in it for me.'

Adaptive:
> 'Gosh, that was kind of him. It will be nice to have a romantic evening together. We can both enjoy these exercises and at least they should make us feel more affectionate towards each other.'

Explaining the rationale for cognitive restructuring

Treat (1987) suggests that the first step in cognitive restructuring in relation to sexual dysfunctions is to provide the couple with a rationale for the procedure. This may be partly achieved through the description of examples which illustrate the influence that thoughts and attitudes may have on sexual desire, arousal and orgasmic ability. The rationale may be more clearly understood if the couple are asked to demonstrate to themselves how positive and negative thoughts lead to different emotional reactions. Each partner is asked to relax, to close their eyes and to imagine a specific occasion with their partner in which they both had a wonderful time together. The couple are instructed to concentrate upon what they can see, hear and feel and are then asked to identify their particular thoughts in that situation. This process is repeated with a negative situation. The aim is to identify the specific thoughts that occurred and to demonstrate how negative thoughts may inhibit sexual responding. The need to replace such thoughts with more positive cognitions can then be emphasized. It is important to explain to the couple that maladaptive thoughts often become a habit, but may be changed if people are able to notice when they occur and if an effort is made to replace the negative thoughts with more positive, logical, rational alternatives.

Different cognitive therapists have different ways of working, but it is suggested here that a useful component of providing the rationale is to outline Ellis's (1958) ABC model, to illustrate the importance of beliefs in determining our thoughts, emotional reactions and behaviours to particular situations (see Chapter 2). Discussion may then follow of some of the common myths that are held concerning sexual functioning, such as those proposed by Zilbergeld (1975). The couple can then be asked to predict the likely thoughts and behaviour, in hypothetical sexual situations, of people who adhere to such beliefs.

Describing different types of maladaptive cognitions

Once the couple have understood the rationale for cognitive restructuring, it is useful to describe some of the common forms of 'faulty'/maladaptive/negative thinking that may occur. The present approach integrates the therapeutic suggestions of various authors such as Beck *et al.* (1979) and Ellis (1958). Examples are provided to the client to illustrate different types of maladaptive thoughts, using situations relevant to sexual functioning:

Overgeneralizations:
   'I will always be like this. I will never be able to reach orgasm.'
All-or-none thinking:
   'Because our sexual relationship is poor, our whole relationship is a disaster.'
Magnifying negatives and disqualifying positives:
   'Having this erectile problem is absolutely terrible. The fact that my partner cares for me deeply and we have a good relationship in other areas is unimportant.' This type of thinking includes: 'catastrophizing' or 'awfulizing'.
Personalizations:
   'Because my partner has difficulty reaching orgasm, she can't find me attractive. She can't love me.'

Other examples of the faulty thinking include:

- Selective abstractions (a tendency to focus on some detail of the situation, taken out of context, ignoring other features of the situation);
- Dichotomous reasoning (a tendency to place all experiences into one of two extreme/opposite categories, e.g. good/bad);
- Shoulds, oughts and musts (these may be identified within self-statements and typically reflect some underlying irrational belief concerning what should, ought, must occur in the client's life, as described by Ellis, 1958).

Further examples of types of faulty thinking were provided in Chapter 2.

Weeks (1987) emphasizes the importance of negative thoughts, rather than faulty, illogical cognitions, in determining sexual desire and arousal. It is proposed that sexual functioning is inhibited by a focus on the negative characteristics of the self, partner and the relationship, with the exclusion of attention to positive characteristics. The negative focus tends to result in negative self-statements which can be identified by the therapist and clients. This approach has the advantage that intervention aims to increase the use of positive self-talk, rather than attempting to challenge the accuracy or logicality of the thoughts. Hence, if the negative thoughts concerning the partner's bad habits or one's own deficits are actually true, these do not need to be challenged, but rather the clients are asked to focus their attention on positive characteristics of the self, partner or the relationship. The following examples illustrate negative self-statements relating to the self, partner and the relationship:

Self:
  I can't do it.
  I'm not attractive any more. My breasts are droopy and I'm very overweight.
  My private parts are disgusting.
Partner:
  He's going bald.
  He's so untidy.
  All he ever wants is sex.
The relationship:
  If we really loved each other, we wouldn't have this problem.
  We're incompatible, it won't work.

Identifying maladaptive thoughts and attitudes

Various methods may be used to identify maladaptive or negative thoughts and attitudes. In many instances these arise spontaneously during therapy sessions and the therapist should be on the constant look-out for their occurrence. Response to assessment questionnaires may also be a valuable source of information. Self-monitoring provides a useful means of obtaining information about the occurrence of negative, maladaptive thoughts in specific situations. For example, recording of actual thoughts before, during and after sensate focus exercises may provide a valuable source of data for cognitive restructuring sessions. The self-monitoring sheets may be brought to the next session and subjected to challenging and restructuring. It is important to explain that self-statements must be recorded exactly, word for word, rather than providing vague descriptions. One of the main challenges for cognitive therapists is to identify which cognitions are relevant to the presenting problem and which are not.

Failure to complete home-based assignments or negative outcomes provide one of the most valuable sources of information regarding negative, automatic thoughts. The couple may be asked to recall their exact thoughts before, during and/or after the exercise. These thoughts may be used to demonstrate the emotional consequences of negative thoughts and the impact upon sexual behaviour. Similarly, the therapist may ask the couple to imagine that they are about to undertake the exercise and ask them to describe the thoughts that occur. For example:

Therapist: 'Michael, I want you to close your eyes for a moment and imagine that it is 8.15 p.m. and you have agreed with Jan to begin the sensate focus, genital pleasuring exercises at 8.30 p.m. Now, really imagine that you are there . . . concentrate on the situation until it feels like this is really happening. What are your thoughts now?'

Michael: 'Oh, hell, I can't go through with this. I really don't want to do this.'

Therapist: 'Continue to imagine the situation. What other thoughts come into your mind?'

Michael: 'I feel ridiculous. I feel like a failure. I shouldn't have to go through all this. All normal men can get erections. It should be natural. Jan must think I'm a real failure.'

Therapist: 'Now, Jan. Can you try this same exercise and really concentrate on your own thoughts. What are you thinking now?'

Jan: 'I hope Michael doesn't ask me to do this exercise. I know he hates having to go through this programme. I daren't ask him myself or he'll probably go off in one of those tantrums. I don't really think he wants sex with me anyway. He probably doesn't find me attractive enough. I am a bit fat and I'm not exactly beautiful.'

Not only does this type of exercise identify a variety of maladaptive self-statements, it also provides the therapist with an insight into some of the underlying attitudes or beliefs of each partner. In the present example, Michael can be seen as adhering to the assumptions that (a) all men must be successful sexually, (b) a problem in sexual responding means that a man is a total failure and (c) sexual competence should be innate and does not have to be learned. Jan in turn holds the belief that a woman has to fit into the stereotype of the perfect woman in order for a partner to find her attractive. It is particularly important for the therapist to investigate whether any themes underlie each partner's maladaptive cognitions, as this may indicate specific areas of unresolved conflict that are contributing to the problem, either in the sexual domain or in the relationship in general. Themes may relate to male–female roles in sex/life, issues of equity, power and control of the relationship, the distinction between sex and affection or intimacy fears. These issues may be tackled through cognitive restructuring, but also through the techniques of relationship enhancement outlined above.

The communication skills training exercises described above, in which the couple are asked to discuss a particular topic and explore the relationship between intent and impact, frequently reveal maladaptive thoughts or attitudes that are relevant to the presenting problem. This technique may be applied to sexual situations, for example:

Problem for discussion: Peter is coming to bed around 1 hour later than Marian.
Peter: 'I go to bed later so that I give you a chance to get off to sleep. You know you need more sleep than me and I tend to keep you awake.'
The impact of the message upon Marian, however, is 'Well I know you're just trying to avoid me. Obviously you don't find me attractive anymore and don't want to make love.'

Given this type of discrepancy between intent and impact, it is possible to explore the actual thoughts and beliefs that underlie such common errors in communication.

Cognitive challenging

Once the individuals are aware of their cognitive distortions and can identify when they occur, the therapist is in a position to commence the teaching of cognitive challenging skills. Initially, this is best conducted in the clinic situation under therapist guidance. Information from self-monitoring sheets, or situations which arise during the session, may be taken as examples for cognitive challenging. Initially, Beck *et al.* (1979) suggest that the clients are asked to state their degree of belief in the truth of a particular thought on a 0–100 scale.

The thought is then challenged, with the therapist asking for evidence for and against the truth or accuracy of the thought. Clients are asked to generate alternative thoughts that provide a more logical, correct interpretation of the situation. They are also asked to search for examples of faulty thinking within their thoughts. Finally, the clients reassess their original thoughts and note their belief in those self-statements. This process may be recorded on specially designed sheets as described by Fennell (1989).

In addition to practice in cognitive challenging within the clinic, the clients may also be asked to carry out home-based assignments as a means of providing evidence for disputing maladaptive thoughts. For example, one client reported the thought that his wife 'never did anything nice to please him and that she obviously didn't care about him'. That week he was asked to keep a record of any pleasing activities or behaviours that she engaged in. This task provided him with evidence that his wife actually did many things in an attempt to please him and that she obviously cared about him a great deal. He was then able to produce a much more realistic appraisal of his partner and their relationship. Fennell (1989) points out that the home-based tasks set should provide a 'no-lose' situation, where even a negative outcome may be beneficial, such as providing valuable information for discussion in the following session. For example, in her home-based recordings, one lady reported the thought 'I cannot get aroused. There must be something the matter with me'. She was set the assignment of having a relaxing bath on her own, to read a short, erotic story and to engage in her favourite fantasy. She was then asked to relax further and engage in gentle, genital self-massage using a gel. During this time she was to concentrate on the feelings of pleasure, but not to try to become sexually aroused. She was also asked to record specific thoughts that occurred before, during and after the exercise. The therapist predicted that this assignment would produce some mild feelings of sexual arousal for this lady and that this would provide evidence to demonstrate that she could become aroused, given the appropriate conditions. If arousal was not experienced, it was predicted that some maladaptive thoughts or attitudes would be identified that could be worked on in the next session.

The presence of the partner within the therapy session may also be valuable in providing evidence to dispute maladaptive cognitions. For example, one female client experienced numerous negative thoughts about self-stimulation in front of her partner and was unable to demonstrate to him the most pleasurable types of stimulation. Her thoughts revolved around her concerns that he would perceive her as disgusting or dirty if she was to do so. When this was raised in the session, he was able to discuss his actual thoughts about the activity and demonstrate that he would not feel negatively towards her.

The examples in Tables 5.1 and 5.2 illustrate the process of cognitive restructuring with sexually dysfunctional clients. The first example relates to the challenging of a specific, negative thought concerning the partner. Challenging took place within a clinic session, in

Table 5.1 Self-monitoring of thoughts and cognitive challenging related to partner

Date	Emotion	Situation	What exactly were you thinking?	What would be a more positive/ rational thought?	How do you feel now?
			How much did you believe each thought (0-100)	How much do you believe them? (0-100)	How much do you believe the original thought? (0-100)
19 Jan.	Angry Rejected Unloved	Husband worked late on my birthday	Damn him! (70) He doesn't care about me at all (90) He never considers my feelings (80)	He has a deadline to meet at work and he has just started this new job. He is worried about doing it badly (90)	A bit calmer Lonely but not angry (30) (50) (40)

Table 5.2 Self-monitoring of thoughts and cognitive challenging related to a sexual situation

Date	Emotion	Situation	What exactly were you thinking?	What would be a more positive/ rational thought?	How do you feel now?
			How much did you believe each thought (0-100)	How much do you believe them? (0-100)	How much do you believe the original thought? (0-100)
21 Jan.	Panicky Anxious Afraid	We are supposed to practise our massage exercises tonight	I wish we didn't have to do this (100) It is only going to lead on to other things (95) Mark is bound to expect to make love (95)	Just keep calm (90) Mark will stick to Dr S's instructions (50) I can tell him of my worries first (70) I can do it (60)	Still a little tense A bit more relaxed (50) (40) (40)

which the client was asked to identify possible alternative explanations for her partner's behaviour. The second example concerns the challenging of negative thoughts which occurred prior to the practice of a sensate focus 2 (genital pleasuring) exercise. Challenging took place in a clinic session in which both partners were present. Both partners were asked to state their thoughts about sensate focus exercises and the woman identified some specific, maladaptive thoughts about the tasks. In the session, Mark was able to list his thoughts about the situation, which provided evidence for cognitive challenging of her maladaptive thoughts. She then felt more able to take part in the home-based assignments.

It is important to mention at this point that some maladaptive cognitions may actually be logical and accurate, even though their occurrence creates negative emotions. For example, a couple may actually have a terrible relationship, or indeed one partner may not feel sexually attracted towards the other. Obviously, there will be times when the therapist realizes that successful treatment of a sexual dysfunction may not be feasible, or that the relationship of a particular couple is so negative as to be beyond help. In such instances therapy may need to focus on problem-solving in order to determine an alternative solution or separation counselling may be required, if this is desired by the couple.

Challenging of underlying attitudes and beliefs

Although it can be difficult for clients and therapists to identify specific maladaptive thoughts, it is often even harder to determine the exact nature of maladaptive attitudes or beliefs. Attitudes tend to reflect certain rules that a person adheres to and which result in consistencies in thoughts and behaviour. To a large extent, attitudes and beliefs must therefore be inferred on the basis of consistent patterns of thoughts or behaviours, or from a self-report of a client regarding the acceptance of a particular attitude or belief. It is often difficult to determine exactly which attitude should be tackled, in that attitudes are frequently hierarchical, with one attitude giving rise to a series of secondary attitudes and so on; see the example in Table 5.3.

Ellis was one of the founders of cognitive therapy and initially outlined his ABC theory of emotional disturbance in 1958. This theory proposed that activating events (A) resulted in emotional and/or behavioural consequences (C) according to the beliefs (B) held about the situation. If these beliefs are irrational, then they may lead to

Table 5.3

Attitude 1	Everything must be perfect at all times		
Secondary attitudes	I must be good at sex	My relationship must be wonderful	My partner must never do anything wrong

negative outcomes in terms of emotions and behaviours. An emphasis is placed on four major types of irrational beliefs, namely *must*urbatory ideology (demands about what should or must happen), *awfulizing* (it is terrible, awful, a catastrophe when things are not the way they should/must be), '*can't bear its*' (the situation can't be tolerated if things are not the way they should/must be), and *damnations* (any person, including oneself, who prevents things from being the way they should/must be is a terrible person who deserves to be damned). These beliefs tend to be unrealistic, irrational and extreme, resulting in negative emotional reactions (such as anger, depression, anxiety or disgust) in situations which do not fit with the rules. Certain underlying beliefs are common in the area of sexual dysfunctions, such as those outlined by Zilbergeld and others (see Chapter 2). A list of these is helpful in assisting the therapist to explore the existence of commonly held maladaptive attitudes and beliefs. Consistently arising thoughts or behaviours should also facilitate the identification of maladaptive beliefs.

Fennell (1989) in reviewing Beck's approach to cognitive restructuring refers to cognitive assumptions, rather than attitudes or beliefs, in describing the rules that underlie negative, automatic thoughts. Both Ellis and Beck assume that beliefs/cognitive assumptions (whatever term is used) may be challenged. The therapist must first identify the underlying rule and then teach the client to challenge this by asking:

- In what way is the belief unreasonable?
- In what way is it unhelpful?
- What would be a more rational, alternative belief?
- What belief would result in a more positive emotional reaction to the situation?

A useful description of the challenging of maladaptive attitudes is also provided within the context of rational emotive therapy (see Ellis, 1977). Ellis teaches clients first to identify and then to dispute irrational beliefs. The aim is to generate more logical,

163

rational beliefs, which in turn generate more adaptive emotional and behavioural responses to the situation of concern. In practice, the challenging of irrational beliefs closely resembles the process involved in the challenging of maladaptive thoughts. Individuals are taught to search for more appropriate interpretations of information, to collect evidence with which to dispute original conclusions and to identify the negative emotions and behaviours that will be produced if the irrational belief is adhered to. Ultimately, a more adaptive belief can be substituted, which can in turn be tested out and hopefully reinforced.

There appears to be a lack of literature concerning the details of application of cognitive restructuring methods in the treatment of psychosexual dysfunctions. Zilbergeld (1975) briefly describes a cognitive challenging approach which he terms 'debunking male sexual mythology'. McCarthy (1984) also mentions the use of cognitive therapy procedures, in order to bring about attitudinal change, but neither of these authors provides specific guidelines for the conduct of cognitive therapy in relation to sexual problems.

Having outlined the methods involved in the conduct of relationship enhancement therapies and restructuring of maladaptive thoughts and beliefs, it is now important to explore those techniques which will focus more directly upon sexual behaviour change.

6

Sexual skill development and techniques relating to specific psychosexual dysfunctions

If sexual responding is viewed as a skill then it may be assumed that such responses may be taught, given an appropriate learning experience. Our knowledge of skill development in other areas of human behaviour suggests that the most effective way of teaching new skills is a combination of instructions, discussion, modelling, practice and feedback about the quality of performance. As mentioned in Chapter 2, individuals rarely have the opportunity of optimal learning experiences in the development of sexual skills, hence it is perhaps not surprising that so many people experience difficulties in sexual responding. The core elements of sex therapy that have been found to be effective in enhancing sexual functioning can be seen to provide situations in which appropriate learning experiences may take place. The ethical limitations upon the forms of teaching that may take place within a clinical setting require that the majority of learning experiences occur within the privacy of the client's home, with their regular partner. The instructions and discussion components take place within the clinic, under the direction of the therapist, with home-based tasks being designed to provide practice of new behaviours and feedback from the partner. Modelling may be used in the form of guidance by the partner for tasks involving physical contact and by the therapist when the skill relates to verbal communication. Tasks are used to teach graduated steps in skill development, using successive approximations to the final goal.

SENSATE FOCUS 1: NON-GENITAL PLEASURING

The non-genital sensate focus 1 exercise was originally developed by Masters and Johnson (1970) and has been adapted in various ways by different practitioners over the past twenty years. The aim of the exercise is to provide an opportunity for couples:

1. To learn to communicate about their feelings and preferred types of physical contact;
2. To learn to focus on their partner's cues and hence to gain knowledge about the forms of physical contact that their partner finds most pleasurable;
3. To learn to relax in situations of close physical contact. This represents one step in a hierarchy, in which systematic desensitization aims to reduce anxiety in intimate situations. In addition, sensual physical contact may be experienced in a non-demanding situation, in which performance anxiety is reduced;
4. To learn to focus attention on physical sensations;
5. To increase the level of positive interactions, which is suggested to increase general satisfaction with the relationship.

The exercise focuses on learning to give and to receive pleasure from massage to areas of the body that are not sexual or genital. Hence the woman's breasts and the genitals are excluded. This exercise would not be commenced unless both partners feel comfortable with direct physical contact to non-genital body areas. For some clients, the level of anxiety or negative affect associated with direct touch to the body would be too great to permit this exercise to take place successfully. It may therefore be necessary to commence with a more gradual systematic desensitization of earlier steps in the hierarchy. This may involve learning to relax and enjoy physical contact while fully dressed, to feel comfortable about seeing the partner's naked body or to expose one's own body to the partner without feeling anxious. Unless these prerequisites exist, then sensate focus 1 exercises should not commence. For the majority of clients, a ban is placed on continuation to intercourse (see discussion in Chapter 5), in order to create a non-demanding situation in which the aims of the exercise can be achieved. The therapist usually explains that self-pleasuring is acceptable, when desired.

The therapist generally describes the aims and methods of sensate focus 1 within the session. The following handout summarizes the main points and may be provided to clients to assist with home-based practice.

Guidelines for home-based task: sensate focus 1

The aim of this exercise is to help you to improve your ability to enjoy the experience of physical contact with your partner and to learn more about the types of touch and contact that your partner likes. Hopefully, the exercise will allow both of you to feel more relaxed and to become aware of and concentrate on pleasurable feelings. You should also find that the tasks help you to build up better communication with your partner.

The expression of physical affection and giving of pleasure through physical contact does not necessarily mean that touch has to involve your sexual parts (genitals). The sensations experienced in all parts of your body are important and it is possible to give and to receive pleasure through touch that is not sexual and does not involve the genitals. There are many different types of touch that can provide pleasant feelings, such as stroking, caressing, kissing, licking, massaging, fondling and tickling, just to mention a few. Different people find different forms of touch pleasurable at different times. It is important to be able to communicate with your partner so that he or she can use the type of touch that you would most enjoy at a particular time. It is also important that you are aware of the pleasant feelings that touch can provide and be able to concentrate on these feelings without feeling tense, embarrassed or distracted by other things.

We suggest that you practise the sensate focus 1 exercises at a time when you are both feeling relaxed, comfortable and not too tired. Some people prefer not to wear any clothes, while others find it better to keep their underclothes on. It is up to you to decide what to wear, but you will need to remove some clothing for back rubs or leg massages. It is best to pick a warm, comfortable place, at a time when you won't be disturbed. Perhaps you could take the telephone off the hook. Some couples tell us that they find it helpful to create a romantic and relaxed atmosphere by dimming the lights, playing some soft music and perhaps having a glass of wine first. Remember, that right from the start, the aim is not to be sexual, but to enjoy the pleasurable feelings.

We suggest that you take it in turns to give and to receive pleasure. It is a good idea to decide in advance who is going to take the first turn in being the 'receiver' and who is going to be

167

the 'giver'. You might feel rather embarrassed about this, so perhaps you could toss a coin in order to decide. Try and work out beforehand when will be a good time to practise the exercises and then really make an effort to stick to this plan. Once you get started it will seem much easier. The person who is giving pleasure should try to explore different types of touch, in order to learn more about the type of contact that their partner finds pleasurable. The 'giver' needs to concentrate on their partner's reaction and should not try to receive pleasure him or herself at this point. Try to experiment with different types of touch, perhaps using massage oils or talcum powders, on different parts of the body. The face, neck, shoulders, back, stomach, arms and legs can be explored, remembering to avoid any touching of the breasts or sexual areas.

The person who is receiving pleasure should just relax and concentrate on enjoying the experience. It is important to give information to your partner about how you are feeling . . . about the type of touch that you find pleasurable and the parts of your body where you enjoy being touched. If your partner uses some form of contact that you do not find pleasurable, it is important to communicate this too, but very sensitively. Your partner will be trying very hard to give you pleasure and it is important that they do not feel hurt or embarrassed when they do not succeed. Always try to give your feedback in a positive way. You can show your pleasure by actually saying that you find something enjoyable, such as 'Oh, I really like it when you stroke me there.' If you need to communicate something that you do not like, and yet want to keep it positive, you could say 'I think I preferred it when you massaged my shoulders . . . I thought that felt wonderful . . . could you do it again, please?' You can also communicate your likes and dislikes to your partner by actually guiding his or her hands and showing your partner what to do. Gradually, you will find these exercises easier to do and we realize that you may find them difficult at first . . . but please try really hard to make them work.

After you have had your first turn at being the giver or receiver for about 10 minutes, it is time to change over. We suggest that you take it in turns as to who will be first to be the giver each time you practise these exercises. Then, try to make each session last about 40 minutes and you should both have two chances at being the giver and two chances at being the receiver. Occasionally, you may feel tempted to break the rules and move on to include sexual areas of the body or even to take part in sexual intercourse. Please try not to do this, as it goes against the whole aim of the exercises. The aim is not to become sexually aroused but to allow you to practise these exercises in a relaxed way, where you do not feel at all pressured to take part in sexual activities. You should feel free to give and to receive pleasure without any sexual involvement.

Once the instructions for sensate focus 1 have been outlined, the therapist should check that the couple have clearly understood the aims of the exercise and the instructions. It is then important to explore any reservations that the couple may have about the assignment, as this may provide material for cognitive restructuring. In addition, the couple may be asked to keep a record of thoughts related to their home-based sensate focus tasks. The following monitoring form may be useful for clients for whom maladaptive, irrational thoughts are suggested to contribute to the sexual difficulty or to resistance to therapy.

Home-based monitoring form: sensate focus 1

Date completed	How did you feel?	What were your specific thoughts?
Before the exercises		
During the exercises		
After the exercises		

For some couples the hardest part of these exercises is actually getting started. This is particularly true if the couple's communication skills are poor, or if particular cognitions are interfering in their attempts. For example, thoughts which may inhibit the start of the exercises could include:

'Why should I make the first attempt? It is always me . . . he/she never makes an effort so why should I?'

'I would really like to make a start on these exercises but I am afraid to ask him in case he says no and I'll feel really foolish and humiliated.'

'I'll wait and see if she makes the first move and then I'll know if she really cares about me.'

Obviously such cognitions will need to be dealt with.

Even if each partner's cognitive activities include the desire and intention to commence the tasks, it may be necessary to work on the communication skills needed to initiate the assignment or to provide appropriate feedback to the partner during the exercises. Modelling by the therapist and role-play of verbal communication in the clinic (as outlined in Chapter 5) may be needed as a prerequisite to beginning the sensate focus exercises. During the teaching of communication skills at this stage, it is suggested that couples make use of skills learned in the general communication skills sessions. Hence they are reminded to make use of 'I' statements, listening skills, perceptual cues and to concentrate on the use of appropriate non-verbal cues.

Similarly, the therapist may be required to take a role in getting the couple to agree to a place and setting in which to carry out the exercises. Some couples will not yet possess the communication skills to resolve issues related to such an intimate topic. It is debatable as to whether the couple should agree to set times and dates when the exercises are to be carried out. Some authors suggest that sensate focus exercises should begin spontaneously, when the couple feel the desire to practise them, whereas others recommend a pre-arranged time. In practice, this decision tends to depend on the couple and they may choose which method they prefer. If the selected approach produces problems, then the therapist may decide to switch to the alternative method.

Sensate focus 1 exercises usually need to be practised two to three times per week, over two to three weeks, before couples are able to master the skills which the exercises aim to develop. It is important that both individuals feel relaxed during the exercises, feel able to ask their partner to take part in them, to be able to focus attention upon their own sensations, to monitor their partner's cues, to know the partner's preferred forms of pleasuring and to be able to communicate their own preferences. For some couples, this learning process may be faster or slower and the rate of progress through therapy will vary. Unfortunately, resistance may be found amongst some couples and these blocks to therapy must be carefully explored in order to identify interfering cognitions, beliefs or skills deficits, which must be overcome before therapy can progress.

SENSATE FOCUS 2: GENITAL PLEASURING

Once the sensate focus 1 exercises have been mastered the therapist may decide to make use of the sensate focus 2 assignment. The aims of sensate focus 2 reflect a continuation of those outlined for sensate focus 1 in that they enable the couple:

1. To learn to communicate about the types of physical contact with the genital areas that produces greatest pleasure (and ultimately sexual arousal);
2. To learn to focus on their partner's cues and hence to gain knowledge about the forms of physical contact that the partner finds most pleasurable (and ultimately sexually arousing);
3. To learn to relax in situations of physical contact of the genitals. In addition, genital physical contact may be experienced in a non-demanding situation;
4. To learn to focus attention on physical sensations, including arousal cues.

The instructions and guidelines for the task are similar to those outlined above for sensate focus 1 and will therefore not be repeated here. A detailed outline of the instructions given to clients is provided below. It is suggested that initial sessions should involve gentle touching and it is important to emphasize to the couple that the aim is *not* initially to produce sexual arousal. In outlining the exercises it is important to discuss with the couple their attitudes towards different types of sexual activities, such as oral sex and internal touching of the vagina by the partner. The therapist should acknowledge that different couples prefer different activities and there are no pressures to take part in activities that are not pleasurable. The couple are then able to select the type of physical contact that they would prefer to use.

171

It is likely that sexual arousal will occur once the couple become skilled at identifying the areas and type of stimulation that their partner finds most pleasurable. When the couple feel confident about genital pleasuring, the therapist is able to discuss different forms of sexual stimulation and skills relating to the production of sexual arousal. This element is particularly important for clients who have minimal knowledge concerning ways of providing sexual stimulation to their partner.

Guidelines for home-based task: sensate focus 2

This exercise is a continuation of sensate focus 1. You are again asked to take it in turns to give and to receive pleasure, but this time you may include the touching of sexual areas of the body. We still ask that you do not move on to have intercourse as the aim is still to concentrate upon pleasurable feelings, rather than trying to become sexually aroused. Even if you begin to feel sexually aroused, we recommend that you do not try to produce orgasm or ejaculation or begin any sexual activities. The aim is to be sensual rather than sexual. The exercises should help you to feel relaxed about being touched by your partner, to be able to concentrate on feelings of pleasure and to allow your partner to know more about the type of touch that you find pleasurable. In the same way, your partner will become more aware of pleasurable feelings and you will learn more about the best ways to provide pleasurable sensations. As a couple, you should also become better at communicating about physical contact.

As before, we suggest that you organize a time in advance when you know that you will not be disturbed and where you can be comfortable and relaxed. Try not to pick times when you are likely to be tired, irritable or stressed. It is very important to set aside the time to practise your exercises, as it is very easy to come up with a variety of excuses which may stop you from doing them. Decide beforehand who is going to have the first turn at giving pleasure and who is to be the receiver. Make sure that you choose a warm comfortable place, and again you might like to use dim lights and relaxing music to set the scene. Some couples have found it useful to practise the exercises in the bath for part of the time.

The person who is giving pleasure should usually begin by using a variety of different types of touch and contact to the parts of the body covered in sensate focus 1, before gradually including the sexual areas (including the breasts). The aim is still to try different types of touch, such as stroking, caressing , kissing, licking, or massaging over different parts of the body, in order to give pleasure to your partner and to discover the type of contact that he or she finds enjoyable. You may like to try different movements or different strengths and speeds of movement, all the time concentrating on your partner's response. Your partner has been asked to let you know what is pleasurable. Listen carefully to what your partner says and try to follow their suggestions. Occasionally, your partner may actually take your hand and guide it in order to show you the type of touch that is most enjoyable. If this happens, please do not try to resist, but relax and allow your partner to show you a particular form of touch. Remember that certain parts of the penis and clitoris may be very sensitive and you should try to vary your touching to include different parts of the body, rather than concentrating only on the sexual areas.

The person who is receiving pleasure should relax and concentrate on the enjoyable sensations. There is no need for you to do anything, other than to enjoy the experience and to communicate to your partner the type of touch that you are finding pleasurable. Try to relax when your sexual parts are being touched and concentrate on the nice feelings, rather than attempting to become sexually aroused. Try not to think about the sexual parts of your body as being different from the rest of your body, so that you can concentrate on sensual body feelings, rather than sexual ones. At this point we would like you to start to guide your partner's hands and show him or her the type of touch that gives you most pleasure. Your partner will be expecting you to do this, so do not feel worried about doing so.

Generally, we suggest that each of you spends around 10 minutes as the 'giver' before swapping over to be the receiver. You may prefer to change over sooner than this if either of you is becoming tired. Ideally, each of you should have at least two turns at being the receiver and giver during the session. Gradually you will find that the communication between you and your partner becomes easier and you will both have learned to enjoy sensual feelings and to know the type of touch that each of you finds most pleasurable.

Note: The assignment outlined above includes a proscription/ban on intercourse and this may need to be modified for some clients (see discussion on page 134).

Sensate focus exercises may form part of the intervention programme for many clients. Once the aims of the exercises have been achieved, the sexual skill exercises tend to become more specialized, and vary according to the presenting problem. The following sections outline some of the commonly used techniques of sexual skill development.

KEGEL EXERCISES

A series of exercises to increase the strength and responsivity of the pubococcygeal muscle was initially developed by Arnold Kegel as a means of enhancing female sexual responsiveness. These exercises have since been applied to enhance female sexual arousal and orgasmic ability. It has been suggested that by learning to relax and contract these muscles and by building up their strength through exercise, the woman experiences an increased awareness of sensations within the vaginal area, increases the level of arousal to stimulation and is more able to experience orgasm during vaginal stimulation. Whether or not these claims are justified is debatable and yet the exercises continue to be incorporated into many intervention programmes. It does appear that the exercises may increase subjective reports of arousal and increase physiological levels of arousal, as measured by vaginal pulse amplitude amongst non-dysfunctional women (Messe and Geer, 1985). This effect was not evident in an attention placebo condition and was dependent upon practice of the exercises. Whilst Kegel exercises may be useful in increasing arousal response, it does not appear that the strength of the pubococcygeal muscle is associated with orgasmic ability in non-dysfunctional women (Chambless *et al.*, 1982). Attempts to improve orgasmic ability through Kegel exercises also proved ineffective (Chambless *et al.*, 1984).

Given that Kegel excercises may result in increases in physiological arousal among non-dysfunctional women there seems to be some support for their use in cases of low sexual arousal. It is possible that the exercises serve to increase the focusing of attention upon sensations in genital areas and may thereby enhance the sexual arousal response. Where intervention aims to enhance awareness of vaginal sensations, Kegel exercises may be justified. The following instructions for Kegel exercises are adapted from those outlined by Barbach (1980) and Heiman *et al.* (1976) and may be given to clients, where appropriate:

Home-based assignment: pubococcygeal muscle exercises

Your pubococcygeal muscle is a large muscle that tightens the rectum and vagina when contracted. Various therapists have suggested that, by strengthening this muscle by exercises, women may become more aroused during sex and more likely to experience orgasm. The exercises also help to make you more aware of the sensations and feelings in your genital area.

The first step in this exercise is to find the pubococcygeal muscle. You may be able to do this by concentrating on the muscles between your legs, taking a deep breath and pulling upwards until you feel a tightness in the area of the rectum and vagina. You can also find the muscle by trying to stop the flow of urine when you are urinating. Try this a few times and you will become aware of the muscle that is contracting when you stop the flow. Once you have identified it, we suggest that you practise the following task when you are in private. Lie down and gently insert a finger into your vagina. Relax for a moment and then contract the muscle against your finger, breathing in as you tighten the muscle. You should be able to feel the muscle tightening around your finger. Then breath out as you relax and repeat the contraction several times. Each time, hold the muscle tight for 3 seconds and then relax for 3 seconds. (We do not suggest that you continue to practise the exercises during urination as this may result in retention of old urine and possible infection.)

Now, remove your finger and continue to relax and contract the muscle. Concentrate upon the feelings of the muscle and be aware of the tightness and relaxation. This exercise can be carried out at any time. Nobody is aware of what you are doing, so you can practise whenever you wish. We suggest that you start off doing ten 3-second squeezes, with each squeeze followed by a 3-second relaxation. Try to do this several times a day. The aim is to gradually build up the length of time that you can hold the tightness and also to increase the number of contractions that you can do in each practice session. See if you can practice holding the muscle tight for a period of 5 seconds and gradually build up to a maximum of 10 seconds. It may take several weeks to get to this stage.

The exercises need to be practised for at least six weeks if you are to build up muscle strength. You might also try the following exercises. Once you are able to hold and relax for several seconds, then try relaxing and contracting as quickly as you can, so that you are only holding and relaxing for around half a second each. Another exercise to practise is to try to push down the pubococcygeal muscle rather than pulling it upwards. This feels as if you are trying to push something out of your vagina.

Once you have mastered each exercise, you should practise each of them ten times, two to three times every day for around six weeks.

BIOFEEDBACK

Research into the use of biofeedback in the treatment of sexual dysfunctions is in its infancy. Feedback may be provided concerning arousal levels as measured by penile circumference or volume and blood flow or blood volume within the vagina (e.g. vaginal pulse amplitude). Given that the majority of practitioners do not have the necessary equipment to conduct such interventions, and that minimal research is available to permit us to draw conclusions about the benefits of such approaches, this area is not covered within the present text. The interested reader is referred to Rosen and Beck (1988) for a review of the area.

USE OF EROTIC MATERIALS

Considerable research is available to demonstrate that exposure to erotic stimuli such as tapes, literature, pictures or films tends to trigger sexual arousal in both males and females. For many non-dysfunctional couples the use of erotic material forms part of their sexual repertoire, serving to enhance arousal levels and to bring an element of variation into their sexual activities. The use of erotic stimuli may therefore be a useful means of enhancing sexual arousal in the treatment of sexual dysfunctions, where inadequate levels of sexual arousal are present.

176

There are two major issues that tend to concern both clients and therapists alike when it comes to the use of erotic materials. The first worry is that exposure to erotic materials (or what is frequently termed pornography) is likely to trigger deviant sexual behaviour. The second issue is a concern that repeated exposure to erotic stimuli will result in a habituation response, in which stronger and stronger forms of stimulation are required in order to produce sexual arousal in the future. Fortunately, evidence is available to dispute both these proposals. The data available concerning the effects of exposure to pornography upon sexual activities do suggest that an increase in sexual behaviour tends to occur, but that this effect is limited to behaviours already within the person's sexual repertoire. Evidence does not generally suggest that new sexual behaviours are triggered, although Rosen and Beck (1988) concluded that exposure to violent pornography may be associated with a negative shift in attitudes towards a greater acceptance of rape myths and an increased tolerance of sexual coercible and aggressive behaviours. Providing that erotic materials are restricted to non-violent, mild stimuli involving non-deviant sexual activities, rather than violent or hard-core pornography, there does not appear to be any evidence to suggest that its use should be avoided.

In terms of habituation effects, Rosen and Beck (1988) concluded that habituation may occur if the same erotic stimuli are presented repeatedly, but if the stimuli are varied then habituation does not occur. Hence, the concern that use of erotic materials may create an insensitivity to subsequent stimulation does not appear to be justified.

Erotic videotapes are readily available for hire and obviously there are many suitable magazines designed for male and female audiences. Some audiences find it unacceptable to look at sexual pictures or to watch erotic movies and may find it more acceptable to read erotic literature. A list of books that women in particular may find sexually arousing is provided by Heiman *et al.* (1976). Two particular books are recommended by the present author:

- *Diary of Anais Nin* by Anais Nin;
- *My Secret Diary* by Nancy Friday.

Both these texts contain short stories which may be used as components of home-based assignments.

THERAPY TECHNIQUES FOR SPECIFIC PSYCHOSEXUAL DYSFUNCTIONS

The methods outlined above are appropriate for use with a wide range of psychosexual dysfunctions where the individualized intervention programme suggests they are applicable. Some techniques have been developed specifically for the treatment of particular sexual problems and these are outlined separately below.

Hypoactive sexual desire

Given that hypoactive sexual desire was relatively neglected until recently, there is a lack of research to inform us as to the best way to treat this dysfunction. If a thorough assessment is carried out, it should be possible to identify those factors relating to the couple, their relationship and their environment which may be making it less likely that feelings of sexual desire will occur. Interventions may be classified into two main types, namely: (1) those that aim to decrease cognitions or situations that are likely to inhibit the occurrence of feelings of sexual desire; and (2) those that aim to increase sexual desire by increasing the couple's exposure to situations that are likely to trigger feelings of sexual desire.

The approaches used to decrease factors which may inhibit sexual desire will vary for different couples, depending upon the inhibitory variables identified during assessment. In particular, marital therapy techniques may be essential in dealing with non-sexual problems within the relationship. The treatment of hypoactive sexual desire has been notoriously difficult, with success rates being poor (Weeks, 1987). Indeed Weeks (1987) concluded: 'The therapist who attempts to treat inhibited sexual desire must be thoroughly trained in all major approaches to marital therapy, have some knowledge of individual therapy (especially cognitive therapy) and be a competent sex therapist . . . The therapist must be prepared to carefully map out the course of treatment . . . The usual treatment formats sex therapists have learned do not apply in treating inhibited sexual desire. The clinician must now create and tailor formats for specific clients with specific aetiological factors. This process is indeed a challenge for the clinician and an impossible task for the sex therapist who has become a technician' (p. 200).

Weeks (1987) placed a major emphasis on the use of cognitive restructuring procedures that are designed to modify irrational or maladaptive cognitions relating to the individual, the partner or the relationship. This approach is also taken by McCarthy (1984), who outlined a cognitive-behavioural approach to the treatment of inhibited sexual desire using semi-structured, written behavioural exercises. Four exercises were included for the couple and four for the individuals. The focus of the individual components included positive self concept, positive body image and attractiveness, positive sexual thoughts, images, fantasies and positive sexual scenarios to act out. The couple components focused on expression of affect, discussions of the characteristics that the couple find attractive about each other, exploration of the degree of trust and desire that each partner wants and the design and acting out of a sexual scenario.

A variety of methods may also be used to create situations in which sexual desire is most likely to be experienced. Where deficits are identified, clients may be trained to use fantasy as a means of generating feelings of desire. For many couples this represents an important element of treatment. Weeks (1987) suggested that 'a lack of sexual fantasy has been an almost universal characteristic of individuals with inhibited sexual desire' and this statement is supported by the empirical evidence of Nutter and Condron (1983). In addition to making the occurrence of sexual desire more likely, Kaplan (1987) also suggested that fantasies may be used to inhibit negative cognitions concerning performance anxiety or negative features of the partner. Clients are instructed to focus exclusively upon their sexual fantasy and to 'tune out' all distracting or inhibiting thoughts. Exposure to erotic materials, such as literature, pictures or videotapes, may also be beneficial in increasing the probability of sexual desire. In addition, situational changes may be used to create trigger situations; for example, the couple may be instructed to organize a regular romantic dinner or arrange for the children to visit friends or relatives on one afternoon per month.

For some couples, it may be found that the lack of sexual desire relates specifically to sex with the partner, with levels of sexual activity through self-stimulation being relatively high. This situation is not unusual; indeed, Nutter and Condron (1983) found that their sample of 25 women referred for problems of inhibited sexual desire reported similar levels of self-stimulation and orgasm to a matched control group. If assessment reveals a normal frequency of self-stimulation, the therapist may suggest that masturbatory activities are reduced during the therapy period, in order to make it more likely that any feelings of sexual desire will lead to sexual interaction with the partner. This is important for those couples in which it has become much more convenient or less stressful for feelings of sexual desire to be produced by self-stimulation, rather than sexual contact with the partner. For example, one woman who was referred to our clinic reported no feelings of desire for sexual contact with her husband, although she was able to become adequately aroused and experience orgasm on the few occasions when she reluctantly agreed to engage in sexual activities. She did not experience negative thoughts or emotions concerning her husband. This woman frequently felt the desire for sexual activity and used a vibrator in order to achieve orgasm at least four times per week, Typically she arrived home from work 2–3 hours before her husband and, by the time he arrived home from work, she would already have used her vibrator to produce orgasm and no further feelings of sexual desire occurred. Her husband was not aware of her masturbatory activities and believed her to be lacking in sexual desire for all situations. Therapy included a temporary ban on self-stimulation during the early stages of intervention. It was also suggested to the husband that he might return home from work early on two evenings per week, with these times being used for home-based assignments.

In this example, several maladaptive beliefs were identified that required restructuring. These can be categorized in relation to the self, partner and the relationship. In relation to the self, this woman reported negative thoughts concerning her own ability to become aroused and to enjoy intercourse with her husband. Whilst finding him physically attractive and desiring to maintain their relationship, she reported negative thoughts concerning the amount of time he dedicated to his work and his low contribution to the housekeeping. These thoughts were found to intrude frequently during the initial sensate focus exercises. With respect to the relationship she believed that there must be something wrong, in order to account for her lack of sexual desire for her husband. This belief was also held by the husband, who reported thoughts such as 'if she really cared for me, then she wouldn't have this problem'. Both partners reported negative thoughts concerning the potential sexual contact, anticipating negative outcomes. Sexual interaction had become an anxiety-provoking situation, in which the husband anticipated rejection if he made an approach and the woman dreaded his approaches for fear of the conflict that resulted when she announced her lack of desire. Intervention included a marital therapy component which focused on communi-cation skills training, problem-solving skills training relating to areas of conflict and an increase in positive interactions (and events) between the couple. Cognitive restructuring methods were also used to challenge maladaptive thoughts and to increase the focus on positive thoughts concerning the self, the partner and the relationship.

This example illustrates an important point made by Weeks (1987), who suggested that of all the sexual dysfunctions low sexual desire is the least tolerated and most likely to lead to conflict within the relationship. Weeks suggested that this occurs because couples typically believe that sexual desire is under the individual's control and that lack of sexual desire is the individual's 'fault'. It is assumed that, if the individual truly felt positively towards their partner, then sexual desire would automatically occur.

Sexual arousal disorders

Surprisingly little attention has been paid to the treatment of sexual arousal disorders in women. As mentioned previously, the tendency to merge problems relating to female orgasm, arousal and desire has led to a relative paucity of data which looks at each of these areas independently. Far more is known about the treatment of sexual arousal disorders in males. For women, the lack of empirical data concerning the most effective forms of intervention means that currently we must rely upon clinical experience and theoretical recommendations concerning the design of treatment programmes.

Female sexual arousal disorders

Given the numerous factors which may inhibit or enhance sexual arousal, a wide variety of treatment approaches may be indicated, according to the characteristics of each presenting couple. As with the treatment of low sexual desire, intervention typically uses techniques which are designed to either increase the probability and degree of sexual arousal or to reduce inhibitory factors. Methods such as fantasy training, use of erotic materials, attention-focusing skills, Kegel exercises (see above) and enhancement of partner skills in providing stimulation may all be used to increase sexual arousal in both males and females. Techniques which aim to reduce factors which inhibit sexual arousal include cognitive restructuring, therapies which attempt to reduce negative aspects of the general relationship, relaxation training and systematic desensitization of anxiety-provoking situations. These techniques are used, as appropriate, in combination with home-based assignments, such as sensate focus exercises and graded exposure to non-demanding sexual situations.

As with the treatment of erectile difficulties, considerable emphasis is placed on the reduction of negative cognitions which may interfere with sexual arousal. Once situations have been created in which sexual arousal is likely to occur (e.g. during the self-pleasuring or sexual fantasy), the individual is instructed to focus attention on pleasurable feelings and positive self-statements. A direct effort is made to inhibit negative and competing thoughts concerning performance, self, partner or the relationship. Generally, this approach is successful in generating sexual arousal during self-pleasuring. Intervention then continues by including the partner in the sexual situation, such as genital pleasuring of sensate focus 2. The same basic procedures are followed throughout successive situations, which may include self-pleasuring in the presence of the partner, partner pleasuring, vaginal containment of the penis with a passive partner and finally intercourse with normal movements.

It is suggested that the move from self-pleasuring to partner pleasuring should include a stage at which the partner observes the woman engaging in self-pleasuring. Some couples find this extremely difficult to do and considerable cognitive restructuring is required before the assignment can be completed. It is often at this stage that numerous negative cognitions are identified, particularly concerning masturbation and male–female roles in sex. The male partner may experience various thoughts and emotions such as:

- Disgust, e.g. 'Women shouldn't touch themselves down there . . . the sight of her showing her pleasure like that . . . women shouldn't be like that . . .'
- Inadequacy, e.g. 'It's a man's job to do that, not hers. I should know how to do that . . . she shouldn't need to show me . . .'

The female, on the other hand, may also experience negative emotions and thoughts, such as:

- Embarrassment, e.g. 'What on earth must he think of me. I feel really uncomfortable doing this. I bet he thinks I'm disgusting.'
- Fear/anxiety, e.g. 'I know I can't do this with him watching. This is terrible . . . nothing is happening anyway . . . I knew I wouldn't be able to do this.'

Frequently, negative thoughts reflect underlying irrational beliefs of the type outlined in Chapter 2 which must be tackled before the couple are able to complete the assignment. Unfortunately, for some couples the beliefs may be so entrenched that it is unrealistic to attempt to restructure them. In such cases it may be more appropriate to adjust the content of therapy to fit in with the attitudes and beliefs of the couple. This is particularly true if strongly held religious or cultural influences make the conduct of a particular exercise inappropriate. The therapist should always be sensitive to the issue of attempting to impose his/her own philosophies and beliefs upon the couple. It needs to be acknowledged that it is difficult to draw right or wrong conclusions regarding what is acceptable in sexual activity between consenting adults. What is perceived as acceptable to the therapist may be totally unacceptable to some couples.

Once the couple has practised self-pleasuring in front of the partner and the woman is able to become sexually aroused in his presence, then they may move on to genital pleasuring by the partner. For some couples, where this step is difficult, it is suggested that the woman intially creates sexual arousal by self-pleasuring and then takes her partner's hand and guides him through types of contact that produce pleasurable feelings. In subsequent sessions, the male may then commence the sexual pleasuring, making use of methods of touch that he has learned from observation and guidance. Oral sex or gels may be used where the couple find this acceptable. When the stage is reached in which sexual arousal regularly occurs as the result of partner stimulation, the couple are ready to progress to include intercourse situations. The couple should be asked to select the most comfortable position for these exercises, with the suggestion that they try the female-above position first. This step should begin with mutual genital pleasuring exercises, until both partners are sexually aroused. Initially, the therapist requests that the couple do not attempt to engage in the normal movements of intercourse, but rather the woman should gradually insert the penis into the vagina when she feels ready. The male is asked to remain passive and to allow the woman to slowly move, exploring the sensations produced by different forms of movement. The penis should be held within the vagina for around 5 minutes. It should then be withdrawn and the exercise repeated on two further occasions. Kaplan (1987) suggested that, if the male becomes too excited, movement should stop or the penis should be withdrawn. Ideally, the male partner (and the female if orgasm is not a problem) should experience orgasm at the end of the session, during partner stimulation. This is important in order that the woman does not concentrate on thoughts about her partner's feelings of frustration and also provides reinforcement for partner contribution to the assignment. As with the treatment of other forms of sexual dysfunction, it is essential that difficulties relating to the relationship or the partner's negative cognitions are overcome, so that he or she may contribute effectively to the therapy process.

Finally, the couple are encouraged to engage in the normal movements of intercourse, following genital pleasuring exercises, initially with the woman taking responsibility for insertion of the penis.

Erectile disorder

Various methods may be used in the treatment of erectile difficulty. Generally, the approach is to progress through a hierarchy of situations, which become successively closer to sexual intercourse, in which the male is able to experience sexual arousal in non-demanding conditions. Initially, the couple are asked not to proceed to sexual intercourse if any erections occur.Similarly, it is usually suggested that the male should *not* try to produce an erection. Rather, the aim is to focus upon pleasurable sensations in order to reduce performance demand and make it more likely that an erection will occur. The male is instructed to relax, to focus on pleasurable sensations, to dismiss negative cognitions and to rehearse positive, arousing statements. It has also been suggested by some therapists that the programme should be carried out early in the morning, which is a time when testosterone levels are greatest and erections are most likely to occur for many men.

The first sexual situation in the hierarchy usually involves the genital pleasuring exercises of sensate focus 2. Pleasuring may include the use of gels or oral stimulation (if the couple wish this), in addition to various forms of partner touching. Initially, the couple are instructed to stop stimulation if an erection occurs, allowing the erection to subside, and no attempt should be made to progress to orgasm. The pleasuring exercises may then be repeated, allowing the erection to return. Gradually, the couple come to realize that it is possible to achieve erections with the partner and that erections will recur even if they are lost.

As therapy progresses to include new sexual situations, the basic instructions should be repeated. Once the couple reach the stage at which erections can be readily produced and maintained, pleasuring may be continued until orgasm is reached. It is suggested that the use of sexual fantasies may be encouraged at this point, in order to enhance sexual arousal. When this step is satisfactorily mastered, the couple may begin exposure to vaginal containment. This commences with genital pleasuring exercises, but when the penis becomes erect the female partner is instructed to slowly massage the penis against the clitoral area, using a gel. This exercise is repeated until the erection can be maintained during clitoral contact.

Once this is mastered, the couple may commence entry into the vagina, initially without movement or any attempt to produce orgasm. Different couples seem to prefer different positions for this exercise. Traditionally, it has been suggested that the female partner should take responsibility for insertion of the penis, using a position with the woman kneeling over the male, facing forwards, with her knees level with the male's chest/waist, in a position that permits easy entry into the vagina. It is important that the woman is sufficiently aroused and lubricated to permit comfortable penetration and these issues should be discussed with the couple in the therapy session. Some couples prefer a sideways position for this task and in some instances the male may prefer to be responsible for insertion of the penis when his partner is ready. Generally, the exercise begins with genital pleasuring, until a firm erection is produced. The female then moves above, into what is called the female superior position. She then takes the penis and gradually inserts it into her vagina, remaining still for several minutes. The couple are informed that it does not matter if the erection is lost. The penis is then withdrawn and the exercises are then repeated two to three times after brief periods of relaxation. Once the erection is being maintained within the vagina for several minutes the couple move on to include gentle thrusting and ultimately to the more natural movements of intercourse. At this stage, it is suggested that the activity may culminate in orgasm.

Various problems may occur during therapy and the therapist should be prepared to deal with them as they arise. Some couples may rush the procedure and attempt to use any erections produced to have intercourse. Even if intercourse is successful, then it is important for the therapist to reassert that the aim of the programme is to gain confidence and to create a situation in which there is no pressure to perform. If the attempt results in loss of erection, then the rationale for the intervention is repeated and the experience is used to illustrate the underlying principles of the programme. Such events also provide valuable discussion material through which to explore cognitions during a continuation of cognitive restructuring.

As with the treatment of most psychosexual dysfunctions, a great deal of input is required from the partner during the home-based exercises. It is therefore essential that the couple's relationship contains the necessary elements to permit successful conduct of the tasks. Good communication skills are required and the woman must feel sufficiently positive about her partner and their relationship, in order to be motivated to contribute to the assignments. It is also important that the female's cognitions and attitudes do not inhibit the satisfactory conduct of home-based tasks. For this reason, the female partner should always be considered during the assessment of cognitions and cognitive restructuring may be necessary in some instances.

Premature ejaculation

The early stages of therapy should ensure that the couple have the skills and relationship to enable a technique such as the stop–start method to be used successfully. If this is the case, it is generally appropriate to move on to methods that are specifically designed to increase ejaculatory control.

The following outline provides a step-by-step guide to the conduct of the stop–start technique and is based on a handout provided to trainees in clinical psychology at the University of Sydney during a course in sexual and marital therapy.

Guidelines for home-based task: stop–start technique

The following exercises are designed for use by individuals or couples where ejaculation tends to occur before you would like it to. One method that can be used to increase the time before ejaculation is called the stop–start technique. This can be broken down into steps, which you work through gradually, as directed by your therapist.

Step 1. We suggest that the first step is carried out by the male on his own. Set aside a time when you have some privacy and when you will not be disturbed. Make yourself comfortable and relax for a couple of minutes. Then, when you feel ready, start to stimulate yourself, but using dry hands, without any form of lubricant or lotion. Concentrate on the pleasurable feelings that are produced and don't try to distract yourself or worry about not being able to control yourself. Try not to let your mind wander off into fantasies during this first step, as the aim is to become aware of sensations and feelings that occur when you become sexually aroused. Try to describe to yourself what these feelings are like and what is happening to your body. In particular, we ask you to notice the feeling that occurs just before you ejaculate. This sensation has been described in various ways . . . such as 'the point of no return' . . . or as one man described it, as like 'being on a water slide and trying to stop'. During step 1, don't try to stop yourself at all and don't try to hold back. Just allow yourself to ejaculate when you feel ready. We suggest that you practise Step 1 once, every day, for two to three days, or until you feel able to notice and describe the sensations, especially those just before ejaculation.

Step 2. *The aim of this step is to allow you to learn better control over ejaculation when you stimulate yourself. As with Step 1, you begin by stimulating yourself so that you become sexually aroused and again you should not use any lotions or lubricants at this point. Do not try to distract yourself or to reduce your arousal. Concentrate on the pleasurable feelings and look out for the feeling that occurs just before orgasm. This time, we would like you to stop touching yourself at the point when the feeling of urge to ejaculate begins. At this point, stop all stimulation and relax for 3 minutes, during which your sexual arousal level will go down. At first you may find that you still ejaculate even though there is no stimulation. Do not feel worried about this, as it may take several attempts before you are able to stop the stimulation in time. If you are having difficulty in stopping the stimulation in time, then try to stop earlier, even if this means stopping as soon as you become sexually aroused.*

When you have relaxed for 3 minutes and your arousal level has gone down, then start the stimulation again. Repeat the process just as you did before, stopping all touch as soon as you feel the urge to ejaculate. Relax again for 3 minutes and repeat the process four or five times, allowing yourself to ejaculate on the last practice.

187

Step 2 should be practised at least six times over the next week. Each time you practise, we would like you to gradually shorten the length of time that you relax for. On the third and fourth practice sessions, you may like to reduce the length of time that you relax from 3 minutes to 2 minutes before you restart the stimulation. Then, in the fifth and sixth practice session you could try relaxing for only 1 minute before you begin the stimulation again.

All our clients are different and some men require many more practice sessions than others. You may need to alter the guidelines to fit your own needs, and do not get disheartened if you require a longer relaxation period or need to stop stimulation very frequently. The aim is ultimately for you to be able to stop stimulation and start again, so that you build up control over ejaculation.

Step 3. *In Step 3, we ask you to begin to use lubricating lotions during stimulation, as this tends to be more arousing than using dry hands. Various lotions may be used, but we suggest a non-perfumed baby lotion, which is not likely to be irritating or produce an allergic reaction. The guidelines are exactly as outlined in Step 2. When you begin the stimulation, do not try to distract yourself or allow yourself to drift into fantasies. Concentrate on the pleasurable feelings and stop touching yourself at the point when the feeling of urge to ejaculate begins. Relax for 3 minutes, during which your sexual arousal level will go down.*

When you have relaxed for 3 minutes and your arousal level has gone down, then start the stimulation again. Repeat the process just as you did before, four or five times, allowing yourself to ejaculate on the last practice.

Step 3 should be practised at least six times over the next week. Each time you practise, we would like you to gradually shorten the length of time that you relax for. On the third and fourth practice sessions, you may like to reduce the length of time that you relax from 3 minutes to 2 minutes before you restart the stimulation. Then, in the fifth and sixth practice sessions you could try relaxing for only 1 minute before you begin the stimulation again.

Step 4. *At this point we would like your partner to become involved, but only to help with the stimulation to begin with. For the time being, we ask that you do not have intercourse together. At first, your partner is asked to touch you in a way that causes you to feel sexually excited. You may need to show her the best type of stimulation for this. The instructions are the same as for Step 1, using dry hands and stopping all stimulation when you feel the sensation of the urge to ejaculate. You will need to work out a signal so that you can let your partner know that stimulation should stop.*

Practise the exercise five or six times over the next week or two, gradually reducing the length of time that you relax before your partner begins the stimulation again. Eventually you will be able to stop and start with only short breaks in between. We realize that this stage is often difficult for your partner, who may feel very aroused and somewhat neglected during the session. To avoid this becoming a problem, we suggest that you begin the session by gently massaging your partner and, if they would like to, bringing them to orgasm first. Remember to be sensitive to your partner's needs and talk about how she is feeling.

Step 5. *Step 5 makes use of the same guidelines as Step 4, but this time your partner should use a lubricating lotion or gel as this tends to be even more arousing. As with all of these steps, you may need to alter the guidelines to meet your own needs. For example, some men require more practice sessions before they move onto the next step, while others may need to increase the amount of relaxation time or stop the stimulation much earlier on. The aim is to be able to communicate with your partner when to stop, then relax and repeat the stimulation. Each session you should relax for a shorter time until the stimulation can continue after just a short break. At each step, we suggest that you do not try to rush things and move on too quickly. It is better to wait until you are confident with each step and have really mastered it.*

Step 6. *When you feel confident with Step 5, you are ready to begin to practise the stop–start method using intercourse. As with Steps 4 and 5, your partner's help is very important. You should begin the exercise by gently arousing your partner so that she becomes lubricated enough to allow intercourse to take place. Then, we suggest that your partner gently stimulates you until you become sexually aroused and your penis becomes erect. At this point you may gently move into a position in which you can slide your penis into her vagina and remove it easily when you need to. Some men find this stage extremely arousing and may ejaculate at the point of entry. If this happens, you may need to add in an extra stage of stop–start in which you move your penis gently against the clitoris area, using a lubricating gel.*

When you are ready, slowly and gently insert your penis into your partner's vagina. Some men will need to withdraw immediately and relax for a couple of minutes before inserting the penis again. The aim is to gradually increase the amount of time that the penis stays within the vagina and also to increase the amount of movement that is possible before ejaculation occurs. At first, you and your partner should remain still and you should withdraw your penis as soon as you feel the urge to ejaculate. Then, relax and insert again when your arousal level is not so high. Gradually decrease the amount of time that you need to relax and also try to increase the amount of time that you can remain inside your partner's vagina. You may gradually feel able to relax and reduce your arousal level without withdrawing. Remember that after you have practised the stop–start four or five times you may end the session by ejaculating.

Some couples prefer to have the woman taking the responsibility for inserting the penis and withdrawing. If you both would prefer to use this method, then we suggest that your partner sits astride you and inserts the penis when you begin to feel aroused. It is then up to you to signal when you begin to feel the urge to ejaculate and your partner may then gently move off your penis and allow you to relax. The stop–start method is then used in the same way as described above. This method helps to make your partner feel really involved in the exercises but it needs very good communication between the two of you.

Step 7. *When you feel confident enough to be able to control ejaculation within the vagina when you are both still, you may both begin moving gently, again using the stop–start method. When you have practised this exercise several times, you may gradually move on to greater movements until you are having a more natural sexual intercourse. It is important to continue to use the start–stop method for several weeks even during normal sexual intercourse until you feel confident in your ability to control ejaculation. From time to time you may find that you are ejaculating too quickly again, especially if you have not had sex or masturbated for some time. We suggest that you try to make sure that you practise Step 7 at least three times each week for the first few weeks after finishing this programme. After that, we recommend that you practise one stop–start session each week for several months, in addition to your usual lovemaking, as it usually takes this length of time for most men to feel really confident about being able to control ejaculation. In the long term, if you find that ejaculation is happening a bit too quickly again, please talk to your partner about this and begin to use the stop–start method again for a few weeks.*

Step 8. So far, we have asked you to concentrate your attention on the feelings of sexual arousal, but we realize that most people use fantasies during sexual activity and it is important for you to learn to control ejaculation when you fantasize. Fantasies are thoughts or daydreams about a situation, in this case a sexual one which tends to make you feel aroused. If you use fantasies, we suggest that you try to use the stop–start method while also being involved in a fantasy. At first you could try to practise on your own while you stimulate yourself. Even though you may be deeply involved in your fantasy thoughts, it is important to notice when you feel the urge to ejaculate and use the stop–start method. It is up to you to decide whether you use fantasy in the presence of your partner.

The 'squeeze technique'

Some couples find it better to use a 'squeeze' method as an adjunct to the stop–start system. The instructions are basically the same as for the stop–start method but instead of just stopping stimulation the penis is firmly squeezed when the urge to ejaculate begins. When the urge to ejaculate is felt, all stimulation should be stopped and immediately the penis should be taken firmly between the thumb and two fingers. The thumb is placed on the frenulum (the V-shaped areas where the shaft of the penis meets the glans), with the fingers being place around the ridge where the shaft of the penis ends. The penis should then be squeezed firmly for about 5 seconds. This should be firm enough that the urge to ejaculate no longer occurs, without causing pain. After a brief relaxation, the exercises should be carried out as described for the stop–start method. Initially, it may be the male himself who is responsible for 'squeezing', whereas the partner takes over responsibility for squeezing from Step 4 onwards as outlined above. When the partner becomes involved, it is important for the male to demonstrate the technique to his partner, showing how hard to squeeze without hurting and yet firmly enough to be effective. It is also necessary for the couple to work out a signal by which the male may communicate when he feels the urge to ejaculate. Ideally, the couple should practise the squeeze method with an erect penis before high levels of arousal occur.

Therapy considerations

Although the stop–start or squeeze techniques have been found to be highly effective in the treatment of premature ejaculation, therapy may take several weeks and even months with some cases. A major difficulty in therapy is the boredom and frustration which may result from a systematic and organized treatment programme. In order to overcome these problems, Kaplan (1987) suggests that one free lovemaking session should be permitted each week, in which the couple are free to have intercourse in their normal manner. In the later stages of the programme a major contribution is required from the partner. It is important the partner finds the sessions positive and rewarding experiences and does not feel used or frustrated. This problem may be reduced if the partner experiences orgasm before or after the exercises are practised.

Kaplan (1987) has outlined a variation of the stop–start method that may be incorporated into the instruction given above. Her technique requests the male to grade arousal on a zero to ten scale (0=no arousal, 10=orgasm). He is instructed to stimulate until a rating of 9 is reached, then to wait for a few seconds until arousal (subjective, not erection) declines to 4–5. The process is then repeated three times, with ejaculation then being permitted. The male is instructed to keep at a level of between 5 and 7 for increasing periods, with stimulation ceasing if a point of 9 is reached.

Inhibited male orgasm

Different assumptions can be found to underlie the two major approaches to the treatment of inhibited male orgasm. The first approach is based on an assumption that anxiety exists in relation to ejaculation during vaginal penetration. Therapy attempts to construct a hierarchy of situations, each of which is selected as being progressively more similar to sexual inter-course. The second approach attempts to create maximal stimulation, based on the assumption that the difficulty is related to inadequate stimulation, an excessively high threshold of stimulation required to trigger orgasm or a lack of ability to perceive the sensations available.

Anxiety reduction methods include relaxation training, desensitization to partner contact through exercises such as non-genital and genital sensate focus, education about sexual issues, creation of non-demand situations and gradual introduction of the partner into situations in which ejaculation occurs. Kaplan (1987) suggested that total inhibition of male orgasm is extremely rare and most cases report difficulty with ejaculation with certain situations involving the partner. The point at which therapy commences varies according to the range of situations in which orgasmic difficulties occur. With situational inhibited male orgasm, graded exposure typically commences with self-stimulation alone, followed by self-stimulation in the presence of the partner, partner manual stimulation, and oral stimulation if acceptable. Once these situations have been mastered, exposure to vaginal intercourse begins. At first, the male may be asked to stimulate himself, with ejaculation occurring in close proximity to the vagina. A graded series of steps are then involved in which the penis is inserted into the vagina just prior to ejaculation, following self-stimulation, with ejaculation taking place inside the vagina. Insertion of the penis then occurs after progressively shorter periods of self or partner stimulation, relying upon the stimulation caused by vaginal thrusting to trigger orgasm. It is suggested that the male-above position is initially used, as this is thought to facilitate ejaculation (Hawton, 1985). Eventually, ejaculation can be triggered without the need for manual stimulation.

In addition to the desensitization aspect of the programme, attempts may also be used to increase the amount of stimulation and awareness of sensation produced. The use of sexual fantasies during all forms of sexual stimulation, including intercourse, is encouraged. Similarly, erotic materials may be used prior to sexual activity. It is important to ensure that appropriate stimulation is being received, hence knowledge of sexual techniques should be ensured. Sensate focus 2 exercises are a useful basis for the acquisition of sexual stimulation techniques and as a means of facilitating attention focusing upon bodily sensations. The use of oral sex or lotions may also be helpful as a means of increasing stimulation levels for couples who find these activities acceptable.

In cases of total inhibition of orgasm, vibrators have been used as a means of providing high levels of stimulation. Whilst these have been effective in triggering orgasm for the first time with some males (see Chapter 7), others may find that the vibrator has an inhibitory effect and may actually result in loss of erection. With all referrals for inhibited male orgasm, it is important to explore the role of maladaptive cognitions and attitudes or homosexual orientation in the maintenance of the problem. Various case histories may be found in the literature which illustrate the role played by fears of pregnancy, negative attitudes towards genitalia, lack of physical attraction towards the partner, hostility towards women or homosexual preferences. Similarly, relationship issues may play an important contributory role (Derogatis, 1983; Schull and Sprenkle, 1980).

Inhibited female orgasm

The approach to the treatment of female orgasmic dysfunction differs depending upon the degree to which the problem is lifelong or acquired, situational or global. Various terms have been used to describe lifelong, total lack of orgasm, with anorgasmia being the most common. Barbach (1980) prefers the term preorgasmic, given that all women start out without having experienced orgasm. The most commonly used approach to the treatment of total anorgasmia involves a technique known as masturbatory training, which was initially developed by LoPiccolo and Lobitz (1972). The rationale for this approach is that the most reliable way for women to experience orgasm is from masturbation rather than coitus, and hence this form of stimulation is suggested to be most likely to trigger orgasm in previously non-orgasmic women. The programme has been developed into a self-help manual (Heiman et al., 1976) which may be used with or without therapist guidance. Various adaptations of the programme have been reported, such as that of Barbach (1980), which is designed for use in a women's group therapy format. Both approaches are based on the masturbatory training model of LoPiccolo and Lobitz (1972) and have been successfully applied in this author's clinical work on a group and individual therapy basis (Spence, 1985).

The initial stage of masturbatory training focuses primarily upon the female and does not typically involve the attendance of the partner at sessions. Barbach (1980) suggests that it is easier to establish orgasmic skills for the woman on her own to begin with, and once the woman is confident of being able to experience orgasm on her own, therapy may begin to generalize orgasmic skills to activities with the partner. The components of therapy are based upon the methods of systematic desensitization, education, physical skill

development and attitude change. Various formats for masturbatory training are available. The original programme outlined by
LoPiccolo and Lobitz (1972) described a sequence of nine steps during
therapy. Barbach (1980) follows this programme closely for the first
four steps and then deviates into a more individualized approach during
the later stages of therapy. The following description is taken primarily
from Barbach (1980) and reflects the approach used by the author
(Spence, 1985). The first step of intervention includes a discussion
about attitudes related to sex activities, sexuality and sexual
responding. Information is also provided about the female body, with
home-based tasks including the practice of Kegel exercises, relaxation
exercises, body viewing and touching of non-genital areas of the body,
in order to determine what forms of touch are pleasurable. A ban
is usually placed on attempts to achieve orgasm at this point. The
second step usually focuses on anatomy and physiology and may use
pictures of genitalia in order to identify the various parts and also
to demonstrate the wide variation in appearance. Information is
provided about sexual responding, and frequently held misconcep-
tions are discussed. The home-based tasks include looking at one's
own genitals and sensual touching.

The third step of the programme typically concentrates upon
discussion related to masturbation; myths, attitudes and methods.
Some therapists (eg. Barbach, 1980) may use films to illustrate
methods of masturbation and also as a form of desensitization.
The use of films depicting masturbation may not, however, be
acceptable in some cultures and the programme appears to be
effective without their inclusion (Spence, 1985). Methods of self-
stimulation are then practised at home, although the aim at this point
is not to progress to orgasm. The fourth step attempts to increase
attention focusing upon pleasurable feelings and encourages women
to make use of fantasies. The women are also asked to read erotic
literature at home, prior to or during self-pleasuring, as a means
of enhancing sexual arousal. Assertion training may also be introduced at this stage. The duration of self-stimulation is gradually
increased and may be carried out for up to 1-hour periods if the woman
is not becoming sore. Clients are asked to experiment with different
movements and positions in order to identify the most arousing forms
of stimulation.

Subsequent components of intervention then tend to vary across
different programmes. Some therapists recommend the introduction
of a vibrator at this point, given that the use of a vibrator is

suggested to be the most likely means of producing orgasm for women. The woman is also encouraged to extend the duration of self-pleasuring, and to begin using fantasy and erotic materials. For most clients, orgasm is experienced for the first time during this phase of therapy. With other women, it may be necessary to deal with various factors which may be inhibiting orgasm, such as fear of losing control, anxiety or negative cognitions about self-stimulation or performance. Once orgasm has been experienced regularly on a self-stimulation basis, a series of exercises are used to generalize the occurrence of orgasm to situations which gradually become closer to intercourse. At first, the woman is asked to carry out her self-pleasuring exercises in front of her partner. This partly serves to demonstrate to the partner the type of touch and stimulation that is needed to produce orgasm, but is also designed to teach the woman to feel relaxed and comfortable about having an orgasm in the presence of her partner. As mentioned above, this stage may be extremely difficult for some couples, particularly if therapy has been conducted with the woman alone up to this point.

The introduction of the partner into therapy usually commences with sensate focus 1 (non-genital pleasuring), followed by sensate focus 2 (genital pleasuring), with an emphasis upon increasing communication skills in relation to sexual matters. Intervention may then move on to prolonged genital pleasuring, in an attempt to produce orgasm from partner stimulation. Given that many women have difficulty in experiencing orgasm from partner stimulation, it may be preferable at this point to suggest that the woman practises self-pleasuring during intercourse. The couple are advised to select a position in which the clitoral area is easily accessible. Once orgasm can be reached in this situation, clitoral self-stimulation is stopped just before the point of orgasm, allowing orgasm to be triggered by vaginal stimulation from thrusting. The aim is then to gradually stop the self-stimulation earlier in the sequence, until orgasm may be triggered by the movements of intercourse, following minimal, direct clitoral stimulation. In practice, only a minority of couples appear to reach this stage of orgasmic ability and the majority are required to rely upon direct clitoral stimulation from the partner, from self-pleasuring or from the use of a vibrator (Spence, 1985).

Whilst this package approach is found to be highly effective in generating orgasmic responding amongst many women who have previously never achieved orgasm, it is not always found to be effective. A study reported by this author (Spence, 1985) found that nine out of 17 anorgasmic women failed to attain orgasm following masturbatory training, even at three-month follow-up, using a programme based on Barbach (1980) and Heiman *et al.* (1976). Examination of the cases that did not succeed reveals some interesting insights into those factors that influence sexual functioning and which are not routinely tackled through the masturbatory training package. For example, one woman in her forties had very entrenched views regarding male–female roles and sexual behaviour. She did not find self-stimulation at all acceptable and it took several weeks before she was able to touch herself. She also experienced a high level of negative thoughts about her genitalia and found them ugly and disgusting. The pictures of female genitalia were tolerated, but she experienced considerable anxiety and revulsion. Although she acknowledged the importance of clitoral stimulation in sexual arousal and orgasm, she consistently returned to thoughts that she *should* be able to experience orgasm from vaginal stimulation alone, during intercourse. This woman was seen in a group therapy format, which was unable to provide the intense cognitive restructuring required. Therapy was also carried out in a format for women without their partners, which made it difficult to deal with the couple's marked communication problems. Her partner also held rigid beliefs concerning male–female roles, not just in relation to sex, but life in general. This woman was unable to pay the $40 deposit for the therapy programme, as her husband kept a record of all her expenditures from the housekeeping allowance and she was afraid to tell him about her attendance at the clinic. This example illustrates the numerous, complex variables that may need to be dealt with, on an individual case basis, if therapy is to be effective.

The approach taken to intervention in cases in which orgasm is achieved in some situations and not others will vary according to the situation in which the woman desires to achieve orgasm. For many women, it may be unrealistic for them to aim to experience orgasm purely from the stimulation provided by penile thrusting, in view of the statistics which suggest that a high proportion of women are unable to achieve orgasm without some form of direct clitoral stimulation during intercourse (Wilcox and Hager, 1980). The approach to intervention with situational orgasmic difficulties has typically involved a greater focus on partner communication, involvement of the partner in masturbatory activities, increasing partner skills in clitoral stimulation and incorporation of clitoral stimulation during intercourse. The general aim of treatment is to extend the range of stimuli that can trigger orgasm, with an attempt to move away from any stereotyped forms of producing orgasm that may have developed. It is suggested here that therapy designed to generate orgasmic ability through penile thrusting alone comes within the domain of sexual relationship enhancement, rather than the treatment of a sexual dysfunction. A programme which is designed to achieve this goal was outlined by Zeiss *et al.* (1977). This approach involves a six-step procedure in which an attempt is made to switch the content of fantasies just prior to masturbatory orgasm to include intercourse situations, to gradually increase partner involvement in masturbatory activities and then to introduce insertion of the partner's penis just prior to orgasm. The point of insertion is then introduced progressively earlier, so that ultimately orgasm is triggered by penile thrusting alone. Zeiss *et al.* (1977) report two successful single cases using this method, but the more general effectiveness of this approach is unclear.

Sexual aversion disorders and sexual phobias

The treatment of sexual phobias and sexual aversion disorders typically involves a combination of relaxation training and graduated exposure to a hierarchy of feared situations (systematic desensitization). Exposure may take place on an in vivo or imaginal basis, or a combination of the two. It is essential that the assessment accurately identifies the presence of underlying fears, as well as the situations that produce a fear response. For example, for some clients, the underlying fear may relate to semen, pregnancy, loss of control, appearance of genitalia or sexually transmitted diseases. In some instances, careful exploration of thoughts and beliefs is required in order to identify the nature of these fears or irrational beliefs.

Although exposure therapies may be effective in many cases, it may be necessary with some clients to conduct intensive cognitive restructuring with regard to maladaptive thoughts and irrational beliefs, as an adjunct to systematic desensitization. Similarly, enhancement of the couple's general relationship may be necessary in many cases. Kaplan (1987) places particular emphasis on fears of intimacy in the development of sexual aversion disorders. The therapist should therefore explore these areas carefully during assessment and treatment.

The following case example was treated by the author and provides a useful illustration of the treatment of a sexual phobia. Mrs T. was a 35-year-old woman who attended the clinic with her partner. They had been married for ten years and had two children aged 7 and 5. The presenting problem was described as a total avoidance of sex by Mrs T. over the past five years. Prior to this point the couple reported a satisfactory sexual relationship, with regular intercourse occurring approximately twice a week. Both partners were able to attain orgasm, with Mrs T. requiring self-stimulation of the clitoris. The marital relationship had originally been satisfactory, but some conflict was now reported by both partners, which mainly related to Mr T.'s desire for a sexual relationship and Mrs T.'s avoidance behaviour.

The problem appeared to have developed over a three-month period after Mrs T. returned home from hospital following the birth of the second child. Initially she had experienced mild post-natal depression and had found intercourse unpleasurable. She reported increasing feelings of revulsion and panic when being touched by her husband, which gradually generalized to all areas of her body. Mrs T. reported classic symptoms of fear when being touched by her husband, including sweating, shaking and dryness of the mouth. If her husband attempted to touch her she would scream, push him away and then leave the room. She reported thoughts such as 'I'll die if he touches me . . . I'll suffocate . . . I've got to get out of here'. Initially, Mr T. had continued his attempts to take part in sexual activities, but had now ceased all initiations. During assessment, Mrs T. produced the hierarchy shown in Table 6.1

This hierarchy clearly illustrates that the feared situations related to being touched in sexual areas. Unlike some cases, the fear did not appear to focus around semen, sexually transmitted diseases, revulsion about genitalia, fears of intimacy or pregnancy. Therapy commenced with relaxation training, and progressed to within-session imaginal desensitization combined with in vivo home-based assignments. Simultaneously, the therapist conducted interventions designed to enhance the general relationship, with a major focus on communication skills. The husband was extremely supportive during treatment, but intervention took almost six months, as each step of the hierarchy could take up to three weeks to complete.

Once the couple were able to engage in non-genital contact while the woman was wearing clothes, therapy progressed to include non-genital sensate focus 1, with clothing, followed by steps with gradually fewer clothes. Eventually, sensate focus 2 could progress. Once this stage was reached, the couple independently moved on to intercourse

Table 6.1

Situation	Degree of fear/anxiety (0–100)
Shaking hands with a previously unknown female	0
Shaking hands with a previously unknown male	0
Being kissed by her children, on the cheek	0
Being pregnant again, if intercourse did not have to occur first	5
Shaking hands with her husband	10
Holding hands with her husband for one minute	15
Husband looking at her, when (she is) nude	15
Seeing her husband nude	15
Being kissed by her husband, on the cheek	20
Having her feet massaged by her husband	30
Touching her own genitals	30
Watching her husband masturbate	35
Touching the semen produced by her husband	35
Touching her husband's penis (flaccid)	35
Touching her husband's penis (erect)	40
Stimulating her husband's penis to ejaculation	45
Being kissed by her husband, on the lips	50
Having her breasts caressed, wearing an overcoat	60
Having her breasts caressed, wearing a thick jumper	70
Having her breasts caressed, wearing a thin jumper	85
Having her genitals caressed, wearing jeans	90
Having her breasts caressed, wearing a bra	90
Having her breasts caressed, no top clothes	95
Having her genitals caressed, wearing panties	95
Having her breasts caressed, nude	100
Having her genitals caressed, nude	100
Having sexual intercourse with her husband	100

during sensate focus 2, although they had been advised not to do so. No problems were encountered during intercourse and it appeared that sexual touching was the major fear source, rather than sexual intercourse per se. Some relapse was encountered during the three-month follow-up phase and it was necessary to reinstitute therapy for several weeks. No further difficulties were then encountered over the following six-month period.

It is interesting to note that no specific cognitions or maladaptive attitudes could be identified in this case, despite repeated attempts by the therapist to elicit them. It remains unclear as to why the problem initially developed, although it is interesting that Kaplan (1988) suggests that a high proportion of sexual phobias involve underlying panic disorders which reflect a biologically determined syndrome. This may have been true for the case outlined above, particularly in view of the onset following childbirth and the initial post-natal depression. Indeed, although there was no evidence of generalized anxiety or non-sexual panic attacks at the time of referral, the description of the fear reaction to sexual touching has many similarities to panic disorder reactions.

Vaginismus

In addition to the individualized cognitive-behavioural and general relationship therapies which are appropriate for any case of sexual dysfunction, the treatment of vaginismus typically includes a programme of systematic desensitization related to vaginal penetration. The approach introduced by Masters and Johnson (1970) commenced with education concerning sexual anatomy and responding. This was then followed by a demonstration of the involuntary vaginal spasm response, with the therapist triggering the response in the clinic during a medical examination. The partner was also requested to trigger the response by attempted insertion of a gloved finger, in the clinic, under the guidance of the therapist. The demonstration of the automatic contraction response to both partners was suggested to be a highly important component of therapy. Intervention then made use of a series of vaginal dilators of increasing size, which formed a heirarchy for in vivo systematic desensitization.

Various adaptations of this procedure have been developed, which make it more suitable for use by a non-medical therapist (who should not be undertaking physical examinations) and which do not require the apparatus of artificial vaginal dilators. Kaplan (1987) suggests that many couples find the use of artificial objects difficult to accept and therefore replaces the use of vaginal dilators with more natural sources of penetration (e.g. own or partner's fingers). This approach is also used by the present author using a hierarchy of steps during desensitization which may proceed as follows:

- Discussion of sexual anatomy and sexual responding;
- Observation of pictures of female genitalia and photographs of the internal sexual anatomy (a wonderful book for this step is produced by the Federation of Feminist Women's Health Centres, *A New View of a Woman's Body*, New York: Touchstone);
- Relaxation training;
- Relaxation plus *home-based*:

  - Visual inspection by woman of her own external genitalia;
  - Touching by woman of her own external genitalia;
  - Placing of her finger at entrance to her vagina;
  - Insertion of a tampon into vagina, using lubrication gel;
  - Insertion of two fingers into vagina, using lubrication gel;
  - Insertion of three fingers into vagina, using lubrication gel;
  - Non-genital sensate focus 1 exercises;
  - Early stage of sensate focus 2 exercises;
  - Touching of external genitalia by partner;
  - Placing of partner's finger at entrance to vagina;
  - Insertion of one of partner's fingers into vagina, using gel;
  - Insertion of two of partner's fingers into vagina, using gel;
  - Insertion of three of partner's fingers into vagina, using gel;
  - Touching of external genitalia by the penis;
  - Insertion of penis by woman into entrance of vagina, using woman-above position and no movement;
  - Deeper insertion of penis by woman, using woman-above position and no movement;
  - Deeper insertion of penis by woman, using woman-above position with gentle movements by the woman;
  - Deeper insertion of penis, using woman-above position with gentle movements by the partner;
  - Normal intercourse and gradual variation of positions, including partner responsibility for insertion.

This type of approach covers the basic aspects of the systematic desensitization procedures. All sexual tasks are conducted at home, preferably on a daily basis. The first stages should be conducted by the woman on her own, so that self-vaginal penetration may be achieved without anxiety, before the partner is introduced into the exercises. Kaplan (1987) suggests it is important to warn the woman that she may initially feel some discomfort during the initial tasks of penetration and that this should be tolerated while relaxing. The clinic sessions may include imaginal desensitization of the hierarchy situations and cognitive restructuring of maladaptive cognitions or beliefs. In addition, it may be useful to teach the client a series of positive, coping self-statements for dealing with each hierarchy situation. This process may be particularly important for those women who hold strong beliefs that their genitals are in some way abnormal, or who have marked fears of pregnancy or sexual diseases. These cases tend to respond poorly to traditional systematic desensitization treatments, in the absence of intensive cognitive restructuring (Scholl, 1988). For some clients, the use of Kegel exercises (see above) may also facilitate the development of control over vaginal contractions and awareness of relaxation versus contraction responses. This may be helpful in order to maximize vaginal relaxation during penetration exercises.

It is also important for the therapist to monitor closely the response of the male partner during therapy. Therapy can be a stressful experience for both partners and the therapist needs to ensure that excessive performance demands are not placed upon the male. It must also be acknowledged that the male is likely to experience fears of causing pain to his partner, hence reassurance is important in order to reduce the possibility that erectile difficulties may occur during treatment.

Psychogenic dyspareunia

Once it has been established that there is no physical basis to the dyspareunia, then it is acceptable to proceed with a psychologically based intervention. The approach taken to treatment is dependent upon the aetiological parameters identified during assessment. Theoretically, genital pain which results from inadequate stimulation or lack of lubrication should not be classified as dyspareunia (according to DSM-III-R) and should be dealt with by ensuring that the couple acquire the techniques necessary to produce adequate stimulation and arousal. Assuming that these factors have been excluded, and no physical explanation can be found, then the pain is suggested to be of psychogenic origin. Psychogenic dyspareunia may therefore be viewed as a chronic pain syndrome, in which the level of pain experienced and pain behaviours (such as avoidance responses, medical visits, use of medication) exceed that which can be explained by physical factors. The approach to treatment strongly resembles that used in the treatment of other chronic pain conditions. Intervention commences with an explanation of the psychological influences over pain experiences, with particular emphasis on the pain-tension–pain cycle and the gate control theory of pain (Melzack and Wall, 1965). A variety of pain management methods are then taught, such as relaxation techniques, attention diversion methods, positive coping, self-talk strategies and reinterpretation of sensations as pleasurable rather than painful. A useful practical guide to the treatment of psychogenic pain conditions can be found in Turk *et al.* (1983).

In addition to pain management methods, intervention should also cover relationship issues and cognitive restructuring, where appropriate. Sensate focus 1 and 2 exercises provide the opportunity for desensitization to situations which have frequently come to trigger fear responses and possibly a vaginismus reaction which will need to be dealt with as described above.

CASE ILLUSTRATION OF THE COGNITIVE-BEHAVIOURAL APPROACH

The following case was selected to illustrate a cognitive-behavioural approach to the treatment of sexual dysfunctions and the importance of an integrated programme which includes a focus on enhancement of the couple's general relationship.

Melanie referred herself to the clinic, requesting help for a sexual problem which she felt was interfering with her marriage. She reported never having experienced orgasm, despite regular sexual activities with her partner, during their 3½ year marriage. She was 28 years old and worked full time as a librarian. Assessment revealed a high level of dissatisfaction with the sexual relationship, a low level of sexual activities other than intercourse, minimal anxiety about sexual activities and adequate levels of sexual arousability on the Hoon *et al.* (1976) Sexual Arousal Inventory. Her ratings of the marital relationship revealed a low score of 81 on the Spanier (1976) Dyadic Adjustment Scale (DAS), which is almost 2 standard deviations below the norm for married couples. Despite the low score on the DAS, she stated that 'I want very much for my relationship to succeed and will do all I can to see that it does.' A high frequency of disagreements between the couple concerning a wide range of areas was reported.

Her attitudes towards self-stimulation were favourable and she had attempted to masturbate and to use a vibrator, but had not reached orgasm. Intervention commenced with individual therapy, along the lines of Barbach (1980) and Heiman et al. (1976). By the sixth session, Melanie reported having experienced orgasm, using her vibrator and subsequently reached orgasm using manual stimulation. The eighth session focused on introducing the partner into therapy, through use of written home-based instructions for sensate focus 1 and 2, with additional suggestions for communication exercises. Although Melanie remained able to reach orgasm through use of the vibrator and self-stimulation, she was unable to trigger orgasm in the presence of her partner with either self or partner stimulation. Interestingly, assessment after session 9 revealed a marked improvement in Melanie's rating of the marital relationship on the DAS to 108, which is within the normal range. However, several areas of conflict within the relationship remained unresolved.

It was clear at this point that both members of the partnership needed to attend the therapy sessions if Melanie was to reach the point of being able to experience orgasm in her husband's presence. Tom agreed to attend and a reassessment of the situation was carried out, with both partners being interviewed separately and together. Several important points emerged at this time. First, it was clear that Melanie's attempt to enhance her sexual responding had produced an improvement in their relationship and had increased the level of positive feeling between the couple. Melanie's lack of orgasmic ability resulted in considerable friction about their sexual relationship. Tom reported feelings of inadequacy related to thoughts about 'not being a good enough lover'. Melanie reported a wide range of maladaptive thoughts during their sexual activities. These included numerous performance anxiety statements and spectatoring thoughts such as 'nothing's happening . . . why can't I feel anything? . . . I'll try tensing the muscles . . . no, . . . it's not going to happen'. Of particular importance were her thoughts concerning Tom's reaction to her: 'I must really try to do it this time. I wish he could do it the way I can. He's been doing that for ages now. I bet his arm is getting tired. Come on . . . hurry up. He must be fed up with this by now. I'm sure he'd rather be with someone else.' Sexual activities had become rather aversive for both partners and intercourse frequently left both of them feeling miserable. The negative emotions tended to carry over to non-sexual situations and arguments frequently occurred about 'silly, little things', such as whose turn it was to do the shopping.

Assessment revealed a low score from Tom on the DAS, suggesting that although the initial intervention had produced a more positive view of the relationship for Melanie, Tom was still very dissatisfied with their marriage. Both partners stated a strong desire to stay together and were highly motivated to improve their relationship in non-sexual, as well as sexual areas. Intervention with the couple therefore commenced with an attempt to increase positive interactions. A menu of pleasant activities was drawn up, from which they were asked to select and carry out two items each week. Melanie and Tom were also asked to practise non-genital, followed by genital, sensate focus exercises. Self-monitoring of cognitions before, during and after the exercises revealed that Melanie tended to focus on negative thoughts about her partner, such as those relating to conflicts that had arisen earlier in the day. She found it very difficult to relax and focus her attention upon the sensation produced by Tom's pleasuring. It was clear that intervention needed to focus on several areas, including:

1. Enhancing the couple's general relationship, with a particular focus on communication and problem-solving skills to enable them to resolve areas of dispute;
2. Increasing Melanie's ability to focus attention upon pleasurable sensations;
3. To reduce interfering, negative thoughts concerning herself, sexual performance, Tom and their relationship;
4. To enhance Tom's ability to provide appropriate stimulation.

The training of communication and problem-solving skills was highly effective, using discussion, modelling and role-play in the clinic, followed by home-based practice. Much of the improvement in their marital satisfaction occurred during the increasing of positive interactions, in which each partner was asked to provide one low-cost, high-benefit event for their partner each day. Relatively minor, pleasing events were found to generate high levels of marital satisfaction.

During the practice of pleasuring exercises Melanie was instructed to concentrate upon erotic cues. She was also encouraged to make use of fantasy as a means of enhancing sexual arousal and blocking out interfering, negative thoughts. The information provided from the self-monitoring sheets was extremely useful during the cognitive restructuring components of treatment. With both partners present, it was possible to discuss any irrational or maladaptive thoughts. For example, Tom was able to demonstrate to Melanie that her thoughts about his becoming bored or tired were unfounded. It was also possible to demonstrate to Melanie that her thoughts concerning Tom's reaction to her stimulating herself in his presence were inaccurate. Her thoughts revolved around a fear that he would think she was dirty or disgusting, whereas Tom described his actual thoughts as realizing that 'if it was OK for men then it should be OK for women'. He, in turn, discussed his negative thoughts about being an incompetent lover and his feelings of stupidity at having to learn from his partner. Discussion about the steps involved in learning any skill and the lack of education that most of us get in relation to sex served to allay these concerns and Tom felt more relaxed about being guided by Melanie or observing her techniques of stimulation. A series of positive, sexual self-talk statements were developed for Melanie to use, in order to focus attention on her sensations, such as . . . 'I must just relax, and concentrate on those feelings. Don't let any worrying thoughts come in . . . I'm just really going to enjoy this today. Tom can have his turn some other time. This is going to be great.'

During the genital pleasuring, Melanie gradually developed the confidence to guide Tom through the forms of stimulation that she found particularly pleasurable. After considerable cognitive restructuring she was also able to stimulate herself to orgasm in front of Tom, on the condition that he was willing to do the same in front of her.

After five sessions, Melanie was able to experience orgasm through self-stimulation with Tom watching. After this had been repeated several times, orgasm was then reached through partner stimulation while Tom was being guided by Melanie. Around the same time, Melanie reported being able to reach orgasm regularly during intercourse, using a vibrator or self stimulation. She was not able to experience orgasm from vaginal stimulation alone, or through vaginal plus partner stimulation, but neither of them viewed this as a problem. The final ratings of their marital relationship revealed high levels of satisfaction on the DAS for both Tom and Melanie. These improvements were maintained at one- and three-month follow-ups. The couple were then advised to recontact the therapist if problems recurred within their relationship, but no further contact was made.

Although single cases of this type demonstrate the effectiveness of a cognitive-behavioural approach in the treatment of some couples who present with dysfunctions, it is important to examine the research literature relating to the general effectiveness of interventions. The next chapter provides a critical examination of the treatment outcome literature.

7

The effectiveness of interventions for sexual dysfunctions

METHODOLOGICAL PROBLEMS IN OUTCOME STUDIES IN THE TREATMENT OF PSYCHOSEXUAL DYSFUNCTIONS

Attempting to review the outcome literature concerning the effectiveness of cognitive and/or behavioural treatments of psychosexual dysfunctions is a frustrating task. The evidence available is fraught with methodological limitations and it is extremely difficult to draw any firm conclusions. The majority of studies suffer from a variety of methodological problems. These include:

- Small subject numbers;
- Absence of experimental control groups (e.g. waiting list/ no-treatment/attention placebo controls);
- Lack of random allocation to conditions;
- No clear-cut definitions of diagnostic criteria to permit replication;
- Absence of, or inadequate duration of, long-term follow-up;
- Inadequate outcome measures, in terms of specific target behaviours and general indices of the sexual and marital relationship;
- Inclusion of a mixture of different types of psychosexual dysfunctions, thereby limiting the conclusions that can be drawn regarding effectiveness of treatment with a specific diagnostic group;
- Inadequate description of therapy methods used.

The methodological inadequacies of most outcome studies place a considerable limitation on the conclusions that can be drawn with regard to the long-term effectiveness of a given therapy approach with any specific psychosexual disorder.

LARGE-SCALE EVALUATIONS OF TREATMENT OUTCOME

The first category of outcome studies to be considered includes the uncontrolled reports of data from clinics which specialize in the treatment of sexual problems. Probably the first report of this type was published by Masters and Johnson (1970). These authors reported the results for the first patients to pass through their clinic and included two to five-year follow-up data. The Masters and Johnson programme involved a two to three-week programme of daily therapy during a residential period away from home. The results were extremely impressive and have rarely been matched by other therapists since. Kolodny (1981) subsequently reported the two to five-year follow-up information for 1872 sexual dysfunctions seen at the Masters and Johnson Institute. The outcome data remained equally impressive, particularly for vaginismus, with a 98.8% success rate, and premature ejaculation, with a 96.1% success rate. The success rates reported for other dysfunctions included primary erectile dysfunction (66.7%), secondary erectile dysfunction (78.4%), ejaculatory incompetence (76%), primary female orgasmic dysfunction (72%) and situational female orgasmic dysfunction (71%). These data were based upon the original criteria for success outlined by Masters and Johnson (1970).

Outcome figures from other centres have not been so impressive (e.g. DeAmicis et al., 1985; Dekker and Everaerd, 1983). The results from a specialist clinic in Oxford, UK, illustrate this point (Hawton et al., 1986). These authors reported a one to six-year follow-up of 140 cases of psychosexual dysfunction who were treated on an outpatient basis, using a modified Masters and Johnson approach. Independent assessors were asked to rate the degree of improvement in the presenting problem on a 5-point scale ranging from 'problem resolved' to 'worse'. Immediately after treatment, 26% of the cases were assessed as being resolved, with another 32% being judged as problem resolved but with some difficulties still apparent. Eighteen per cent of cases showed some improvement, 22% no change and 2% were assessed as being worse. If the independent assessor ratings of 'resolved' and 'resolved but with some difficulties still apparent' are taken as successes, then the success rate for various dysfunctions was found to be highest for vaginismus (81%), erectile dysfunction (68%), premature ejaculation (64%) and female impaired sexual interest (56%). The worst outcome occurred for ejaculatory failure (20%), but this sample only involved five cases (Hawton and Catalan, 1986).

At follow-up, 75.7% of cases responded, which brings into question the likely status of clients who did not complete the follow-up contact. Of those who were available at follow-up, 75% reported recurrence of the presenting problem at some point, but most of these dealt with the problem successfully. In terms of specific disorders, the long-term results for vaginismus were excellent, supporting the results of the Masters and Johnson Institute. There was also a relatively good outcome for erectile dysfunction, with the problem being assessed as being resolved or resolved/some difficulty for 13/18 men. The results were relatively poor for premature ejaculation, with only 2/8 men being assessed as successful at follow-up, compared to 6/8 at post-treatment. Female impaired sexual interest was also found to show relapse during follow-up. These data are obviously much less impressive than those reported by Kolodny (1981), particularly for the treatment of premature ejaculation. If this disorder is excluded, the results are, however, generally consistent with other studies carried out in outpatient settings (e.g. DeAmicis et al., 1985; Dekker and Everaerd, 1983).

One must therefore ask why other centres report much lower success rates for most forms of psychosexual dysfunction. As mentioned above, the variation between studies in the criteria used for success makes it difficult to make direct comparisons. Similarly, there are many variations in procedure between different centres and differences in the clientele that could account for the discrepant findings. The Masters and Johnson Institute specializes in residential treatment, with therapy being conducted over a three-week period on a daily basis. Therapy is conducted by two therapists, using a carefully structured approach, and clients are freed from the stresses and interference of work and family throughout treatment. Clients are also followed-up by telephone after they leave the centre, which provides a booster to therapy. The fees charged by the Institute also suggest that the client group may be somewhat different in terms of socio-economic status compared to clients attending some government or university-funded clinics. It is possible that behavioural treatments of psychosexual dysfunctions are more effective with couples from higher socio-economic status backgrounds. An alternative explanation for the less spectacular results of more recent studies is that the problems being presented by clients are becoming increasingly complex, as proposed in Chapter 5, and a basic behavioural approach is inadequate for many couples (Halgin *et al.*, 1988).

The discrepancy between the findings of Masters and Johnson (1970) and Kolodny (1981) compared to those of subsequent researchers has led to investigation of the various parameters that could explain the different results. Several studies have investigated the impact of parameters such as the spacing of sessions (daily versus weekly) and single-therapist versus co-therapy teams. Evidence suggests little difference in outcome according to the variation in these aspects of treatment (see later), leading to the general suggestion that the techniques introduced by Masters and Johnson are suitable for use in an outpatient clinic, on a weekly basis and by a single therapist (Libman *et al.*, 1985). Although it is apparent that the treatment of sexual dysfunctions can be effective in the outpatient setting, it is also clear that the results of most studies fail to match those reported by Masters and Johnson (1970) and Kolodny (1981). So far as I know, no study has yet attempted to compare the effectiveness of a programme identical to the Masters and Johnson Institute (i.e. fee-paying, residential, daily treatment with a co-therapy team) with the same treatment applied on a non fee-paying, outpatient, single-therapist, weekly session basis. Such a study would be important, as it would investigate the degree to which the highly successful results of Masters and Johnson can be accounted for by the situation and format in which therapy occurs.

MASTERS AND JOHNSON VERSUS OTHER APPROACHES

Although the traditional Masters and Johnson approach to therapy may not be so effective when applied on an outpatient basis, it is probably the most frequently used technology in the treatment of psychosexual problems. Its effectiveness has been compared with a variety of alternative therapy approaches. For example, Crowe *et al.* (1981) compared the effectiveness of traditional Masters and Johnson therapy with a combination of marital therapy and relaxation training. Forty-eight couples took part in the study and were classified as presenting with erectile dysfunction, anorgasmia and loss of libido. These couples were randomly assigned to either

(a) a modified Masters and Johnson approach, involving a co-therapy format; (b) a modified Masters and Johnson approach, involving a single-therapist format; (c) marital therapy plus relaxation, with a co-therapy format; or (d) marital therapy plus relaxation, with a single-therapist format. Therapy involved five to ten sessions lasting 30–40 minutes at two-weekly intervals. Improvements were found for all four forms of therapy on measures of sexual satisfaction, level of libido, and self and therapist ratings of target behaviours. No improvements were found for marital satisfaction and no differences were found between the various forms of therapy. Crowe *et al.* (1981) suggest that this study and others in which alternative approaches have also been shown to be equally effective to the Masters and Johnson approach all have in common the inclusion of an intervention which produces anxiety reduction. These studies included systematic desensitization (Mathews *et al.*, 1976) and Valium (Ansari, 1976). The led Crowe *et al.* (1981) to suggest that the effective element of Masters and Johnson's therapy may be anxiety reduction and that alternative methods of generating anxiety reduction may be equally effective. This proposal does not stand up to scrutiny for certain types of sexual problems. For example, anxiety reduction methods such as systematic desensitization have been found to be of little benefit in the treatment of primary female orgasmic dysfunction (Andersen, 1981). This is hardly surprising, as such methods are unlikely to be effective unless anxiety concerning sexual situations is present in the first place and Andersen (1981) found little evidence of anxiety in most of her anorgasmic sample. Anxiety reduction appears to play a much greater role in the treatment of disorders in which sexual anxiety is more likely to be present, such as sexual aversion disorders, vaginismus, erectile failure or dyspareunia.

EXPLORING THE PARAMETERS OF TREATMENT

Numerous studies have been carried out to assess whether different therapy formats influence the effectiveness of therapy for psychosexual problems. Parameters such as level of therapist contact, use of bibliotherapy (i.e. self-help literature), group versus individual couple therapy, couple versus one-partner treatment, co-therapy verus single therapist, massed versus spaced sessions and same-sex versus 'opposite-sex therapist have all been subject to

213

examination. To date, the state of the research literature does not permit many conclusions to be drawn. For example, it is not necessarily valid to apply the results found with one form of sexual dysfunction to a different type of sexual difficulty. Hence, the findings that a particular format for treatment may be beneficial for global, female orgasmic dysfunction does not mean necessarily that the same approach will be helpful in the treatment of erectile difficulty. Those studies that have included a range of different sexual problems have typically failed to include sufficient subject numbers to permit conclusions to be drawn about specific types of sexual problems. Furthermore, the finding that a particular format of treatment produces beneficial changes for one client does not mean that the same approach will necessarily be effective for a different client with the same type of sexual difficulty. We are still a long way from being able to match the most effective format of therapy for a given couple or client.

Minimal therapist contact/bibliotherapy

The majority of studies which have used minimal therapist contact have also used bibliotherapy, which makes it difficult to separate out the effective components if treatment is successful. The form of minimal therapist contact has also varied considerably, ranging from contact only at the onset and termination of the therapy phase, to four therapy sessions, or even weekly telephone contact, which further limits the conclusions that can be drawn.

Bibiotherapy with minimal therapist contact has been found to be effective for some clients in the treatment of premature ejaculation (Lowe and Mikulas, 1975; Trudel and Proulx, 1987; Zeiss, 1977). Interestingly, the Zeiss (1977) study found that bibliotherapy alone was not effective, whereas it was almost as effective as individual-couple therapy if combined with a brief weekly telephone contact. A combination of four treatment sessions plus bibliotherapy was found to be as effective as 15 therapy sessions, in the treatment of global anorgasmia using a masturbatory training approach (Morokoff and LoPiccolo, 1986). The effectiveness of bibliotherapy and minimal therapist contact in the treatment of female orgasmic dysfunction was also demonstrated by Tripet-Dodge *et al.* (1982) and Libman *et al.* (1984). A more recent study, however, suggests that minimal therapist contact and bibliography may be less effective in changing the more complex aspects of the couple's relationship. Trudel and Laurin (1988) investigated the benefits of using the Heiman *et al.* (1986) masturbatory training self-help manual with minimal therapist contact. Five cases of primary and 12 cases of secondary female orgasmic dysfunction were allocated to either a 15-week waiting-list condition or bibliotherapy plus weekly telephone contact. The treatment group reported increased sexual arousal, sexual pleasure and increased sexual repertoire. No changes were reported, however, in terms of orgasm frequency, marital happiness ratings or interpersonal communication skills. Given that the majority of cases in the Trudel and Laurin (1988) study experienced situational orgasmic difficulties in achieving orgasm with their partner, it seems possible that more intensive therapist intervention is required to deal effectively with communication and partner skills. It seems sensible to suggest that brief therapist contact combined with bibliotherapy would be inappropriate for very complex cases of psychosexual dysfunction. Admittedly, this proposal is made on the basis of clinical intuition rather than any empirical evidence. The group design nature of most empirical studies tends to mask the fact that some clients do not respond positively to minimal therapist contact.

Group therapy formats

Group formats have been used for couples and individuals in the treatment of sexual difficulties. The group format has the obvious advantage of being less costly in terms of therapist time (assuming that the group intervention is effective). Barbach (1980) also suggests that the group situation has the benefits of providing support from other members, cohesiveness, the opportunity for learning from the experience of others, peer pressure, and prompting and reinforcement from other group members. All these factors are suggested to facilitate attitude change, compliance with homework assignments and behaviour change. The experience of group participation may also provide a desensitization experience in relation to discussion of sexual matters and may increase confidence and skill in communication about sexual topics. The group format obviously has its disadvantages too. The amount of attention that can be paid to a given individual or couple is generally reduced and the group situation makes it difficult to tailor the intervention to the needs of the couple or individual.

215

Group (three to four couples) therapy has been found to be as effective as therapy sessions attended by one couple in the treatment of combined premature ejaculation and secondary female orgasmic dysfunction (Golden *et al.*, 1978). Both therapy formats led to significant improvements in latency of ejaculation and range and frequency of female orgasmic response at post-treatment. No significant differences were found between group and couple therapy at follow-up. Unfortunately, this study did not include a no-treatment or attention placebo comparison group, which limits the conclusions that can be drawn as to the effectiveness of either procedure.

Group interventions have also been found to be effective when used with individual members of the partnership or single persons. Minimal differences between group and individual therapy have been found in the treatment of premature ejaculation (Perelman, 1977), total anorgasmia (Ersner-Hershfield and Kopel, 1979) and sexual anxiety (Nemetz *et al.*, 1978).

A study reported by Spence (1985) compared the effectiveness of group versus individual treatment of primary and secondary female orgasmic dysfunction. Twenty-five women who were categorized as experiencing primary orgasmic dysfunction and 25 women who were categorized as experiencing secondary orgasmic dysfunction were randomly allocated to either group intervention, individual therapy or a waiting-list control condition. Intervention for the 'primary' women was based on the masturbatory training approach of Lobitz and LoPiccolo (1972). The content of therapy for the 'secondary' subjects included extending the range of situations in which orgasm occurred, increasing communication with the partner in relation to types of stimulation (through home-based sensate focus exercises) and gradual introduction and then phasing out of masturbatory activities with the partner and during intercourse. Both group and individual therapy produced improvements in subjective ratings of satisfaction with the sexual relationship and orgasmic ability, which were not evident for the waiting-list control. Individual therapy was found to be more effective in producing orgasm during intercourse (by any means) for the 'secondary' cases, particularly by the three-month follow-up. The individual therapy approach was also found to be marginally more effective in terms of number of 'primary' clients who achieved orgasm by any means. Interestingly, all conditions including the waiting-list demonstrated improvements in sexual arousal. No improvements were evident in terms of increased range of sexual activities or reductions in heterosexual anxiety. In terms of the marital relationship, improvements were greater for primary subjects with the individual therapy approach, whereas the secondary women showed greater marital satisfaction following group therapy. This study therefore suggests that, although both group and individual therapy approaches are superior to no intervention on measures of orgasmic ability, the individual therapy approach was helpful to a greater number of women in comparison to group intervention.

Massed versus spaced sessions

The original daily therapy approach introduced by Masters and Johnson (1970) is not particularly suitable for application on an outpatient basis, where weekly or bi-weekly sessions have traditionally been used. Indeed, it has been suggested by some therapists that daily sessions do not permit adequate opportunity for the practice of home-based assignments. This may be true if therapy occurs on an outpatient basis, in which clients return to their homes, work and family demands. The Masters and Johnson Institute clients attend on a residential basis in which the opportunity for 'out of session' practice is built into the programme and competing demands on time are reduced. It must be borne in mind, therefore, that studies which compare weekly versus daily sessions, or massed versus spaced sessions, on an outpatient basis do not represent evaluations of the relative effectiveness of the original Masters and Johnson approach, which requires massed sessions on a residential basis.

Unfortunately, several studies which have investigated massed versus spaced therapy have also varied the number of therapy sessions involved or the duration of therapy. It is therefore difficult to determine whether differential treatment effects are the result of variation in spacing of sessions, number of sessions or length of therapy. For example, Clement and Schmidt (1983) compared the use of 17 sessions over three weeks, using a mixed sample of sexual dysfunctions, with 35–40 twice-weekly sessions over 18 weeks. No differences in outcome were evident on a variety of measures. Carney *et al.* (1978) compared 16 weekly sessions with five, monthly sessions using a mixed sample of sexual problems. Therapy involved a Masters and Johnson approach combined with either testosterone or diazepam. No difference in outcome was evident between the more versus less frequent

217

forms of treatment. This study did not, however, include a no-treatment or attention placebo control condition, which limits the conclusions that can be drawn.

Of the studies which have held the number of sessions constant, Heiman and LoPiccolo (1983) compared 15 sessions held on a daily basis with 15 sessions in a weekly format. Subjects included 69 lower-middle class couples, presenting with a variety of sexual problems. Therapy followed the Masters and Johnson format and was conducted by co-therapy teams. Although no differences between daily and weekly therapy were found on many outcome measures, of the ten significant differences found, nine favoured the use of weekly sessions, particularly for secondary female orgasmic dysfunction and erectile failure. This suggests that different types of sexual problems may respond differently to massed versus spaced sessions. Hence the results of studies such as Ersner-Hershfield and Kopel (1979) indicating massed (two sessions per week for five weeks) versus spaced (one session per week for ten weeks) sessions to be equally effective in the group treatment of primary female orgasmic dysfunction should not necessarily be generalized to other types of sexual dysfunction.

Co-therapy versus a single therapist

The relative effectiveness of one therapist versus a co-therapy team is probably the most well-researched aspect of therapist characteristics. Although Masters and Johnson have emphasized the importance of a mixed-sex, co-therapy team, this is very costly in terms of therapist time, and two, opposite-sex therapists may not be available in many therapy clinics. It is therefore encouraging to find that most studies which have researched one therapist versus mixed-sex, co-therapy teams find little difference in outcome. For example, Crowe et al. (1981) compared the effectiveness of a modified Masters and Johnson approach or marital therapy plus relaxation when applied by either one therapist or a co-therapy team. Improvements were found for all forms of therapy on self and therapist ratings of the target behaviour, sexual satisfaction, self ratings of libido and assessors' ratings of relationship satisfaction. No differences were evident for one versus two therapists and the matching of sex of the therapist with that of the person with the main presenting problem did not appear to influence outcome. Heiman *et al.* (1985) also compared a single-therapist versus co-therapy approach. Sixty-five couples with mixed sexual problems were randomly assigned to either one therapist or to a co-therapy team. No difference in outcome between these formats was evident on measures of satisfaction with the sexual relationship, sexual adjustment or symptom remission. Consistent with the Crowe *et al.* (1981) results, no difference was found whether or not the sex of the therapist matched the client with the presenting problem.

The studies available to date appear to have focused upon the impact of one therapist versus co-therapy using a couple format for treatment. It remains to be determined whether the use of a co-therapy team is preferable for group treatment. Research is also needed to determine whether some forms of sexual difficulty respond better to one therapist.

Involvement of the partner

The emphasis of the Masters and Johnson (1970) approach has also included the involvement of the partner. For some couples, sexual dysfunctions are present for both partners and hence inclusion of both members of the partnership makes sense. For others, it is possible to suggest that the presenting problem occurs in one partner. This goes right against the philosophy inherent in the Masters and Johnson approach, which states that any sexual dysfunction reflects a problem of the partnership, rather than any one individual, and that intervention must focus on both partners in order for therapy to be successful. This approach is certainly logical for couples for whom the sexual problem reflects just one aspect of dysfunction within their relationship. It is possible, however, that for some cases individual therapy may be adequate. Obviously, some clients will present for therapy who do not have partners and a couple format will not be feasible. In other instances, one partner may be unwilling to attend and any intervention would have to proceed on an individual basis.

Zilbergeld (1975) described a successful approach to therapy for men without partners or whose partners were unwilling to attend. Intervention focused on the development of sexual skills during masturbatory activities, assertion training and cognitive challenging of male myths. This study did not, however, employ experimental control groups and did not include systematic evaluation using psychometrically sound outcome measures. Ersner-Hershfield and

Kopel (1979) compared individual therapy in groups with couple therapy in groups in the treatment of primary female orgasmic dysfunction. Minimal difference was found in therapy outcome on measures of marital satisfaction, sexual behaviour and pleasure for the male or female partner, whether or not the partner was included in sessions. It seems that partner involvement may not therefore be necessary in the treatment of female primary orgasmic dysfunction. Whilst partner involvement seems to be less important in the early stages of masturbatory training, it seems likely that inclusion of the partner in sessions would be helpful in the later stages of therapy when the partner is included in home-based assignments. It would be useful to investigate whether this is the case, particularly in terms of the ability of the programme to produce orgasm during partner stimulation and intercourse.

OUTCOME STUDIES WITH SPECIFIC SEXUAL DYSFUNCTIONS

Many studies have been conducted which investigate the effectiveness of behavioural and/or cognitive therapy approaches in the treatment of specific psychosexual dysfunctions. These will be reviewed briefly below.

Hypoactive sexual desire disorder and female sexual arousal disorder

The initial failure to recognize disorders of interest/desire and arousal, particularly in women, as problems distinct from each other and from orgasmic dysfunction, has meant that there is a paucity of research into the treatment of these disorders. Much of the relevant literature has tended to select samples on the basis of labels such as 'sexual unresponsiveness' which include a combination of low sexual desire and low sexual arousal (e.g. Carney *et al.*, 1978; Dow and Gallagher, 1989). Although some authors (e.g. Golombok and Rust, 1988) have produced evidence to suggest that most cases presenting with sexual dysfunctions demonstrate an overlap between symptoms relating to sexual desire, arousal and orgasm, there is a need for empirical outcome studies concerning the treatment of specific populations in which problems of desire or arousal predominate.

Carney *et al.* (1978) reported a balanced factorial design which compared testosterone therapy plus a psychological therapy approach, with diazepam plus psychological therapy, in a sample of 32 couples in which the woman presented with 'sexual unresponsiveness'. The psychological treatment was based on the Masters and Johnson approach, using an initial ban on intercourse and a prescribed graded sequence of undemanding sexual skill exercises, leading ultimately to intercourse. The design of the study also allowed for the comparison of 16 weekly with five, monthly therapy sessions. Allocation to groups was random, with each condition containing half high and half low sexually anxious women. The results indicated that, irrespective of the degree of anxiety, testosterone plus psychological therapy was superior to diazepam plus psychological therapy on measures of subjective quality of intercourse, pleasant feelings associated with sex, decreased vaginal discomfort in coitus, frequency of sexually exciting thoughts and frequency of orgasm. No difference was found between the monthly and weekly treatment conditions. Given that the study did not include a no-treatment or attention placebo control condition, or psychological treatment only, it is difficult to determine the true effectiveness of the programme, or the relative contribution of the drug/behaviour therapy components. At first glance, it may be suggested that testosterone was beneficial for these clients, but an alternative proposal is that diazepam may have actually inhibited the benefits of psychological treatment, with testosterone producing little additional benefit.

This possibility led Mathews *et al.* (1983), using a similar patient sample, to compare testosterone (same form and dosage as Carney *et al.*, 1978) plus psychological therapy with placebo plus psychological therapy. This study also involved a balanced factorial design, in which the frequency of sessions and single versus co-therapy formats were compared. The results demonstrated no additional benefits for testosterone therapy over and above those produced by the behavioural treatment plus placebo medication.

Although it would appear therefore that testosterone does not add anything to the effectiveness of psychological intervention, it is still possible that testosterone does result in some enhancement of sexual desire and arousal, but that this does not exceed the benefits of psychological treatment. In order to examine this hypothesis, Dow and Gallagher (1989) randomly assigned 30 couples in which the woman presented with 'general sexual unresponsiveness' to either testosterone only, testosterone and psychological treatment or placebo plus psychological treatment. The treatment methods matched those used in the two studies outlined above, in order to permit comparison of results. Outcome was assessed by independent ratings and self-report at post-treatment and four-month follow-up. The subjects in the testosterone condition attended sessions at times and for durations equivalent to other therapy conditions. The results indicated that the psychological therapy plus placebo, and psychological therapy plus testosterone conditions were superior to testosterone alone on numerous outcome measures. Minimal difference was found between psychological therapy plus placebo and psychological therapy plus testosterone, suggesting that the most active contributor to the successful outcome was the psychological treatment. Improvements were found in measures of sexual anxiety, marital status, sexual attitudes, general sexual satisfaction, sexual interest and sexual pleasure. Although testosterone was less effective than psychological therapy, some benefits were evident for this group, including improvements in self-reported sexual responsiveness and sexual pleasure and independent assessors' ratings of frequency of sexual interest and adequate vaginal response. The lack of a waiting-list control or placebo-only condition makes it difficult to draw conclusions about this result, as it is not possible to exclude placebo effects or spontaneous remission. As it turned out, maintenance of improvements was poor for the testosterone-only group at the four-month follow-up, whereas the benefits were generally maintained for the subjects who received therapy which included the psychological treatment. It seems, therefore, that behaviour therapy is superior to testosterone treatment for women who are referred with problems of arousal and desire.

Unfortunately, the exact characteristics of the samples used in these studies are unclear and they appear to include a mixture of clients with low sexual desire, minimal pleasure, low arousal and low frequency of sexual activities. Future studies need to separate out the components of desire and arousal, in order to determine whether different treatment approaches may be more appropriate for disorders of desire versus disorders of arousal. It is also unclear from the studies outlined above what proportion of their sample would be assessed as having overcome the sexual problem and could be judged as successful cases. Although statistically significant changes were evident, the clinical significance of the results is unclear. Future studies should also include some means of demonstrating the proportion of clients who can be considered as successfully treated.

Erectile disorder

Success rates in the treatment of primary erectile disorder suggest that this dysfunction is relatively difficult to treat compared to situational (secondary) erectile problems. For example, Kolodny (1981) reported a success rate of 66.7% for the treatment of primary impotence. This compares to a success rate of 78.4% for secondary erectile dysfunction (Kolodny, 1981). Given that the vast majority of males presenting with erectile difficulties report problems of a secondary nature (i.e. the problem tends to be situational and not lifelong), research has tended to focus on secondary erectile dysfunction. The effectiveness of behavioural and cognitive treatments of secondary erectile dysfunction has not been particularly impressive and long-term follow-up results have been poor. For example, Kilmann et al. (1987), in a review of the literature, concluded that the erectile problem is typically resolved in only about 52% of cases and that maintenance of improvements over time is poor. Heiman and LoPiccolo (1983) suggested that the relatively poor results from psychological treatment of secondary erectile dysfunction may reflect the unintentional inclusion of organic cases in some studies. These authors pointed out that identification of organic causes for erectile failure has been difficult in the past and it is only recently that methods have been available and routinely applied in order to exclude those cases with organic aetiology. If organic cases can be excluded, leaving those genuine cases of psychogenic cause, it is likely that the effectiveness of behavioural and cognitive therapies will improve.

For example, Kilmann et al. (1987) randomly assigned 20 couples presenting with erectile dysfunction to one of five conditions, namely communication skills training, sexual technique training, a combination of communication skills and sexual techniques, an attention placebo control and no intervention. All conditions did, however, initially receive 4 hours of sex education which covered anatomy, the human sexual response, methods of stimulation and myths of sex. The no-intervention control was therefore somewhat confounded. All men undertook an extensive medical and physiological screening in order to exclude organic cases. The communication skills condition covered effective listening, self-assertion, intimate communication, sexual initiations and refusals, impact of sex role stereotyping, sexual self-image, sexual attitudes, communication about sex and conflict resolution. Intervention methods included discussion, modelling, role-play and home-based assignments. No sexual skills were taught and home-based tasks did not include pleasuring exercises. The sexual technique training included Zilbergeld's masturbation training, partner exercises and sensate focus exercises. All non-sexual, marital and partner issues were avoided. The combined therapy involved an abbreviated version of each of the above approaches, for the same 8×2 hours of therapy. The attention placebo condition included an extended version of the sex education procedure, combined with relevant literature to read at home. The validity of this procedure as an attention placebo is rather questionable and the positive results for this condition are perhaps not surprising. Each treatment condition was found to have a positive impact upon marital satisfaction and sexual adjustment on the Sexual Interaction Inventory, with no differences between therapies on outcome measures. The extremely small subject numbers in each condition, however, do not permit sound conclusions to be drawn as to the relative effectiveness of the different forms of therapy. If the therapy subjects are combined, 81% (13/16) of men were found to reach or exceed the criteria for successful penetration on 80% or more of intercourse attempts. This success rate is encouraging and suggests that careful screening of organic problems may indeed lead to better results for behavioural and/or cognitive therapies.

Cognitive therapy on its own does not appear to be effective in producing long-term improvements in erectile functioning, although short-term benefits may be found. Munjack et al. (1984) selected 16 couples presenting with secondary erectile dysfunction. These couples were randomly assigned to six weeks of bi-weekly rational emotive therapy (RET; Ellis, 1958) or to a six-week waiting-list control. Assessments were conducted for two weeks, before and after treatment and at six to nine months follow-up. The results showed that RET resulted in significant reductions in sexual anxiety, increased attempts at intercourse and a greater number of successful penetrations. These improvements were not found for the waiting-list control. Interestingly, no changes in irrational beliefs were found. At follow-up many of the benefits of RET had been lost, with intercourse only being achieved with an adequate erection on 25% of occasions. It seems therefore that, although cognitive restructuring methods may be valuable in the short term, additional methods are required if the benefits are to be maintained. It also remains to be shown whether cognitive restructuring is effective in enhancing the gains of behavioural approaches and whether the benefits produced by methods such as RET are as great as those produced by other techniques, such as behaviourally based sexual skills training approaches.

Premature ejaculation

The behavioural treatment of premature ejaculation is now recognized to be highly effective. Kolodny (1981) reported a long-term success rate of 96.1% for 432 cases at the Masters and Johnson Institute. It is unclear what criteria were used by Kolodny to define success, given that success was originally defined by Masters and Johnson (1970) as the ability to achieve ejaculatory control for a sufficient length of time during intravaginal containment to satisfy the partner in at least 50% of coital connections. This definition is clearly inadequate as it is also dependent upon the orgasmic performance of the partner. Unfortunately, it is very difficult to produce a satisfactory criterion for defining successful outcome for premature ejaculation. Various criteria have been used in different studies, which makes it hard to compare results across projects.

Golden *et al.* (1978) demonstrated extremely positive results for the treatment of premature ejaculation using a modified Masters and Johnson approach, in either group or individual couple therapy. Both therapy formats led to significant improvements in latency of ejaculation and range and frequency of female orgasmic response at post-treatment. Unfortunately, this study did not include a no-treatment or attention placebo comparison group, which limits the conclusions that can be drawn. Minimal therapist contact combined with bibliotherapy has also been found to lead to successful outcomes in the treatment of premature ejaculation (Lowe and Mikulas, 1978; Trudel and Proulx, 1987; Zeiss, 1977). Kilmann and Auerbach (1979) in a review of the literature at that time, concluded that success rates of 90–98% are typically reported for behavioural treatments of premature ejaculation. This figure is in keeping with the figure of 96.1% success reported by Kolodny (1981) in the two to five-year follow-up at the Masters and Johnson clinic. Not all studies, however, have reported such positive results in the treatment of premature ejaculation. Hawton *et al.* (1986), for example, reported only a 64% success rate in their sample. The degree to which this discrepancy may reflect differences in client samples, method used to determine success, therapy methods used or skills of the therapists is unclear.

225

It is possible this discrepancy in success rate may reflect the proposition of Halgin *et al*. (1988) that cases presenting for treatment of sexual problems in more recent times tend to be more complex and difficult to treat, as the more simple cases have been dealt with through self-help approaches, or their development prevented through the greater availability of sex education material in the media.

Inhibited female orgasm

The treatment of female orgasmic problems has been widely researched. Nevertheless, the outcome literature is not without its problems. In particular the lack of consistency in criteria used to assess outcome and variation in evaluation measures used makes it difficult to compare the results of different studies. As with any form of sexual problem, the issue arises as to whether outcome should be based on subjective ratings of satisfaction with the sexual relationship, or more objective measures of some aspect of overt behaviour. The sensible approach would seem to be to aim for both of these goals, but the question as to which behaviours reflect successful therapy then arises. In the case of primary/global/lifelong orgasmic failure, success may be determined by various measures, such as a single occurrence of orgasm (the woman is then technically no longer anorgasmic), by the ability to achieve orgasm regularly (by any means) or by the ability to achieve orgasm regularly in specific situations (e.g. during coitus). Questions then arise such as, should therapy be judged to be successful if the woman is able to attain orgasm by any means (such as only with a vibrator) or should some specification be included about manual self-stimulation, partner stimulation or ability to generalize orgasm to intercourse situations?

The problem in defining success is equally difficult in the treatment of secondary orgasmic dysfunctions, in which the woman typically is able to attain orgasm through some form of self-stimulation, but is unable to generalize this to situations involving partner stimulation or intercourse. Should success include being able to attain orgasm with a partner using a vibrator, or during intercourse with a vibrator? Some authors such as Wakefield (1987) have suggested that the generally accepted definition of successful orgasm held by most of the adult population would refer to orgasm which is triggered through penile thrusting alone and not orgasm that occurs during intercourse that is triggered by self-stimulation of the woman using a vibrator.

Views such as this have led other authors (e.g. Wilcox and Hager, 1980) to point out that the vast majority of women require some form of clitoral stimulation in order to experience orgasm during intercourse and that to aim for orgasm through penile thrusting alone is unrealistic in many cases. Debate as to the most appropriate way to determine success in the treatment of female orgasmic difficulties should be borne in mind when interpreting the outcome study literature.

Numerous studies have demonstrated that masturbatory training approaches can be successful in triggering orgasm for the first time in previously anorgasmic women. The degree to which orgasm is then experienced consistently, and is generalized to partner stimulation or intercourse is variable. For example, McMullen and Rosen (1979) allocated 60 women who had never experienced orgasm to either videotaped modelling of a masturbatory training programme, written instructions for the same programme or a waiting-list control. Therapy was conducted on an individual basis. No difference was found between the videotaped modelling and written text formats of the programme, with 24 of the 40 therapy clients experiencing orgasm by post-treatment. Only 13 out of the 40 women were able to attain orgasm during intercourse (by any means). Both approaches to treatment produced improvements in sexual attitudes, adjustment and responsiveness. This study illustrates the relative difficulty in generalizing orgasm to intercourse situations, with the results being in keeping with those of Spence (1985), which found that only 5 of 17 primary cases generalized orgasm to intercourse by the three-month follow-up.

Wakefield (1987) presented an extremely critical review of two early studies by Wallace and Barbach (1974) and Ersner-Hershfield and Kopel (1979), which reported exceedingly impressive results in terms of the proportion of women achieving orgasm and being able to generalize this to intercourse. Wakefield pointed out that both of these studies included some women who were already able to achieve orgasm on rare occasions at the onset of intervention and who were therefore technically not anorgasmic in the sense of never having experienced orgasm. He also noted that both studies accepted orgasm by any means in partner-related activities as being successful generalization. This could include self-stimulation with a vibrator whilst the partner is watching, which Wakefield suggested is not what the majority of the population would consider to be a successful outcome with the partner. Wakefield reanalysed the results of the Ersner-Hershfield study to exclude those women who were technically already orgasmic and to separate out different forms of stimulation with the partner. The reanalysis revealed that 14/15 women experienced orgasm through self or partner stimulation following treatment. By follow-up, only 3/15 women were able to experience orgasm during partner manual stimulation and no women were orgasmic during coitus, even if self or partner stimulation was used. These results present a much less impressive picture than Ersner-Hershfield and Kopel's (1979) original conclusion that 82% of the total sample incorporated orgasm in couple activities at ten weeks follow-up. It seems, therefore, that generalization of orgasmic skills to coitus is relatively difficult to achieve using traditional masturbatory training approaches.

The effectiveness of masturbatory training has been compared with a traditional Masters and Johnson approach. Riley and Riley (1978) compared the use of these two methods with 35 primary anorgasmic women. Directed masturbation training was found to result in orgasm for 18/20 women (90%) compared with 8/15 women (53%) in the Masters and Johnson approach. Orgasm was found to generalize to intercourse for 17/20 women in the masturbatory training condition (15 of whom did not involve a vibrator) compared to only 7/15 in the basic Masters and Johnson approach. These results are particularly impressive and this may reflect the involvement of the partner throughout the directed masturbation programme, which tends not to be the case for many studies which have followed the masturbatory training method of Lobitz and LoPiccolo (1972). Riley and Riley's (1978) approach to masturbatory training also placed greater emphasis, in the later stage of intervention, on the systematic incorporation of orgasm into intercourse situations using a vibrator, the use of which is then stopped progressively earlier in coitus.

Masturbatory training has also been compared with systemic desensitization in the treatment of primary orgasmic dysfunction. For example, Andersen (1981) found that only 1/10 women became orgasmic after systematic desensitization to sexual stimuli, which was the same result as found for the waiting-list control, whereas 4/10 women in the directed masturbation programme experienced orgasm. The use of systematic desensitization only makes sense if sexual anxiety levels are high, and this was not the case for some women in the Andersen (1981) study. The relatively poor results for masturbatory training in this study is also interesting. The lack of partner involvement may be partly responsible, but it is unclear why the results should have been so poor. A further study which investigated the effectiveness of systematic desensitization in the treatment of organic dysfunctions was reported by Sotile and Kilmann (1978), who selected their sample on the basis of sexual anxiety in addition to orgasmic difficulties. This study demonstrated significant reductions in anxiety and improvements in sexual adjustment and orgasmic functioning, for both primary and secondary female orgasmic dysfunction following systematic desensitization. Unfortunately, the results are presented in such a way that it is unclear how many women were helped by the approach, making comparisons with other studies difficult.

Considerable research has also been conducted into the treatment of secondary female orgasmic dysfunction. Early studies tended to report relatively poor results in terms of ability to experience orgasm during intercourse, even with clitoral stimulation. For example, McGovern et al. (1975) found that the programme outlined by Lobitz and LoPiccolo (1972), which focuses on anxiety reduction, masturbatory skill training and couple communication, produced minimal improvements in six women with secondary orgasmic dysfunction. It seems likely that this approach is adequate for the treatment of secondary orgasmic dysfunction and is more appropriate for cases of primary anorgasmia. Recent studies have reported more positive findings, suggesting that many women who are able to attain orgasm through self-stimulation are able to generalize this skill to coitus. Kilmann et al. (1986) selected 55 women who reported a coital orgasm frequency of less that 50% of occasions, with or without clitoral stimulation, of at least five months' duration. Subjects were randomly assigned to either communication skills training, sexual skills training, combined communication skills plus sexual skills training, an attention placebo control or no treatment. All subjects received a detailed sex education programme first. Therapy was conducted in groups, for two session per week over five weeks (20 hours). Couples in all treatment conditions reported improvements in the number of women who exceeded the 50% of occasions criterion for coital orgasm and improvements in sexual satisfaction ratings, compared to no treatment. By six-month follow-up, however, no difference was evident between the treatment subjects and the controls. Interestingly, this study found that success levels were greater for couples with poor relationship adjustment across all therapy conditions, which contrasts markedly with the results of studies such as Hawton et al. (1986) with mixed samples of sexual dysfunctions.

Milan et al. (1988) attempted a two to six-year follow-up of 66 couples for whom secondary orgasmic dysfunction was the presenting problem (and which probably included the Kilmann et al., 1986

Only 58% of couples responded, producing 38 couples whose data could be used. The mean pre-treatment frequency of coital orgasm was 9.2% of occasions, compared to 34% at the two to six-year follow-up. Although the follow-up result reflects an improvement upon pre-treatment levels, it is still lower than the criterion of 50% of occasions which was set as the criterion for secondary orgasmic dysfunction at the start of the study. A decrease in coital frequency was evident between post-treatment (8.2 occasions per month) to 5.5 occasions per month at long-term follow-up. It appears therefore that long-term maintenance of therapy improvements may be a problem in the treatment of secondary orgasmic dysfunction. Ten of the 38 couples in the sample had sought further help for marital or sexual problems and it seems likley that couples who separated, divorced or who had failed to benefit from therapy in the long term may not have responded to the follow-up request, which casts further doubt on the long-term effectiveness of intervention.

Systematic desensitization and a modified Masters and Johnson approach, involving sensate focus and sexual skill exercises, have been found to be beneficial for couples in which secondary female orgasmic dysfunction is present (Everaerd and Dekker, 1982). This study allocated 48 couples to either sexual skills training, systematic desensitization, a combined approach or no treatment. Minimal change was found for the combined treatment or no treatment whereas both sexual skills training and systematic desensitization when used in isolation were found to significantly improve sexual functioning and satisfaction with the general relationship and to reduce sexual anxiety. Contrary to predictions, only the systematic desensitization method resulted in maintenance of improvements in sexual functioning at six-month follow-up. The systematic desensitization approach used, involved generation of hierarchies which were individually tailored to each couple. Couples were then trained in relaxation skills, followed by clinic-based imaginal desensitization and in vivo desensitization to the sexual situations on the hierarchy. It would seem that this approach is useful in enhancing sexual functioning of couples who complain of secondary orgasmic dysfunction, but Everaerd and Dekker (1982) do not state how many women were able to attain coital orgasm in what proportion of intercourse occasions. Comparison with other studies is therefore difficult. It is also unclear as to how many women in the sample experienced anxiety in sexual situations at the onset of intervention and whether changes in sexual functioning were associated with anxiety reduction. The particularly poor results for the combined systematic desensitization plus sexual skills training is also worthy of note. It appears that combining the two approaches may lead to a reduction in the time spent on each therapy component, thereby reducing the effectiveness of intervention.

Inhibited male orgasm

The relative infrequency of presentation of cases of inhibited male orgasm makes research into this area difficult and there is a marked lack of controlled outcome studies. It is necessary to rely upon the uncontrolled case studies or samples from specialist clinics. Kolodny (1981) reported a 76% success rate for 75 cases of this disorder at the Masters and Johnson Institute, using a combination of sensate focus exercises, intensive stimulation by the partner and gradual introduction of intercourse activities. The majority of men presenting with problems of inhibited orgasm were reported to be able to achieve orgasm during masturbation, but not with their partner. This population is obviously different from those who have never been able to achieve orgasm by any form of stimulation.

The effective use of vibrators as a means of producing intensive stimulation has been reported in the treatment of total inhibition of male orgasm. Schellen (1968) reported successful ejaculation in 17 out of 21 patients attending a clinic in the Netherlands. None of these males was able to ejaculate during masturbation or intercourse, but they experienced nocturnal emissions, hence, organic aetiology was considered to be unlikely. The men ranged in age from 25 to 47 years and all reported a history of failed therapy attempts, such as hormone therapy or psychotherapy. Although Schellen reports that 17/21 men were able to achieve ejaculation through vibrator stimulation, it is not reported how many men achieved orgasm during coitus.

Geboes et al. (1975), cited in Jehu (1979), also reported the successful use of vibrator stimulation for males who had previously been unable to ejaculate through self-stimulation or intercourse. Nocturnal emissions were present for all 72 men and organic aetiology was only identified in four patients. The sample were allocated (it is not clear if this process was random) to either masturbatory education/training, psychotherapy, high doses of hormone therapy or electrovibrator stimulation. Only small numbers were allocated to the first three conditions. The vibrator stimulation method was effective, achieving 'positive results' for 41/55 men, compared to 4/4 (100%) in the masturbatory

231

education conditon, 4/7 (57%) in the psychotherapy sample and 3/6 (50%) in the hormonal treatment group. Unfortunately, the lack of specification of the criteria used for assessing positive results, likely lack of random allocation and low subject numbers in three of the therapy conditions makes it difficult to draw conclusions about the effectiveness of the various treatments used in this study. All that can be said is that the use of electrovibrators offers promise in the treatment of inhibited male orgasm.

Vaginismus

There is also a marked absence of controlled outcome studies concerning the treatment of vaginismus. The rate of referral of this disorder is typically low, making empirical studies difficult. Uncontrolled studies generally report high success rates from the use of graduated exposure to a hierarchy of dilators (Dawkins and Taylor, 1961; Fuchs et al., 1975). Lamont (1977) describes a series of 80 cases of vaginismus. Fourteen of these case received assessment only, with the remainder being treated by systematic desensitization, using a graded hierarchy of natural and artificial dilators, plus a ban on intercourse. Successful penetration with coital pleasure was achieved for 53 cases, with another nine cases being classed as technical successes in which penetration was achieved but was not pleasurable or no partner was available. Only four cases were judged to be unsuccessful, indicating a high success rate, in keeping with that reported by Masters and Johnson (1970). It is interesting to note that, during the course of treatment, 15/66 of the male partners reported situational erectile failure and 6/66 men experienced premature ejaculation. These male sexual problems also had to be dealt with in order for therapy to be successful. The interaction between vaginismus and male sexual dysfunction is fascinating and the cause–effect relationship between them is unclear.

Scholl (1988) also reports an uncontrolled study of the treatment of 23 women, all of whom were referred for problems of unconsummated marriages resulting from vaginismus. Twenty of the 23 women completed therapy successfully, with 19/20 women continuing to have coitus at the one-year follow-up. Therapy involved relaxation training, self-administered use of dilators at home, Kegel exercises and a ban on intercourse. The weekly sessions focused on systematic desensitization using verbally induced imagery in a graded hierarchy. Once the dilator hierarchy had been completed at home, partner involvement commenced, followed by gradual introduction to intercourse situations. A greater number of therapy sessions were required to produce successful outcome associated with problems of longer duration of the disorder, previous surgery, thoughts of anatomical abnormality, negative attitudes towards the genitals and negative parental attitudes towards sexuality. Fewer therapy sessions were associated with a desire for pregnancy, presence of an assertive husband and sexual knowledge of the woman.

Sexual aversion disorder/sexual phobias

Much of the research into the treatment of sexual anxiety or avoidance can be found under the unfortunate labels of 'frigidity' or 'essential sexual dysfunction'. One of the earliest studies was reported by Lazarus (1963). Lazarus' definition of frigidity stated that 'frigid women may be placed on a continuum extending from those who basically enjoy coitus, but fail to reach orgasm, to those for whom all sexual activities are an anathema' (p. 327). Although such a definition clearly covers an enormous range of female sexual problems, the cases cited by Lazarus involved women with high levels of sexual anxiety and avoidance. Lazarus reported 16 single cases which were successfully treated using relaxation and systematic desensitization to hierarchy items presented verbally to the imagination. Wincze and Caird (1976) reported a series of single cases, labelled as 'essential sexual dysfunction', in which 'the primary complaint was excessive anxiety associated with most or all aspects of sexual behaviour and the inability to derive erotic pleasure' (p. 335). Seventy-five per cent of the 21 women were also anorgasmic. This study found videotaped desensitization to be superior to systematic desensitization in terms of reductions in heterosexual anxiety at post-treatment and three-month follow-up. Both methods were superior to no treatment. The impact upon orgasmic ability was limited, with only 25% of the non-orgasmic women becoming orgasmic.

Videotaped desensitization combined with relaxation training has also been found to be effective in reducing sexual anxiety when used in a group format. Nemetz *et al*. (1978) allocated 22 women with severe anxiety which precluded their enjoyment of sex to either a waiting-list control, group videotaped desensitization or individual sessions of videotaped desensitization. The procedure involved exposure to a series of 45 videotaped vignettes which depicted a graded series of sexual situations. Clients observed the videotapes in the clinic and were asked to practise the viewed activities at home. These activities included sensate focus exercises. Significant reductions in sexual anxiety were found for both therapy conditions, which were not evident for the waiting-list group. Significant improvements were also found in terms of sexual behaviour and orgasmic ability. Unfortunately, the majority of therapists do not have access to the type of videotaped material required for treatment of this type; however, it is important to note that imaginal plus in vivo desensitization does appear to be effective with many couples, as shown in the Wincze and Caird (1976) study, without the need for videotaped material.

PROGNOSTIC FACTORS

Several studies have attempted to identify factors which predict outcome in the treatment of psychosexual dysfunctions. These studies have varied from those that include a variety of disorders within the therapy sample, to those that have explored prognostic factors with specific diagnostic groups. Hawton and Catalan (1986) examined the factors that were associated with outcome amongst a large sample of mixed psychosexual disorders. This study initially excluded from treatment those cases of severe marital distress, excessively low motivation, diagnosable psychiatric disorder, alcoholism or current pregnancy. The exclusion of these factors removed these variables from strong consideration as predictor variables in the study. Hawton and Catalan (1986) found several factors to predict drop-out from treatment, including lower socio-economic status, lower motivation rating of the male (not the female), poorer general relationship and poor progress by the third treatment session. These authors then divided their sample into those that could be classed as successful versus those that could be classed as unsuccessful. The type of dysfunction was found to be an important predictor of outcome, with vaginismus being most successful (81%), followed by erectile dysfunction (68%) and premature ejaculation (64%). The poorest result was found for ejaculatory failure (20%) but this sample only included five cases. Other important predictors of success included adherence to home-based tasks up to the third session and the quality of the couple's general relationship, with better outcome being associated with a better marital relationship, particularly as assessed by the woman. The therapist's pre-treatment rating of motivation, particularly for the male, and initial quality of the sexual relationship were also found to be associated with positive outcome. No evidence was found for the influence of age, duration of the problem, or extent of religious beliefs on outcome.

The quality of the couple's marital relationship has been found to be an important predictor in several studies (e.g. Abramowitz and Sewell, 1980; Whitehead and Mathews, 1986) but this has not always been the case. For example, Kilmann *et al.* (1986) found the *poor* marital relationship prior to the onset of treatment was associated with *successful* outcome in the treatment of secondary female orgasmic dysfunction. In this study, it is possible that those couples whose relationships were poor tended to be those couples whose communication skills were weak and who therefore benefited most from the focus on communication skills training which was inherent in the therapy approaches used. Alternatively, it is possible that those couples with good-quality marital relationships, in which the woman was unable to experience orgasm with the partner or during intercourse, tended to be those for whom the woman represents the lower end of a biologically determined continuum of ease of attaining orgasm and for whom sexual and communication skills training are less likely to be effective. It is suggested, therefore, that the link between poor general relationship and poor outcome may not hold for all forms of psychosexual disorder. Nevertheless, the case is retained for a focus on the treatment of difficulties within the general relationship, as an adjunct to the treatment of psychosexual dysfunctions, if therapy is to be successful for the many clients who present with combined sexual and marital difficulties.

Whitehead and Mathews (1986) compared 26 improvers and 22 non-improvers in a sample of women for whom the main complaint was one of lack of sexual interest and enjoyment. In this study the most significant predictors of outcome included the pre-treatment assessor's and clients' ratings of the general relationship, greater ratings of pleasant feelings and lower levels of unpleasant feelings during sex, male ratings of self and partner as sexually attractive and the woman rating herself and her partner as more loving. In relation to the general relationship, certain aspects were found to predict outcome. A greater level of arguments/rows/silences, incompatibility of interests and goals and lack of overt affection were associated with negative outcome. Interestingly, inability to discuss and communicate feelings was *not* found to predict poor outcome. In terms of compliance, non-responders were found to make fewer positive attempts to move through the treatment stages or to conduct home-based practice, which demonstrates the importance of compliance with set assignments. This is in keeping with the findings of McMullen and Rosen (1979) that time spent in doing home-based tasks was associated with success in the treatment of primary female orgasmic dysfunction.

The primary prognostic factors to emerge from these studies can be summarized as follows: positive outcome has generally been found to be associated with better quality of the relationship, higher levels of motivation, higher socio-economic status (lower socio-economic status predicting greater therapy drop-out), higher male rating of self and partner as being sexually attractive, higher female rating of self and partner as loving and greater adherence to therapy assignments. Hawton and Catalan (1986), in reviewing the literature concerning prognostic factors, identified previous sexual responsivity and positive rating of the partner as sexually attractive as being predictive of positive outcome, whereas the presence of psychiatric disorder, longer duration of sexual dysfunction and poor motivation were predictive of poor therapy outcome. These factors should be borne in mind during assessment and tackled during the therapy process, in order to maximize the chance of successful outcome.

THE EFFECTIVENESS OF THERAPY COMPONENTS

Research into the relative effectiveness of the various components of cognitive and/or behavioural treatments of psychosexual dysfunctions is still in its infancy. The majority of treatment approaches have incorporated a wide range of therapy techniques and it is difficult to determine which components are actually exerting an active therapeutic effect. The techniques have included increasing sexual knowledge, training in sexual skills, graduated exposure to a range of sexual situations, relaxation training, creating non-demand situations (e.g. a ban on intercourse), sexual communication skills training, marital therapy (e.g. non-sexual communication skills training, problem-solving skills, increasing positive interactions), increasing exposure to erotic materials, enhancing the use of fantasy, Kegel exercises, cognitive restructuring of maladaptive thoughts and beliefs, to mention just a few. Although the literature is limited it is possible to draw some tentative conclusions about the role played by various components of therapy programmes in the treatment of psychosexual dysfunctions.

Increasing sexual knowledge

Methods such as therapist instruction, audio-visual materials and literature have been used in order to increase sexual knowledge. The importance of this therapy component is unclear, although a recent study reported by Kilmann *et al.* (1986) used a four-session sex education programme for secondary anorgasmic women prior to the onset of the main therapy programme. It is interesting to note from this study that the sex education procedure on its own produced improvements in sexual functioning on the Sexual Interaction Inventory across the sample and even improved orgasmic status for a minority of women. Although sex education on its own was insufficient to produce marked clinical improvement for the majority of cases, the finding that it did produce some benefits suggests that it is likely to contribute to the effectiveness of therapy programmes. The same sex education procedure was also found to produce benefits for some clients in a sample of men with erectile problems (Kilmann *et al.*, 1987). Improvements in terms of coital success, decreases in sexual anxiety and improvements in sexual functioning were found following the four-session sex education programme.

Training in sexual skills

The effectiveness of training in sexual skills is rather difficult to analyse given that the methods used in training tend to overlap with sex education and graduated exposure to sexual situations, particularly with in vivo exposure. Kilmann *et al.* (1986, 1987) evaluated the effectiveness of sexual skill training, using sensate focus exercises and graded skill assignments, and found this approach to be successful, at least in the short term, in the treatment of erectile failure and female secondary orgasmic dysfunction. The longer-term effects of sexual skills training were poor for the female secondary orgasmic dysfunction clients.

Graduated exposure to a range of sexual situations

Graduated exposure to a hierarchy of sexual situations may be conducted through imaginal, in vivo or videotaped desensitization. Several studies have demonstrated the effectiveness of this approach in reducing sexual anxiety (see studies discussed above) but the results are less impressive if changes in sexual activities are taken as the outcome measure. For example, Wincze and Caird (1976) found poor results in terms of changes in orgasmic ability for either videotaped or imaginal systematic desensitization for women treated for 'essential sexual dysfunction' in whom the primary complaint was excessive anxiety associated with most or all aspects of sexual behaviour and the inability to derive erotic pleasure. Both methods were superior to no treatment in terms of reductions in sexual anxiety. Graduated exposure may therefore be an important element in treatment when reductions in sexual anxiety are required but appears to be inadequate in terms of producing changes in specific sexual behaviours.

A proscription on intercourse

This topic was reviewed in Chapter 5, in which it is concluded that proscription on intercourse is not essential for many cases (Takefman and Brender, 1984).

Sexual communication skills training

Sexual communication skills training has been found to be effective in the short term as an isolated therapy approach in the treatment of both erectile dysfunction and secondary orgasmic dysfunction (Kilmann et al., 1986, 1987). It seems likely that improvements in communication skills represent one of the crucial elements involved in the success of sensate focus exercises. The Kilmann et al. studies also demonstrate that sexual communication skills training is effective even when used without the sexual skills training element of sensate focus, when compared to a waiting-list control. The long-term results were poor for the female, secondary orgasmic dysfunction clients, suggesting that maintenance of therapy gains may be a problem for communication skills training approaches.

Marital enhancement methods (with sexually dysfunctional clients)

Zimmer (1987) investigated the benefits of combining marital therapy with the behavioural treatment of secondary forms of male and female sexual dysfunction. Twenty-eight couples were randomly assigned to either nine sessions of relaxation and information followed by nine sessions of behavioural sex therapy, nine sessions of marital therapy followed by nine sessions of behavioural sex therapy or a waiting-list control. The results indicated that both treatment conditions showed clinical and statistical improvement at post-treatment and three-month follow-up, but treatment gains were more pronounced and comprehensive for those who had received the combined marital and sex therapy programme.

Increasing exposure to erotic materials

Gillan (1977) conducted a study which demonstrated that erectile performance in males and sexual arousal in females may be enhanced by exposure to erotic stimulation. In this study, ten females who complained of low sexual arousal and 14 men with erectile difficulties were randomly assigned to either no erotica (a discussion condition), or exposure to audiotaped erotic or visual erotic stimulation. After six sessions, both groups receiving erotic stimulation showed a significant increase in the frequency of sexual intercourse, pleasure during intercourse and satisfaction with their sexual relationship, whereas the control condition showed no change. The female subjects also reported an increase in sexual arousal responsiveness following erotic exposure, but no change in orgasmic status, suggesting that this approach is insufficient in the treatment of anorgasmia. For the men, 66% showed regular erections following erotic exposure treatment, with the remaining 33% requiring further treatment with a Masters and Johnson approach. Improvements were found to be maintained at one-month follow-up, with minimal difference between audio and visual forms of erotic stimulation. Given that this follow-up period is relatively short, future research is needed in which longer-term follow-up is included. In the meantime, it appears that the use of erotic materials may be a useful component in therapy for many clients as a means of enhancing sexual arousal.

Explicit erotic audio-visual material has also been used for the purposes of sexual education and desensitization. Neidigh and Kinder (1987) cautioned against the indiscriminate use of audio-visual sexual material in the treatment of sexual dysfunctions. These authors pointed out that there is very little empirical evidence to support its use with specific populations and suggested that its use may actually be detrimental in some instances. They are particularly critical of the use of videotaped sexual scenes in the treatment of sexual anxiety or orgasmic dysfunction and suggest that similar results may be obtained by alternative methods. For example, McMullen and Rosen (1979) reported no difference in outcome between videotaped exposure and use of written instructions of the transcript of the films in the treatment of female anorgasmia. It is therefore likely that the crucial component of therapy in this study was the provision of information, rather than any form of learning through modelling or desensitization to visual sexual material. Neidigh and Kinder (1987) also cited a study by Wincze (1971) in which exposure to 12 explicit films produced an increase in anxiety following an initial positive response to traditional systematic desensitization. They suggested that explicit, sexual audio-visual material should be used with caution, taking into consideration whether alternative methods of equivalent benefit may be available and the suitability of such an approach for a particular couple or client.

Cognitive restructuring of maladaptive thoughts and beliefs

The limited evidence available does suggest that cognitive restructuring can be effective in the treatment of sexual dysfunctions, at least with cases in which strong maladaptive cognitions can be identified. Bishay (1988) reported four single case studies in which cognitive restructuring was used following an assessement that indicated a traditional Masters and Johnson/behavioural approach to be inappropriate. The cases included two women with vaginismus, one case of inhibited male orgasm and one case of sexual avoidance. All four cases were successfully treated using cognitive restructuring methods. Regretfully, minimal description is given as to the process involved in cognitive challenging.

Cognitive therapy on its own does not appear to be effective in producing long-term improvements in erectile functioning. Munjack *et al.* (1984), in a small sample of couples presenting with secondary erectile dysfunctions, found that RET resulted in significant reductions in sexual anxiety, generated increased attempts at intercourse and more frequent successful penetrations compared to the waiting-list control. Interestingly, no changes in irrational beliefs were found. At follow-up much of the benefits of RET had been lost, with intercourse only being achieved with an adequate erection on 25% of occasions. It seems that, although cognitive restructuring methods may be valuable in the short term, additional methods are required if the benefits are to be maintained. The sample of men involved in this study, however, were not selected on the basis of exhibiting negative or maladaptive beliefs. It may be suggested that cognitive restructuring is more likely to be of value for those clients whose presenting problem is associated with maladaptive cognitions or beliefs. This proposition would be worth exploring. The effectiveness of cognitive restructuring procedures with other forms of psychosexual dysfunction also warrants examination.

SUGGESTIONS FOR FUTURE RESEARCH

It is clear from this review of the literature that there is still an enormous amount of research required in the area of cognitive and behavioural treatments of psychosexual disorders. Although it appears that behavioural approaches can be extremely effective in the treatments of some dysfunctions, the results are less impressive for other disorders such as erectile dysfunction. Research is needed to determine effective ways of dealing with these more difficult cases. In particular there is a need to evaluate the benefits of combining cognitive and behavioural approaches with such cases. The following areas also emerge as being worthy of further research:

- Effectiveness of different approaches in the treatment of disorders of sexual desire;
- Effectiveness of different approaches in the treatment of disorders of female sexual arousal;
- Effectiveness of cognitive and/or behavioural approaches in the treatment of dyspareunia;
- Effectiveness of cognitive and/or behavioural approaches in the treatment of inhibited male orgasm;
- Relative effectiveness of therapy components which have traditionally received little attention (e.g. fantasy training or use of erotic materials to enhance arousal);
- Effectiveness of programmes which attempt to match intervention to the characteristics of the presenting problem, versus a package therapy approach;
- Effect of modification of therapy formats with different forms of psychosexual dysfunction.

These suggestions represent just a few of the research issues that remain to be explored in relation to the treatment of psychosexual disorders. Although considerable research remains to be carried out, the empirical evidence available to date suggests that cognitive and behavioural methods are effective in producing improvements in sexual functioning for many clients. The majority of studies have, however, been limited to young to middle-aged, heterosexual, non-disabled clients. The following chapter now explores the use of cognitive and behavioural methods in the treatment of psychosexual disorders with 'special' populations.

8

Sexual dysfunctions among special populations

Sexual dysfunctions may be experienced by any individual at any stage of adulthood, irrespective of their health, sexual orientation or level of intellectual functioning. The approach taken to the treatment of sexual difficulties is essentially the same for all people, but a chapter related to 'special' populations is warranted for three reasons. First, sexual difficulties occur more frequently amongst certain populations such as the elderly, the physically handicapped or those with certain diseases or illness. Second, a therapist attempting to treat a psychosexual difficulty with a client with special characteristics needs to be aware of the many factors which may influence that person's sexual functioning which may not be applicable to other clients. These factors may be particularly important in enabling the therapist to understand the aetiology of the disorder. Third, the factors that make the person special may require that the therapist adapt the therapy programme to the particular needs of that individual, if therapy is to be successful.

When it came to write this chapter, it was difficult to decide which groups to include as being 'special'. There are obviously numerous criteria that could be used in order to place adults into particular groupings. The method selected here is arbitrary and reflects the author's own experience in having to deal with particular clients for whom there is a need for specific knowledge and adaptation of therapy. These groups of people include the elderly, the physically disabled (with a particular focus upon spinal injuries), the physically ill, homosexual clients and the intellectually handicapped.

ELDERLY CLIENTS

A large number of books and articles have been written on the topic of sexual behaviour and the sexual problems of the elderly and much has been said about the need for intervention for such problems. Unfortunately, the literature concerning psychological treatment of psychosexual disorders amongst older persons has been based primarily upon subjective opinion and common sense, rather than upon empirical evidence. There is an enormous need for controlled outcome studies which investigate the effectiveness of cognitive and/or behavioural approaches to the treatment of sexual dysfunctions in the elderly. It would have been nice to have been able to provide a succinct review of the literature, but the lack of research means that we know very little about the most suitable forms of therapy for older clients. What follows is an outline of the information that therapists should be aware of when they work with the elderly and suggestions regarding those factors that should be taken into account in the application of therapy programmes. It is important to emphasize here that the characteristics of older persons vary enormously and it is difficult to generalize from the results of any group studies to an individual client who may request therapy for a sexual dysfunction. This point should be borne in mind when attempting to generalize the findings of research to any given individual.

Sexual behaviour among older people

For the present purposes, the term elderly will be applied to persons over the age of 65 years. This population has been increasing in size considerably over the past fifty years in most Western societies, partly as the result of a dramatic increase in life expectancy but also as a reflection of the general increase in population size earlier this century. In addition, the tendency towards smaller family size in more recent times has produced a situation in which the proportions of persons over the age of 65 years is increasing markedly with respect to the rest of the population. The improvement in health care means that the majority of elderly persons may live healthy, active lives well into their 70s.

The point is made repeatedly throughout the literature concerning sexual behaviour and the elderly that there is a tendency for younger individuals, including many people in the helping professions, to assume that the sex lives of older people are very limited or non-existent (Butler and Lewis, 1977; Croft, 1982). Furthermore, it has been suggested that many older people also adhere to this myth, believing that it is normal for sexual interaction to end during the later years and that it is somehow abnormal for an older person or couple to remain sexually active (Thienhaus, 1988). Several consequences are proposed within the literature to result from these beliefs, such as the failure of many health professionals to explore the occurrence of sexual difficulties for older patients, hence leaving many older couples to suffer in silence. Older people are also unlikely to seek help when sexual difficulties arise, if they feel embarrassed to admit to desiring a sexual relationship and fear a negative response from the practitioner. Although sexual dysfunctions occur more frequently amongst older people, the elderly typically present less often for treatment of sexual problems (Wise, 1983), suggesting that the elderly may indeed be reluctant to seek help for sexual difficulties. Finally, the myth that older people do not have sexual relationships may even encourage some older people to cease their sexual activities, if they believe such behaviour to be unacceptable. In extreme cases, the anxieties and guilt produced by sexual desires and activities may even contribute to the development of a psychosexual dysfunction.

Whilst such attitudes and consequences may have been true twenty years ago, and indeed still persists today amongst some sections of the population, it is suggested here that older people, the general population and health professionals alike are coming to realize that sexual relationships amongst the elderly are extremely common, normal and desirable. This is reflected in the increasing numbers of older clients who are seeking help for sexual problems (Renshaw, 1983) and can also be seen with attitudinal surveys of younger people. For example, Weg (1983a) in reviewing the literature concerning the attitudes of younger people to the sexual behaviour of the elderly concluded that the younger people no longer think of sex for older people as being negligible or unimportant. Increasing age and limited education were identified as being most associated with negative attitudes to sex amongst older persons. Weg (1983) did conclude, however, that even the elderly themselves are showing a more positive attitude. Persons making up the elderly population in research studies obviously change over the years and the elderly now include those persons who were aged in their mid-40s during the 'swinging sixties'. It is perhaps not surprising, therefore, to find a shift in attitudes, as the sample gradually includes decreasing numbers of persons brought up during the Victorian influences upon Western cultures and increasing numbers of those whose sexual relationships developed in a more liberal environment.

245

It is encouraging to find a shift in attitudes towards greater acceptance of reality. It has been known for years that many older people have active and satisfying sexual relationships. Although Kinsey and colleagues paid very little attention to the older population, the limited statistics produced did illustrate this point. However, it was also demonstrated that the frequency of sexual activity declines with age and that sexual problems increase in frequency. Since this early research, several large-scale studies have been conducted into the sexual behaviour of older men. As with most survey research in the area of sexual behaviour, the samples have been biased by low response rates and it is therefore difficult to estimate the degree to which the individuals studied reflect the behaviour of the general population. Response rates have typically been less than 50% and one wonders whether the responders are somehow more liberal in their attitudes and behaviour compared to those who refused to participate in the research.

The Duke study (Pfeiffer and Davis, 1972) is one of the most commonly cited projects in this area. This involved a prospective study of 260 black and white volunteers from 1955 to 1966 who were followed up at three to four-year intervals. The results indicated that, although sexual interest and activity declined with age, sexual interest and activity continued for many individuals into their 80s and 90s, with around 50% of males maintaining an interest in sex and 20% remaining sexually active. Those persons who were most sexually active in their earlier years continued to be the most sexually active in their later years.

Starr and Weiner (1981) reported the result of a survey of 800 persons in the USA aged 60–90 years. A response rate of 14% was reported for questionnaire completion following a presentation to groups of elderly persons entitled 'love, intimacy and sex in the later years'. It seems unlikely that this sample was very representative of the elderly population at large, hence the results should be interpreted with caution. It was clear that the vast majority of respondents still had a strong interest in sex. Eighty per cent were still sexually active, with only 8% of males and 30% of females not experiencing some form of sexual interaction. The average frequency of intercourse for those who were sexually active was 1.4 times per week, which was interesting in that this was the same frequency reported by Kinsey *et al.* (1948) for their 40-year-old sample. Kinsey's 40-year-olds would have been Starr and Weiner's 70-year-olds, suggesting that patterns of sexual behaviour may be maintained with age. The study also demonstrated relatively liberal attitudes for the majority of elderly respondents concerning masturbation, sex without marriage, oral sex and nudity.

The tendency for women to report lower levels of sexual activity than men is found consistently throughout the research literature. It is important to note that a marked imbalance exists in the numbers of males and females in the ageing population. Women far outnumber men from age 65 onwards, and this imbalance increases with age. Hence, if women seek similar age partners, there are fewer males available for sexual activity, whereas males have a greater choice of partners. Social mores also view it to be more acceptable for an older male to have a sexual relationship with a younger woman than it is for an older woman to have a sexual relationship with a younger man. The lower numbers of sexually active women may therefore reflect lack of opportunity, rather than a deliberate choice to cease sexual relationships.

The results of a study by Brechner (1984), also in the USA, examined 4246 persons aged 50–93. The response rate was approximately 50%, which is considerably better than the Starr and Weiner study. Unfortunately, the majority of respondents were aged between 50 and 70, with only 79 respondents being in the 71–80 year group. The proportion of individuals who were involved in sexual relationships declined steadily from age 50 to age 80, with men tending to be more sexually active than women. Even in their 70s, however, 65% of women and 79% of men remained sexually active. Similarly, the proportion of the sample who currently masturbated was found to decline with age, but around one half of men and around one third of women in their 60s and 70s still engaged in this activity and the vast majority of the sample held positive attitudes towards masturbation. Although sexual enjoyment and desire was found to decline with age, the majority of respondents who were still sexually active found it pleasurable.

Several other surveys have been conducted but space limits the coverage that can be provided here. One recent study does warrant a mention though. Bretschneider and McCoy (1988) studied the sexual interests of 100 white men and 102 white women, aged between 80 and 102 and who lived in retirement homes. The results again demonstrated the higher level of sexual interest and enjoyment of sex for men compared to women and that past enjoyment of sex correlated with current enjoyment and frequency. These authors did not find an association between previous frequency of sexual intercourse and current frequency of coitus. They suggest that current physical and social factors begin to play an overriding role in determining the occurrence of sexual intercourse amongst older people in institutional settings. Of particular importance in this study was the finding that the vast majority of older people regularly engaged in activities involving touching and caressing with the opposite sex. High levels of affection, intimacy and fantasy activities were also reported. Fewer individuals engaged in masturbatory activities, with sexual intercourse being the least prevalent form of sexual expression, but even this activity was currently being experienced by 63% of men and 30% of women, at least occasionally. This evidence supports the proposition of Croft (1982) that many elderly persons show a shift in the way that they express sexual interest in their partner, away from sexual intercourse towards touching, fondling and companionship aspects of sexuality.

The Bretschneider and McCoy (1988) study is also interesting in that it examined the occurrence of sexual dysfunctions. Amongst the sexually active men, 33% reported occasional or usual inability to maintain an erection and 28% reported difficulty in reaching orgasm. For the women, 30% reported infrequent experience of orgasm, 30% lack of lubrication and 25% reported lack of drive/interest. It is likely that those individuals with severe sexual dysfunctions would have been amongst those who were no longer sexually active (and who were not included in this sample), hence the figures provided for frequency of sexual dysfunction are likely to grossly underestimate their true prevalence.

Two other studies have recently examined the occurrence of sexual difficulties amongst older people. Weizman and Hart (1987) studied a sample of 81 men aged 60–71 years and who were patients at a community health centre in Israel. All men were married, healthy, with no marital problems or psychopathology. Unfortunately, these criteria are likely to lead to a population that is unrepresentative of older persons in general and which will underestimate the prevalence of sexual problems. Nevertheless, 36% of males were found to exhibit erectile dysfunction. Strangely, no difference was found in the incidence of erectile difficulties between the 60–65 year versus 66–71 year age groups. This result is not in keeping with a study reported by Mulligan *et al.* (1988), who compared two groups of elderly male veterans in geriatric ambulatory care with younger men from a general medical clinic. The 225 respondents represented 65% of the sample approached. In this study, erectile dysfunction was found to increase with age, but interestingly the authors found that, if age was controlled for using a regression procedure, sexual dysfunction was more related to health status. It is concluded that, although sexual dysfunction is more common in the aged, this is more related to illnesses which tend to occur with increased age, rather than ageing per se. This finding supports the statement of Comfort (1980): 'It can be said with confidence that impotence is never a consequence of chronological age alone. Its increasing frequency with age is due to a variety of causes' (p. 886). The failure to find an increase in erectile difficulties in the Weizman and Hart (1987) study can probably be accounted for by the exclusion of unhealthy or unhappily married males from the sample. There is no doubt that the prevalence of sexual difficulties does increase with age but, as Comfort points out, this is due to factors other than age per se.

Less is known about the occurrence of sexual disorders in elderly women. The Bretschneider and McCoy (1988) paper provides some insights, but further studies are needed in order to demonstrate in more detail the type of dysfunctions most commonly experienced. Evidence from Starr and Weiner (1981) suggests that women who have been orgasmic in their younger years tend to remain orgasmic if they continue to be sexually active. The most common problems cited in the literature for older women concern hypoactive sexual desire and arousal, with poor lubrication and dyspareunia being relatively common problems following menopause. However, as will be seen in the following section, many women are able to continue to be fully responsive well into their ninth decade of life. The limited evidence available seems to indicate an increase in sexual dysfunction with age and certainly demonstrates a marked decline in sexual activities for the majority of women from age 65 onwards. The extent to which this reflects a lack of available partners is unclear. A recent study reported by Osborn et al. (1988) suggests that the increase in prevalence of sexual dysfunction in women begins during middle age. A survey of 436 women aged 35–59 in the UK demonstrated a significant increase in sexual dysfunction with age. In the total sample, 17% reported impaired sexual interest, 17% vaginal dryness, 16% infrequency of orgasm and 8% reported dyspareunia.

In summary, studies concerning sexual behaviour and the elderly have demonstrated the following points:

- Although sexual interest and activity tend to decrease in later life compared to earlier years, many older people continue to have active and enjoyable sexual relationships.

- Older males tend to show greater levels of sexual interest and activity than older females.
- Sexual activity patterns in old age tend to reflect the person's patterns in earlier years.
- Although physiological changes in sexual responding occur with age, these are insufficient to explain the decrease in sexual interest and activity found amongst many elderly people.
- The physiological changes in sexual responding which occur with age do not on their own result in sexual dysfunction.

Factors affecting the sexual functioning of older people

As mentioned above, sexual dysfunction is not part of the normal ageing process. Rather, sexual dysfunctions tend to occur as a consequence of the many health and psychosocial influences which tend to affect the lives of older people. In order to understand the effects of ageing on sexual functioning, it is necessary to review the normal physiological changes in sexual responding which occur with age. These changes do not, on their own, lead to sexual dysfunctions.

Physiological influences

The following summary of age-related changes in the physiological aspects of the human sexual response is based on information from a variety of sources which include Brechner (1984), Croft (1982), Rousseau (1986), Thienhaus (1988), Tsitouras (1987), Walbroehl (1988) and Weg (1983b). These changes are not uniform and tend to vary across individuals. In males the changes also tend to occur gradually, without the specific climactic period of change that is normally found in women. For example, the physiological changes amongst ageing males generally include a gradual decrease in testosterone levels and increase in levels of luteinizing hormone (LH) and follicle-stimulating hormone (FSH). Oestradiol levels show little change. The alteration in the balance of circulating sex hormones results in decreased sperm production, some loss of muscle tone and strength, decreased size of the testes, enlargement of the prostate gland and a reduction in the viscosity and volume of seminal fluid. The consequence of this latter change is a decrease in the force of the ejaculate. In terms of the changes in sexual responding, older men tend to experience a reduction in the speed of attaining an erection, with some reduction in the intensity of sensations and the feeling of ejaculatory demand. More intense stimulation may be required in order to attain an erection, but the duration for which the erection may be held tends to increase. The penis may be less stiff when erect than was the case in the man's younger years and it becomes more common for erections to be lost during sex. Detumescence typically occurs faster. The orgasm phase tends to shorten, with fewer contractions, and the refractory period of non-responsiveness to further stimulation tends to increase up to periods as long as 24 hours in some males. For some men a decrease in the consistency of orgasm occurs, so that ejaculation may not occur during every occasion of intercourse. It is important to note that, despite these changes, the erectile and orgasmic capacity of the elderly male generally remains intact, although it is perhaps not so reliable as in the younger years.

The physiological changes in women occur much more rapidly, beginning around the mid 40s for most women. The changes commence with an alteration in the hypothalamic–pituitary interaction which is associated with a decrease in follicular responsiveness and hence reduced fertility. This stage is typically followed by an increase in irregular cycles and the onset of phases of increased and decreased oestrogen levels. Levels of FSH begin to rise, with oestrogen levels then tending to decline. Pre-menstrual uterine proliferation decreases, until it becomes minimal and the maturation of ovarian follicles decreases. The non-reproductive effects of the decreased oestrogen levels at this time may include lowered bone and protein synthesis and disruption of the salt–water balance. Gradually, menstruation ceases, although irregular bleeding may continue for two to three years for some women. Oestrogen levels typically remain lowered with elevated levels of FSH and LH. Some women may experience feelings of depression, irritability and fatigue, or negative symptoms such as hot flushes as they pass through the climacteria. General body changes include loss of skin elasticity, redistribution of fatty tissue (resulting in some loss of firmness of the breasts) and decreased muscle tone.

The consequences of these changes in terms of sexual functioning vary for different women. Genital changes include the loss of vulvar substance and reduction in the fullness of the labia majora. The cervix, uterus and ovaries shrink and the vaginal mucosa begins to thin. The vaginal length tends to decrease and its capacity for expansion is reduced as the result of loss of elasticity. A decrease in the vasocongestive response is frequently found, which is associated with increased time required in order for lubrication to occur or a reduction in the amount of lubrication produced. The clitoral response generally remains intact, although tumescence of the clitoral area tends to be slower and there may be an increase in the time taken to reach orgasm, with a decline in the number of contractions experienced. There does not appear to be any reduction in the consistency of orgasm for women and, despite the changes involved in menopause, satisfying sexual relationships are still viable for many women. Unfortunately, some women may experience pain during intercourse as a result of the thinning of the vaginal walls. A condition known as oestrogen-deficient vaginitis may also occur, which is associated with pain and lack of lubrication. Fortunately, these conditions may now be dealt with through appropriate medical treatment. Butler and Lewis (1977) suggest that around 60% of women experience no marked physical or emotional symptoms associated with menopause. The majority of those who do experience problems only report mild or moderate symptoms such as headaches, hot flushes, depression or fatigue. These symptoms, if severe, can typically be dealt with successfully through treatments such as carefully administered hormone replacement therapy.

The main point to emerge from this summary is that, for older persons, the normal physiological changes which occur with ageing do not in themselves prevent sexual responding. The sexual response of the elderly may be different from the pattern in younger people, but the basic responses of sexual arousal and orgasm remain. It may take somewhat longer and require more stimulation, but an enjoyable sexual relationship is nevertheless feasible. Why then are sexual dysfunctions more common amongst older persons and why do many older people cease their sexual activities? Several answers may be proposed. First, health problems tend to be experienced more commonly amongst the elderly, which may result in sexual disorders. Second, numerous psychosocial influences may act to impair satisfying sexual relationships in the elderly. These health and psychosocial variables will now be explored in more detail.

Health influences

There are a variety of medical conditions which tend to result in sexual difficulties and these were reviewed in Chapter 2. Suffice it to say here that conditions such as diabetes, endocrine, vascular and neurological disorders or arthritis all tend to be more prevalent amongst older people and may interfere with sexual functioning whether directly or indirectly. Medication may also impair sexual responding, with antihypertensive medication being a causal factor in the sexual difficulties of many older men. Fear of triggering a heart attack may lead some older males to avoid further sexual relations following survival from myocardial infarction. For others, the avoidance of pain from conditions such as arthritis may play an important role. Appropriate medical assessment is therefore essential with older persons, as for any client referred with a sexual dysfunction. In some instances it may be possible to reverse the condition with medical treatment and thereby enhance sexual responding. Unfortunately, in other cases, the disorder may not be reversible and the aim of therapy with the sexual problem may become one of encouraging alternative modes of sexual expression or prosthetic intervention (Mulligan, 1989).

Although medical conditions undoubtedly contribute towards the increased incidence of sexual dysfunctions amongst elderly persons, it is important to note that the majority of older people are in good health, are active and independent (Wise, 1983). Health problems on their own are therefore insufficient to explain the decline in sexual activity and increased level of sexual difficulties amongst older persons. It is therefore necessary to examine the psychosocial factors that may play a contributory role.

Psychosocial influences

Myths regarding sexuality and ageing. Unfortunately, older people tend to be subject to various forms of 'ageism'. The commonly held belief within society that sex, beauty and physical attractiveness are attributes of the young but not the old is suggested to lead to attitudes among the elderly themselves that being old means being unattractive and an end to sexual activity (Wise, 1983). Comfort (1980) suggested that these myths have a considerable influence over the sexual behaviour of the elderly. The social expectation that older people do not have sexual relationships is likely to present considerable difficulty for those individuals who feel sexual desire and who are continuing their sexual activities. They may experience guilt or anxiety about their sexual behaviour, which may in turn encourage them to conform to social expectations of asexuality. The lack of understanding of health professionals may also make it difficult for older people to reveal any difficulties that occur in sexual responding, making it less likely that problems will be resolved. For many older people, the myths concerning lack of sexual behaviour in the elderly may provide a welcome excuse to give up an activity that has become difficult or stressful.

Butler and Lewis (1977) suggested that very few older people have a good understanding of the normal physiological changes that occur with ageing. As a result, normal changes such as lengthening of the time required for arousal to occur, or reduction in the number of contractions experienced, may be interpreted by some older people as a sign of sexual inadequacy. Masters and Johnson (1970) emphasized the problems that may arise if older people are uninformed about the normality of changes in sexual responding. They suggest that anxiety may occur if the changes are interpreted negatively. Anxiety may, in turn, act to inhibit sexual arousal and responding, creating sexual difficulties, particularly in terms of erectile responding. What starts off as normal, occasional difficulties in attaining or maintaining an erection may then result in a psychosexual disorder, as erectile failure becomes more consistent.

Life circumstances. Various factors concerning the older person's life circumstances also need to be mentioned, in order to understand their influence upon sexual behaviour. In particular, the marked excess of females compared to males in the older population produces difficulties for many older women, as the result of unavailability of partners. Croft (1982) pointed out that women are far more likely than men to be widowed. In the 65–74 age group, only 8.9% of men are widowed, compared to 42% of women. This discrepancy is even more pronounced in the 75 + age group, in which 23.5% of men and 69.7% of women are widowed and without a new partner. Whilst it is relatively acceptable for men to have much younger partners, this is less socially acceptable for women in our culture. As a result, many older women do not have the opportunity for sexual interactions.

Institutional living or living with one's younger family may also present limitations upon the opportunity for sexual activity for some older people. The lack of privacy and the negative attitudes of institutional staff or younger family members regarding sexual behaviour of the elderly often serves to inhibit the sexual lives of older persons (Croft, 1982). Croft pointed out that some younger people, including younger professionals, frequently forget the fact that older people have probably been sexually active for the past 40–50 years. For some reason it is assumed that sexual interests and behaviours should suddenly cease, as the result of longevity.

Changes in the marital relationship. It is also important to understand changes in the lives of older people that may contribute towards sexual difficulties. Life after age 65 years is frequently linked with retirement, which brings with it a series of changes to which the couple must adapt (Butler and Lewis, 1977). Partners must often spend significantly greater amounts of time together than had previously been the case and new interests must be developed. A period of adjustment is required, in which each partner works out his or her new role in the altering relationship. This period can be difficult for some couples and may place a considerable stress upon their relationship, which in turn may influence their sexual functioning. Retirement has been suggested to be one of the critical points in the lifespan of couples' relationships at which marital conflict becomes more likely.

The other factor that needs to be taken into account, for any long-term relationship, is the need to prevent boredom with activities that have been carried out so many times before. In addition, many older couples were brought up at a time in which open communication about sexual issues was limited and their attitudes and communication skills concerning sex may therefore be restricted. Taken together, these influences may make it very difficult for some couples to develop or maintain an interesting and varied sexual relationship.

The cosmetic changes in physical appearance which accompany ageing may also have a strong influence on the sexual relationship (Felstein, 1983). The unfortunate societal attitudes which equate beauty and sexual attractiveness with youth may influence the ageing couple. Concerns about one's own physical attractiveness towards one's partner may develop and such worries and beliefs are likely to have a negative impact on sexual responding. It is interesting to note that Starr and Weiner (1981) demonstrated that most people over the age of 60 described their ideal sexual partner as being someone of similar age to themselves. Only 2.3% of older men preferred a partner of age 29 or younger. Hence, older couples do not typically succumb to the social stereotypes of the younger ideal sexual partner. Discussion of fears concerning lack of sexual attractiveness may form a vital part of intervention for some older couples. Evidence such as that produced by Starr and Weiner (1981) provides a useful basis from which to allay fears of loss of sexual attractiveness to the partner.

Implications for assessment

The assessment process closely resembles that outlined in Chapter 4, but with a greater emphasis on those factors which are frequently associated with the development of sexual dysfunctions in the elderly. It is essential for the assessor to determine whether a sexual dysfunction is present or whether the changes in sexual responding are purely a reflection of the normal ageing process. If this is the case, a sexual dysfunction cannot be said to be present and the role of the therapist then becomes one of reassurance and of making suggestions for methods of facilitating sexual functioning, rather than the treatment of a sexual disorder. Stone (1987) points out that older people may develop sexual problems in the same way as any younger person, which are totally independent of ageing. Furthermore, some older people may present with sexual problems which have always been present, such as primary female orgasmic dysfunction. Such a problem is obviously not age related and yet it is still important to take into account characteristics of the couple that relate to their age when designing and implementing the therapy programme. A detailed past sexual history is therefore necessary in order to determine the extent to which current patterns of sexual behaviour are recent or reflect long-term patterns of responding.

In addition to the cognitive-behavioural assessment, it is obviously essential for older clients to be referred for a thorough medical evaluation. The greater probability of health problems makes it even more important that this aspect of assessment is carried out.

Implications for intervention

One of the primary goals of intervention for older couples is to provide information to dispel some of the many myths concerning sexual functioning in old age (Masters and Johnson, 1970). Hotvedt (1983) summarized the major myths which need to be tackled during therapy, namely:

1. In later years, we are not sexually desirable.
2. In later years, we are not sexually desirous.
3. In later years, we are not sexually capable.

Subsidiary attitudes also need to be worked on, such as acceptance of sex for pleasure once procreation is no longer possible. Rather than viewing changes in sexual functioning as 'dysfunctional', it is suggested that older people should be encouraged to accept the changes in their pattern of sexual responding as normal and to make the adaptations necessary in order to continue an enjoyable sexual relationship. This may require some changes in the type of stimulation used and alteration in the patterns of sexual behaviour. For example, Butler and Lewis (1977) suggested the need for slower but longer sexual activity, longer foreplay, increased strength of stimulation and use of lubrication gels. These authors also emphasized the need to teach communication skills in order for couples to learn what methods produce greatest pleasure and arousal for their partner. The need for effective communication becomes increasingly important as changes in sexual responding occur and old patterns of sexual behaviour may become less satisfactory. It will be easier for couples to make the necessary adaptation if they can communicate about sexual matters with their partner. In addition, Stone (1987) suggested the need for some elderly couples to develop effective substitutes within their sexual relationships. This is particularly important for older couples for whom ill health results in sexual difficulties and alternative methods of sexual expression may be required.

Several authors have stressed the need for training of health professionals regarding the normal sexual behaviour of elderly people and the sexual difficulties that may occur with ageing. Croft (1982) placed considerable emphasis on the need to train health professionals to communicate better with elderly people about sexual issues, in order to make it more likely that the elderly will reveal any sexual problems that are occurring. Routine questioning and creation of an atmosphere in which it is communicated that it is acceptable for older people to talk about sex and to reveal difficulties is likely to facilitate disclosure of sexual problems (Kellett, 1989). Croft (1982) summarized a programme for teaching health professionals to communicate with older people about sexual issues. Components included examination of one's own beliefs bout sex and the elderly, interpersonal skills required to initiate ommunication about sexual topics with older people, creation of an atmosphere conducive to disclosure, and listening for non-verbal and indirect cues of sexual concerns. The need for adequate sexual knowledge about normal changes in sexual functioning in order for professionals to identify the occurrence of sexual dysfunctions was also emphasized.

A major concern for many older people is a fear of loss of physical attractiveness to their partner. For the majority of couples, this concern is unfounded but it may be revealed as a problem during assessment or therapy. As part of the cognitive restructuring process related to this issue, it is helpful to present research data (e.g. Starr and Weiner, 1981) which demonstrates that older people typically select a person of their own age as their preferred sexual partner.

Adapting therapy to the needs of the older client

Although the treatment of sexual difficulties with older clients is generally based on those methods which are used in the treatment of sexual difficulties with younger clients, it is important for the therapist to be sensitive to some of the characteristics of older people that may influence the therapy process. As mentioned previously, it is important not to generalize to any given client, as each older person will bring with him or her a unique set of characteristics which need to be taken into account if therapy is to be successful. Of particular importance are the client's attitudes and beliefs regarding sexual behaviour. The need for a careful assessment of the cognitive aspects of sexual responding is perhaps even more important for older couples than it is for younger clients. Although the ageing of the population means that an increasing number of people who are now being classed as elderly have lived through a period of relatively liberal attitudes towards sexuality, there are still a significant number of older persons who were raised under the influence of Victorian, conservative attitudes about sex. For many older people, there will be certain sexual activities which they do not find acceptable. Similarly, discussion about sex with a therapist may be very difficult for some older persons. The therapist needs to be sensitive to these issues and to adapt the style and the content of intervention to the needs of the individual or couple. Conservative attitudes towards topics such as oral sex, nudity or female roles in initiation of sex need to be explored during assessment. Such attitudes then need to be taken into account in the design of the therapy programme. For some older people, where their attitudes are entrenched and represent a lifetime of conditioning, it may be easier to adapt the content of treatment, rather than commence a cognitive restructuring process in order to bring about change in attitudes and beliefs. Furthermore, an ethical issue exists concerning the need for therapists to respect the rights of a client to hold different attitudes about the relative rights and wrongs of particular sexual activities (Brown and Sollod, 1988). Jonsen (1980) suggested that the therapist should only attempt to change the client's value system when this is necessary in order to eliminate the sexual dysfunction. If alternative means of therapy can be found, which leave the value system intact and which can successfully treat the sexual problem, then this is ethically preferable. A practical example of attitudes/beliefs that may interfere with the conduct of therapy using particular approaches is the reluctance of some older female clients to participate in the squeeze technique in the treatment of premature ejaculation or self-stimulation exercises in the treatment of female orgasmic dysfunction. Stone (1987) provided a case illustration in which an older female partner refused to carry out the squeeze on her partner. Therapy progressed by shifting to an approach in which the male partner was responsible for this action during the programme.

Associated with difficulties in communication regarding sexual matters is the difficulty that many older people have regarding intimate and emotional expression (Stone, 1987). This has implications for those interventions which are designed to tackle the more general aspects of the relationship, such as communication skills training which frequently focuses on the expression of intimacy and emotions. Stone suggested that this may be extremely difficult for many older couples, whose goals for treatment tend to be more practically and behaviourally orientated towards increasing sexual functioning, rather than changing some of the long-term aspects of their general relationship. For these couples, Stone proposed that an educational and practical skills-orientated approach is most suitable, rather than attempting to change long-term patterns of communication and attitudes towards expression of intimacy.

Stone (1987) also pointed out the need to take into account the cognitive difficulties of some elderly people, such as memory or attention limitations. Fortunately, this does not apply to the majority of elderly clients, but the therapist should be aware of possible cognitive limitations and should adapt the content of therapy accordingly. Shorter sessions, with clear written instructions, may be helpful for some older people. Similarly, the greater probability of sensory handicaps should be born in mind and taken into account in the administration of therapy. Other factors that need to be considered include the negative attitudes of some older clients to the concept of psychological therapy and also the difficulty that they may experience in having to divulge personal information to the therapist if he/she is much younger and/or of the opposite sex.

Outcome studies

Little controlled research has been carried out concerning the effectiveness of psychological treatments of psychosexual problems amongst older people. The minimal outcome data available to date have involved case reports or uncontrolled outcome statistics from clinics. Masters and Johnson (1970) reported the results of treatment for 56 couples in which the male partner was aged 50–79 years. These authors found an overall failure rate of 30.3% for the programme, with results being particularly poor for older females with orgasmic dysfunction. The best outcome data were reported for premature ejaculation and secondary erectile dysfunction.

Stone (1987) described a series of cases in which sexual dysfunctions amongst elderly couples were successfully managed using psychological approaches, but no outcome data were reported. Whitlach and Zarit (1988) presented a detailed case study of a couple aged 74 and 72 who presented with erectile dysfunction of two months' duration. No previous sexual problems had been reported and the general marital relationship was positive. Several health factors were present that could have been associated with organic pathology, but the man experienced erections during exposure to erotic stimuli suggesting that the capacity for erectile responding remained. The couple received eight, weekly therapy sessions which focused on education, cognitive restructuring, a ban on intercourse for one week, sensate focus exercises, use of erotic literature to enhance arousal and partner stimulation using a teasing method. The emphasis of cognitive restructuring and education focused on changing the male partner's beliefs that older people do not have sex lives and that age makes erections impossible. As therapy progressed, erectile functioning returned, but it was necessary to tackle fears about the reduced strength of erections. Therapy also focused on changing beliefs about the necessity of erections in order to have an enjoyable sex life.

Although cases of this type allow only limited conclusions to be drawn concerning the use of cognitive-behavioural approaches in the treatment of psychosexual dysfunctions with older people, they provide valuable clinical information for therapists working with elderly clients.

SEXUAL PROBLEMS AMONG THE MENTALLY HANDICAPPED

Until recently, very little attention had been paid to the topic of sexual behaviour amongst the mentally handicaped. This neglect was undoubtedly a reflection of societal attitudes concerning sexuality amongst people with limited intellectual abilities. There is a tendency for parents and institutional staff who care for mentally handicapped people to have a rather protective attitude when it comes to sex. This may partly reflect historical views concerning restrictions upon the rights of mentally handicapped persons to bear children and also the fears of caretakers regarding the possible sexual abuse of those who become sexually active. Fortunately, these views are gradually changing and, with the push towards 'normalization', it is becoming increasingly accepted that the mentally handicapped have rights which include the ability to form sexual relationships. The major focus related to the sexuality of mentally handicapped persons has been upon the need for sex education, rather than on the provision of intervention services for this population. As a result, very little has been written about assessment of and intervention with the sexual problems of mentally handicapped people. The minimal literature available is limited to uncontrolled case reports and the clinical opinions of those experienced in this area.

Before progressing further, it is important to clarify the population included under the term mentally handicapped. For the present purposes the term mentally handicapped will be taken to refer to people of IQ less than 70, who also show impairment of adaptive functioning as defined by DSM-III-R. Around 3% of the adult population fall into this category, with approximately 95% of these people falling into the mild and moderate categories of mental handicap. The majority of mild and moderately mentally handicapped individuals are capable of sexual responding and indeed show a desire for sex and sensual contact (Craft, 1987). However, investigation of the sexual attitudes of mentally handicapped people reveals a marked lack of knowledge of the facts concerning sexual matters, fears and anxiety about sex and conservative values regarding sex and marriage (Craft, 1987). In a previous paper, Craft (1983) reviewed evidence

261

to demonstrate the conservative sexual values and feelings of guilt among the mentally handicapped. Craft suggested that this reflects the influence of society, which implies that mentally handicapped people should not be educated about sexual matters and that they should not engage in sexual activities. These factors, combined with lack of skill of many mentally handicapped people in developing and maintaining relationships with the opposite sex, makes it difficult for satisfactory sexual relationships to occur (Monat, 1982). Furthermore, if sexual relationships are established, the lack of knowledge regarding what should occur means that very few mentally handicapped people realize when a sexual dysfunction is present (Craft, 1983).

The lack of sexual knowledge and maladaptive attitudes concerning sexual relationships for mentally handicapped people is also likely to contribute towards the development of sexual difficulties for couples in which either or both partners are mentally handicapped. Although there is a marked lack of empirical data, Andron (1983) suggested that sexual dysfunctions are extremely common amongst mentally handicapped couples. Her work in group counselling of mentally handicapped couples revealed a high level of sexual disorders for both the male and female partners. Andron reported case information for ten couples, for whom a variety of sexual dysfunctions were evident, with problems existing for both partners in most of the couples. She pointed out that the sexual dysfunctions were never complained of until they came to light under careful questioning and group discussion on the topic of sexuality. Orgasmic difficulty was the most common problem for the women, along with lack of lubrication and arousal. For men, erectile dysfunction was the most common disorder, followed by premature ejaculation.

Andron noted the extremely limited range of sexual activities in which the couples engaged and also their lack of knowledge about techniques needed to create an enjoyable sexual relationship. For example, few of the individuals knew that a woman could have an orgasm, or that the clitoris existed. Other couples were not aware that thrusting was necessary after penetration. Foreplay was rarely used and there was a lack of knowledge as to what this involved. The communication skills of the sample were extremely poor, which tended to exacerbate the sexual problems of each couple. In keeping with the conclusions of Craft (1983), Andron reported the severe guilt and anxiety about sexual activity experienced by most of the individuals, reflecting a lifetime of negative influence from others concerning sexuality for mentally handicapped people. Most individuals experienced discomfort regarding nudity and masturbation and there was a marked lack of acceptance of the idea that sex can be used for the purpose of receiving pleasure, rather than purely for procreation. Andron pointed out that the sexual difficulties for most of the couples tended to be exacerbated by problems within the general marital relationship. Although this study involved only a small sample size and cannot be suggested to reflect the sexual relationships of mentally handicapped people in general, it provides a good illustration of the types of influences and sexual difficulties that may be experienced.

Implications for intervention

There is a marked absence of empirical data to suggest the most appropriate therapy approaches for treatment of sexual dysfunctions amongst the mentally handicapped. Until evidence is available, it would seem appropriate to make use of the methods which have been found to be successful with other populations. Obviously, the intellectual limitations resulting from being mentally handicapped must be taken into account in the development and implementation of therapy programmes. The learning difficulties of individuals will limit the amount of information that should be presented at each session and will also influence the way in which information is best presented. The use of pictures, films or even model dolls may be helpful in explaining concepts that are difficult for the person to understand if presented verbally. Pipecleaner dolls may provide a useful method of demonstrating positions or actions that are otherwise hard to describe or display pictorially.

In terms of the content of treatment, the educational aspect is likely to be of considerable importance for many clients. Many programmes are available which provide guidelines for sex education with the mentally handicapped (e.g. Kempton and Caparulo, 1983; Monat, 1982). These authors also emphasized the need for adequate education of parents and staff who work with mentally handicapped persons. Attitude change of caretakers (parents/staff/counsellors/health visitors/social workers) and the clients alike, with respect to sexuality in the mentally handicapped, is important. Therapy should include a focus on the acceptability of normal sexual relationships for mentally handicapped people and the need for privacy. For many mentally handicapped clients, there will be a significant need for long-term support from community agencies, in order to maintain a satisfactory relationship within which sexual activity can occur. The need for adequate counselling regarding contraception will also be important. This is an issue of particular concern for parents of mentally handicapped couples, for whom the topic of parenthood is likely to be of considerable interest. Undoubtedly, many mentally handicapped couples require a great deal of community support if they decide to produce children. Fortunately, the majority of children produced by intellectually handicapped parents are not intellectually handicapped themselves (Craft, 1983). Nevertheless, Craft pointed out that evidence confirms that many mentally handicapped persons experience considerable difficulty in raising their children and, although the right to produce children should remain, the couple should receive appropriate counselling so that they have full knowledge of what is going to be involved and the problems that may occur.

Whilst these topics diverge somewhat from the issue of therapy for sexual dysfunctions, they are closely intertwined and need to be considered during any intervention programme. This is particularly true if both members of the partnership are mentally handicapped. For those couples in which only one partner is of limited intellectual ability, therapy is more likely to progress along the lines outlined in previous chapters, making the necessary modifications to the presentation of the programme to take into account the special needs of the mentally handicapped partner.

SEXUAL PROBLEMS AMONG THE PHYSICALLY ILL AND PHYSICALLY HANDICAPPED

A great deal has been written recently about the sexual difficulties experienced by those with numerous forms of illness and physical disability. The list is now so extensive as to prevent adequate coverage of each disorder separately. Suffice it to say that recent articles have discussed sexual difficulties amongst the following disorders:

- Epilepsy (Pietropinto and Arora, 1988a);
- Men with only one testicle (McClure, 1988);
- Dermatological disorders (Pietropinto and Arora, 1988b);
- Couples undergoing fertility programmes (Ansbacher and Adler, 1988);

- Thyroid disease (Porte *et al.*, 1987);
- Post-traumatic stress disorder (Scrignar, 1987);
- Burns patients (Renshaw, 1988);
- Arthritis patients (Roth, 1989);
- Cardiovascular disease and myocardial infarction (Dhabuwala *et al.*, 1986; Gould, 1989);
- Physical disability (DeHaan and Wallander, 1988);
- Spinal injuries (Boller and Frank, 1982);
- Cancer (Balducci *et al.*, 1988);
- Prostatectomy patients (Fisher, 1987, Vikram and Vikram, 1988);
- Male diabetes (Bernstein, 1989; Maatman *et al.*, 1987);
- Female diabetes (Bahen-Auger *et al.*, 1988; Prather, 1988);
  . . . to mention just a few!

Given that space precludes coverage of each of these areas, it is perhaps more sensible to look for some of the common themes that emerge from the literature concerning sexual functioning amongst the physically ill or disabled. The sources of influence upon sexual functioning that need to be take into account closely reflect those areas that should be considered in the assessment of a healthy or non-disabled client. In addition, it is important to consider the physical limitations placed upon sexual functioning, cognitive factors which influence sexual responding and the client's knowledge about the way in which the physical disorder may influence sexual functioning.

It is helpful to break down sexual problems amongst the physically ill or disabled into four categories, namely:

1. Sexual problems resulting primarily from the direct effect of a physical disorder upon sexual functioning. This category may result from certain forms of spinal injuries, diabetes, vascular disorders, hormonal/endocrine disorders, neurological deficits and some forms of cancer.
2. Sexual problems which are primarily the result of treatment for a physical disorder. Such treatments may include medications (e.g. certain cardiovascular drugs), surgery (e.g. certain forms of prostatectomy) and some cancer treatments (e.g. radiation and chemotherapy).
3. Sexual problems which are caused primarily by psychosocial factors resulting from a physical disorder. For example, avoidance of sexual activity or erectile failure following myocardial infarction (heart attack) may be due to fear of

triggering a second heart attack, rather than a direct, physical consequence of the illness.

4. Sexual problems which result from the interaction of physical factors and psychosocial influences. In practice, it is often hard to separate out the effect of physical and psychosocial influences, and the vast majority of sexual problems which are primarily caused by a physical disorder are exacerbated by psychosocial variables (Anderson and Wolf, 1986).

Given the extensive coverage of the wide range of physical injuries, congenital defects and illnesses that may impair sexual functioning in Chapter 2, this chapter will focus primarily upon the psychosocial factors that influence sexual behaviour for the physically ill or disabled. Whilst the reader is referred back to Chapter 2 for coverage of vascular, endocrine and neurological causes of sexual dysfunction, it is also suggested that those seeking more detailed information should consult Palmeri and Wise (1988) and Schover and Jensen (1988). The latter text is particularly recommended, as it presents an excellent discussion of issues relating to assessment and treatment of sexual problems amongst those with a chronic illness.

Psychosocial factors which influence sexual functioning in the physically ill or disabled

Sanders and Sprenkle (1980) made the important point that the fact that a person belongs to a particular special group, whether this concerns age, health status, intelligence or sexual orientation, does not change the importance of a satisfactory sexual relationship. This point is equally applicable to the physically ill or disabled, whether their physical disorder is lifelong or acquired. Although some physical disorders may impair sexual drive, the vast majority of people with physical disorders experience sexual desires and place great importance on sexual relationships. No matter how much the physical disorder impairs arousal or orgasmic capacity, generally it is still feasible to develop some alternative form of sexual expression and enjoyment, as long as sexual desire exists. Unfortunately, psychosocial influences often act to inhibit attempts to maintain or develop sexual relationships. The sexual problems experienced may involve either lack of sexual activity or dysfunctional response when sexual activities are attempted. These effects may result from a variety of influences, including maladaptive cognitive factors concerning sexual activity and self image, the impact of the physical disorder on the marital relationship generally, the partner's reaction to the disorder and general psychological status (e.g. depression or anxiety).

Cognitive factors

A wide range of cognitive factors may interfere in the development of and satisfaction with the sexual relationship for many people whose sexual difficuties are related to a physical disorder. It is also important to examine the way in which the partner's thoughts, attitudes and beliefs may influence the sexual relationship, rather than focusing purely upon the person with the physical disorder. Many of these maladaptive cognitive influences result fom a lack of factually correct information, which leads to acceptance of myths and misinformation. Some of the most commonly cited maladaptive thoughts and beliefs reported in the literature concern the following:

Sexuality and masculinity/feminity issues. Various fears and negative attitudes concerning the loss of masculinity or femininity may occur following a serious illness or in association with physical disability. This is particularly true if the disorder has resulted in impairment of fertility or genital structures. Concerns of this type may also occur for individuals who are placed in a position of dependency if they hold strong beliefs about male/female roles which can no longer be maintained.

Negative thoughts about sexual performance. Fears about the impact of the disorder on the ability to respond sexually have been suggested to play an important role in the development of sexual problems in many illnesses. Negative thoughts about inability to perform may exacerbate the impact of some disorders, such as diabetes, in which psychogenic factors have been suggested to overlay many organic cases of erectile dysfunction. In some cases, performance anxiety may be so severe as to actually cause psychosexual dysfunction.

Sex and the sick/disabled role. For some individuals the effect of the physical disorder is to create an attitude of 'disability', in which previous activities are relinquished and the person's behaviour changes to fit the stereotype of an inactive, disabled person. This may be reflected in thoughts that sick people *cannot* have a sexual relationship or that ill or physically disabled people *should not* engage in sexual activity. These views are tied up with the myth that ill or disabled people do not engage in sexual activity, are not desirable as sexual partners and do not desire sexual activity.

Self and partner concerns about physical attractiveness. Many physical disorders or their treatments result in changes in cosmetic appearance which are considerably different from social stereotypes of what is considered to be 'sexually attractive'. For example, some forms of spinal injury may result in atrophy of the penis and testicles. Some physical injuries produce loss of a limb. Certain forms of treatment may also produce changes in appearance, such as weight loss or hair loss following radiation therapy in cancer treatment, scars following operations, or removal of a breast following breast cancer. Catheterization or ileostomies may also be required for some conditions. The impact of physical appearance may produce cognitive difficulties for both partners. The ill or disabled partner may experience negative thoughts about his or her body image. Similarly, the non-disabled person may have difficulties accepting their partner's appearance as being physically attractive. Negative thoughts of this type are likely to inhibit sexual responding, hence attempts to produce more positive, adaptive forms of thinking are important. This may involve encouraging a focus on other aspects of the person and also challenging societal stereotypes regarding why a particular shape or form should be designated as sexually attractive.

Anticipation of pain. For many individuals who experience chronic pain conditions (e.g. arthritis or low back pain) sexual activity may be avoided for fear of producing pain. Through education, it may be feasible to develop alternative positions and forms of sexual activity that reduce the experience of pain. This also requires the reduction of negative thoughts about the occurrence of pain and generation of more positive, coping self-talk.

Irrational beliefs concerning creation of further injury. Negative thoughts and beliefs concerning the risk of further injury are particularly common amongst heart attack survivors. Thoughts of this type are likely to inhibit sexual activity and responding for both partners. This issue is dealt with in greater detail below.

Other irrational beliefs. A wide range of other maladaptive thoughts or beliefs may result in impairment of sexual functioning. As for most of the examples given above, such thoughts tend to result from ignorance or misinformation about the conditions. Examples include beliefs that effects of radiation can be transmitted to a partner through intercourse or even that cancer is infectious.

General marital relationship

Illness and physical disability obviously have a marked effect upon the couple's relationship generally. Numerous stressors exist, such as change in roles within the family as one person may become more dependent upon another, increased time spent together as the result of convalescence, the physical strain of caring for another person, the limitations and demands imposed by equipment (e.g. catheters) and financial problems, to mention just a few. The impact varies for different couples as they learn to adapt to the changed conditions. The degree to which couples are able to maintain a positive relationship in difficult times will depend upon their skills in the areas of problem-solving and communication and the state of their relationship prior to the physical problem. It will not pass your notice that these are the same skills that are important in determining marital satisfaction under normal circumstances. Deficits in these areas will make adaptation extremely difficult and this is particularly true in relation to the sexual aspect of the couple's relationship. Each partner needs to be able to express his or her fears about their sexual abilities or their physical attractiveness, to discuss alternative forms of sexual activity and to develop innovative solutions to overcome limitations imposed by the disorder (e.g. catheters or ileostomy bags). Without these adaptations, avoidance of sexual activity or development of sexual dysfunctions is likely. For those couples whose sexual relationship was previously unsatisfactory, the physical disorder may provide a convenient excuse for giving it up altogether.

General psychological status

Many chronic illnesses and disabilities may have a negative impact on the general psychological state of the individual (and the partner) which, in turn, may impair sexual responding. Depression and anxiety are the most commonly cited forms of psychopathology that accompany chronic illness (Anderson and Wolf, 1986). The negative influences of depression and anxiety upon sexual functioning are well established, and are associated with impairment of sexual desire and arousal. Lack of sexual interest may also be the result of fatigue or generally feeling ill, hence these factors must also be taken into account when assessing the impact of a physical disorder upon sexual functioning. Depression and anxiety may be associated with a wide range of non-sexual fears and reactions. These may include fears about the future, fears of being without one's partner, anger (why me?), and negative cognitions about the self, the future and the world. General psychological difficulties of this type warrant intervention, irrespective of their impact upon sexual functioning.

Implications for prevention and intervention

A strong interaction exists between biological and psychosocial factors in the determination of sexual functioning in the physically ill or disabled (Anderson and Wolf, 1986). Even where biological causes are present, this is rarely the only influence over sexual responding. Hence, psychological intervention may play an important role as an adjunct to physical therapies. Indeed, evidence suggests that psychological intervention may even enhance sexual functioning when used as an isolated treatment for some cases which are of organic origin. For example, Abel (1984; cited in Anderson and Wolf, 1986) demonstrated that behavioural treatment involving sensate focus exercises enhanced sexual satisfaction for 80% of a sample of men with organic erectile difficulty. Sufficient erectile responding was obtained in 20% of the sample to permit intercourse to take place. This study illustrates the way in which psychological factors may exacerbate an organic problem and how organic influences do not tend to produce an all-or-none effect for many cases. For some of these men at least, behavioural therapy produced psychological changes which were of sufficient magnitude to override the effects of the organic impairment. There is a strong need, therefore, for psychological programmes at both preventative and remediation levels for individuals with medical conditions that are known to be associated with sexual problems.

It seems likely that many sexual problems could be prevented if adequate counselling could be provided at the onset of physical conditions that are known to be associated with sexual difficulties (or during childhood and adolescence for those whose conditions develop early in life). Unfortunately, health professionals tend to be rather biased in their attention towards the physical causes of sexual dysfunction, with psychological factors being relatively neglected (Anderson and Wolf, 1986). As a result, counselling is frequently not provided for preventative purposes following a physical disorder, such as spinal injury, myocardial infarction, cancer or diabetes, despite their known association with sexual disorders (Anderson and Wolf, 1986; Boller and Frank, 1982). Health professionals tend to wait until sexual problems develop before offering services and even then there is a relative bias towards physical intervention rather than examination of the contribution of psychosocial variables. Many sexual problems could be prevented if individuals were provided with adequate information about the limitations imposed upon sexual functioning, alternative methods of sexual expression and graduated sexual interaction exercises to encourage the couple to return to or commence a sexual relationship. This should be routinely provided by the health professional team.

Various suggestions may be made as to why inadequate sexual counselling is provided to people with physical disorders. It has been found that the extent to which professionals, including physicians, provide sexual counselling to their disabled clients depends on a number of factors, including degree of knowledge, reading, attendance at workshops and communication skills (Malloy and Herold, 1988). Hence, lack of education is likely to account for the failure of many health professionals to provide sexual counselling to physically ill or disabled clients. It is also likely that many health professionals feel uncomfortable about discussing sex with a patient and feel that this is a private topic that will cause embarrassment to all. Clearly there is a great need for adequate training of health professionals concerning the influences of physical disorders upon sexual functioning and in basic counselling skills.

Components of prevention/intervention programmes

Empirical research in this area is still in its infancy, hence suggestions as to the most appropriate form of intervention must rely on the suggestions of practitioners and the limited outcome data available. Schover and Jensen (1988) provided a detailed outline of a cognitive-behavioural approach to the prevention and treatment of sexual difficulties with chronically ill patients. Many of the suggestions made are equally applicable to other forms of illness or physical disability. The components of intervention can be summarized as follows.

271

Education. A major component within programmes developed for sexual counselling of the physically ill or disabled involves the provision of information about the disorder and the way in which sexual functioning is influenced. For example, Mooney *et al.* (1975) provided an excellent self-help guide to enhance the sexual functioning of the physically disabled. Information is provided about the impact of various forms of spinal injury upon sexual responding. The text also aims to demonstrate that, while a physical disorder may impair some aspects of sexual activity, it does not totally prevent sexual pleasure being given or received. Explicit pictorial descriptions are provided regarding methods of stimulation that may be used in order to generate sexual arousal and alternative methods of sexual expression are described, which do not focus exclusively upon the genitalia.

Information is vital for those individuals who fear the consequences of sexual activity. For example, myths and misinformation are common amongst myocardial infarction (MI) survivors who fear that sex may trigger off another heart attack. Many individuals express this fear following MI (Renshaw, 1983) and patients typically show a 40–70% decrease in sexual activity (Schover and Jensen, 1988). Renshaw cited evidence to suggest that the probability of recurrence of MI as the result of sexual activity is exceedingly low and that any person who is capable of walking up two flights of stairs comfortably should not be harmed by sexual intercourse. Schover and Jensen (1988) were somewhat more cautious and acknowledged that careful medical evaluation is essential before it is concluded that sexual activity will not be harmful. Although these authors reported that sexual activity rarely results in a heart rate in excess of 120 beats per minute, this level may exceed the ischaemic threshold for some individuals. Education concerning the bodily changes involved in sexual arousal is also important for MI survivors. The possibility of misinterpretation of sexual arousal cues as being an indication of cardiac symptoms needs to be prevented.

At all stages of intervention, the participation of the partner is important. As with the sexual difficulties of most couples, the issue is seen to be a reflection of the interaction of both partners. The provision of information, challenging of maladaptive thoughts and beliefs and development of compensatory skills is equally applicable for both members of the partnership.

Permission. Closely linked to the provision of information is the therapist's giving of permission to the client to take part in a particular sexual activity. Often the mere suggestion that a particular activity is safe, and/or is an acceptable activity to engage in, is sufficient to encourage a couple to participate in the behaviour.

Cognitive restructuring. Given the many maladaptive thoughts and beliefs that may impair or prevent sexual activity, cognitve restructuring plays a vital role in any prevention or treatment programme. This goal may be attained to a great degree through the provision of information (as described above). However, for some people the beliefs are so well entrenched that a more intensive cognitive restructuring approach is necessary. For example, Schover and Jensen (1988) outlined case studies in which irrational beliefs about cancer being infectious had to be restructured in order to prevent sexual avoidance by the partner of a cancer patient. Mooney *et al.* (1975) placed considerable emphasis on the need for acceptance of sexual activity as being normal amongst physically disabled adults. Restructuring of cognitions concerning physically handicapped persons as sexually attractive and responsive individuals were also emphasized as was the need to overcome negative thoughts about the presence of equipment such as catheters. The acceptance of alternative modes of sexual expression for those who are physically unable to engage in traditional forms of sexual activity should also be a focus of cognitive restructuring.

Graduated sexual task assignment. Exercises designed to teach new sexual skills which enable the couple to adapt their sexual relationship to the limitations of the physical disorder are important. Graduated assignments also play a valuable role in desensitizing the couple to sexual activity which may have ceased, never started or become an issue of extreme anxiety. Sensate focus exercises have been suggested to serve both these purposes and may form a valuable part of therapy for physically ill and physically disabled couples. Non-genital and genital pleasuring exercises also provide a forum in which the couple may develop the necessary communication skills for enhancing their sexual relationship. For the physically disabled person, the exercises also allow the couple to discover new forms of producing sexual arousal or pleasure.

For some couples anxiety concerning sexual contact may require a more structured systematic desensitization approach with a detailed hierarchy of situations. Exposure to non-sexual and yet intimate situations may be required initially, such as assistance with bathing. This activity may also be useful as a component of preventative programmes, as part of routine exposure to close physical contact.

Increasing sexual arousal. Various methods have been suggested in order to enhance sexual arousal where a physical disorder impairs the normal arousal response. For example, the use of erotic imagery or erotic literature/films may enhance erectile functioning for some men whose organic erectile problems may be influenced by psychological factors. This approach may also be helpful for women with lubrication difficulties associated with menopause. Similarly, the use of imagery and erotic literature or movies may generate sexual arousal for some people with spinal injuries for whom arousal may still be triggered by cognitive mediation. Mooney *et al.* (1975) described a method of sensory amplification in which individuals are instructed to focus their attention on a particular form of physical stimulation and concentrate on amplifying the sensation. These authors also suggested that sensations may be substituted or transferred in imagination (fantasy) from areas which still have sensation to genital areas in which feeling has been lost. The degree to which these methods are successful remains to be empirically demonstrated, but their use may offer hope for some quadraplegics.

Enhancement of general marital skills

The training of communication and problem-solving skills is also important for couples who show difficulties in this area. Methods as outlined in Chapter 5 play an important role in enabling the couple to adapt their sexual relationship to take into account the influences of the physical disorder.

Physical treatments for sexual dysfunctions of organic aetiology

Given the significant interaction between organic and psychological factors in the development of sexual dysfunctions, cognitive-behaviour therapy has an important role to play as part of a multidisciplinary approach to the treatment of organic sexual problems. Although physical approaches may be highly effective in enhancing sexual functioning for some patients, it is equally important that the psychological aspects of the disorder are tackled. If the cognitive-behaviour therapist is to work within a multidisciplinary team, it is important that he or she has a basic knowledge of what is involved in the physical treatments being used. For this reason, a brief summary is included of commonly used physical procedures. The majority of physical procedures have focused on the remediation of erectile dysfunction in males, with much less attention being paid to physical treatments in women.

With respect to physical interventions with sexual dysfunctions, Schover and Jensen (1988) criticized the widespread use of invasive physical treatments, which are frequently applied indiscriminately, irrespective of organic versus psychogenic influences. These authors emphasized the possible dangers of invasive methods (e.g. injections or surgery) that are not warranted if alternative, effective behavioural treatments are available. Only when behavioural and non-invasive procedures have been found to be ineffective should invasive physical procedures be considered in the treatment of psychosexual disorders.

Hormonal treatments

Although hormone replacement treatments have been reported to be relatively effective in reducing severe symptoms during menopause, there is relatively little evidence to suggest that hormone treatments (e.g. testosterone therapy) are particularly effective for increasing sexual arousal and desire amongst women who report difficulties in this area (Dow and Gallagher, 1989). The majority of research studies, however, have not selected clients on the basis of low levels of specific hormones and hence it really remains to be determined whether hormone treatments are effective for women who have relatively low levels of a given sex hormone.

The evidence concerning the use of hormonal treatments in disorders of sexual desire and arousal in men is also confusing. Again, studies have not typically selected subjects on the basis of demonstrable hormone abnormalities and it is perhaps not surprising to find conflicting results with regard to the effectiveness of hormonal interventions.

Drug-induced erections

Various drugs, such as papaverine hydrochloride, are now available which have a vasoactive effect when injected into the corpus cavernosum (Marshall, 1989). The use of such drugs requires experienced medical involvement in order to establish the correct dosage. When used appropriately, papaverine injection results in penile tumescence and erection within around 20 minutes, which is maintained for 1–3 hours. Ejaculation is unaffected and the erection may be used for sexual intercourse. The risks include excessively prolonged erections (and the dangers therein) in around 8% of cases (Nellans *et al.*, 1987). This side effect may be reduced by careful estimation of correct dosage. The approach has also been used successfully with self-injection. Whilst this approach offers promise in the restoration of erectile capacity which has been lost as the result of disorders such as diabetes and neurological impairment, some couples do not adapt to the use of the injection procedure. The approach is less suitable for the treatment of erectile problems which result from vascular disorders involving excessive drainage of blood from the penis, as the problem of inadequate build-up of blood within the penis remains.

Vacuum constrictor devices

Vacuum constrictor devices are designed to mechanically draw blood into the corpora of the penis in order to produce a state of erection. Various devices are available, the most common of which involves two constrictor rings placed in tandem around the penis. Erection may be achieved in 2–3 minutes. The technique is non-invasive, safe and provides an inexpensive alternative to surgical implants. Nadig and Becker (1984) reported that 72/75 diabetic men with erectile dysfunction were able to achieve penile rigidity sufficient for penetration. At 3–16 months follow-up, 24/31 men reported regular use of the method and both partners were satisfied with the sexual relationship.

Penile prostheses

Excellent summaries of penile prosthetic devices are provided by Smolev (1983) and Schover and Jensen (1988). Different forms of prosthesis are available, reflecting progress in design and differences in cost. The rigid form of prosthesis was originally introduced in the 1950s and was made from acrylic or similar material. This method provides permanent rigidity to the penis, which needs to be flexible enough to bend downwards to be retained within strong elasticated underclothes. When free, the penis hangs at a 45° angle in a state of erection that is somewhat shorter and thinner than the penis would normally be when erect. Over the years the composition and design of rigid prostheses have changed. The majority now include a pair of curved cylinders made of silicon rubber filled with silicone sponge. These are inserted into the twin spaces created by dilating the spongy tissues of each corpus cavernosum. Complications of this method include occasional reports of infection, irritation, oedema, pain and extrusion through the skin, with problems being reported in around 5-10% of cases (Schover and Jensen, 1988; Smolev, 1983). Some patients also report dissatisfaction with the length and diameter of the erection produced.

Adaptations of the rigid prosthesis have included a hinged version which permits the penis to bend more easily at the base. This is designed to provide easier concealment of the penis when the erection is not needed, which may be a source of worry for some couples with the rigid version. An inflatable form of penile prosthesis is also available. This is much more costly, but is designed to overcome the problems of concealment altogether and to permit greater size of erection. The method generally involves a pair of hollow rods inserted into the corpus cavernosum. The cylinders are empty during the flaccid state and when filled with fluid result in penile erection. The fluid is stored in a balloon reservoir which is placed outside the bladder in the rectopubic space under the rectus muscles. A small pump is placed in the scrotum above the testicles. Manual pumping through the scrotal sack results in a release of fluid from the storage reservoir into the cylinders of the penis, causing erection. A valve on the pump is then squeezed to activate the deflation valve. Results with the inflatable prosthesis have been relatively good, although problems such as malfunction or infection are reported to occur in 5-15% of cases (Schover and Jensen, 1988; Smolev, 1983).

Very recently, a self-contained version of the inflatable prosthesis has been developed which involves two connecting cylinders, each attached to its own pump and reservoir. The cylinders extend from the base of the penis along the shaft. When the fluid is stored within the basal cylinder, the penis is flaccid. If the fluid is then pumped into the next chamber in the penile shaft, erection occurs. The surgery involved in the self-contained version is less invasive and the device involves fewer separate parts. Given that the device is relatively new, its advantages remain to be determined.

Vascular treatments

Vascular surgery may be possible for some individuals whose erectile difficulties are associated with diminished blood flow to the penis. Surgery may involve large vessel reconstruction or corporate revascularization and has been reported to be successful in re-establishing erectile functioning for some males (Bennett, 1989). Schover and Jensen (1988) concluded that, in general, penile revascularization has not been particularly successful. They suggest that this may be partly due to the combination of neurological and vascular disorders for many patients, and vascular improvement does not mean that neurological improvement will also occur. In addition, Schover and Jensen noted the complexity of the operations involved for many men, with complex microsurgery being required.

HOMOSEXUAL CLIENTS

It is clear that homosexual clients, both male and female, may experience the same forms of sexual dysfunction as heterosexual clients (McWhirter and Mattison, 1980; Reece, 1988). The same organic and psychosocial influences over sexual functioning apply. McWhirter and Mattison (1980) described the role played by communication problems, performance anxiety, negative sexual attitudes and general relationship difficulties amongst their male homosexual clients. It is not surprising to find then that the approach taken to treatment of sexual difficulties amongst homosexual individuals or couples typically involves those therapy components that would be used in the treatment programme for any other person (Masters and Johnson, 1979; McWhirter and Mattison, 1980).

In terms of the incidence of sexual dysfunction amongst gay men, relatively little is known. Bell and Weinberg (1978) surveyed a gay male sample in San Francisco and reported problems of premature ejaculation to be most common (27% of respondents), with 21% reporting difficulty in maintaining an erection and 14% reporting lack of orgasm. These percentages differ somewhat from those found for different sexual disorders presenting for therapy amongst homosexual males. Reece (1988) summarized studies amongst gay men and concluded that secondary erectile failure was the most frequently presenting problem and inhibited orgasm was also common (22–59% of presenting problems). It seems therefore that although problems relating to premature ejaculation are common amongst homosexual males, this problem is less likely to lead to the person seeking the help of a therapist. In comparison, problems of inhibited orgasm are more likely to lead to a request for therapy. It is interesting to note the higher incidence of inhibited orgasm amongst homosexual men, compared to the incidence amongst heterosexual males.

Reece (1988) pointed out that in order to conduct an adequate assessment and intervention, the therapist requires an understanding of the differences in patterns of sexual activities between homosexual compared to heterosexual couples. Gay men, for example, present frequently with difficulties concerning disorders of desire relating to anal intercourse or oral sex. Negative cognitions concerning these activities may impair the desire, arousal or orgasm phase of sexual responding. Reece also pointed out the impact that the AIDS epidemic has had upon the sexual functioning of gay men, and the fears and anxieties that this has produced.

Much less has been written about the sexual problems of homosexual women. Barbach (1980) suggested that the sexual problems of lesbian women are more similar to than different from heterosexual females. Barbach pointed out that sexual activity and responding has relatively little to do with sexual orientation. In practice, however, the sexual problems of homosexual individuals or couples, whether male or female, may be closely linked with feelings of guilt, uncertainty and confusion over their sexual orientation. For those homosexual people which have come to accept their sexual orientation and to feel comfortable with it, negative thoughts and attitudes about sexual orientation will not tend to impair sexual responding. Many homosexual clients do not reach this stage of acceptance, however, and experience a wide range of negative cognitions concerning homosexual activity. Such cognitions need to be overcome in order to resolve problems of sexual desire and arousal. This issue is less of a problem for the treatment of orgasmic difficulties with homosexual women, given that orgasmic ability can be relatively easily established through self-stimulation programmes (e.g. Barbach, 1980). When the aim of intervention is to transfer orgasm to situations involving a partner, the issue of conflicts concerning sexual orientation may again be important.

Implications for intervention with homosexual clients

Although the basic components of the treatment of psychosexual difficulties with gay or lesbian clients are likely to be the same as those involved in therapy with heterosexual clients, the therapist needs to take into account the unique behavioural and cognitive characteristics of this population. These characteristics emerge in relation to the following:

Behaviours. The typical patterns of sexual activity, such as greater use of anal intercourse by males (and the physical and psychosocial problems that may be experienced in relation to this activity), oral sex and mutual masturbation for homosexual couples must be taken into account.

Cognitions. Although performance fears and negative thoughts concerning the self, partner and the relationship may occur as for any couple, the role of negative thoughts concerning sexual orientation must be explored. Most homosexual people have experienced lifelong negative social pressures concerning homosexuality and it is not surprising to find negative thoughts, guilt and anxieties about homosexual activity amongst some clients.

The general relationship. The nature of the relationship in which sex takes place also needs to be taken into account. Reece (1988) noted that sex is much more likely to take place outside a primary relationship for gay men. The degree to which such activity is accepted by the primary partner needs to be explored, given that some individuals may be distressed by their partner's sexual activities with other men. For many homosexual clients, there may not be a primary partner and intervention must progress as for a single person. The difficulties imposed by societal attitudes upon the relationships of those clients who are involved with a primary partner (e.g. the reactions of parents and colleagues) also need to be considered. Despite the specific characteristics that apply to homosexual relationships, the approach to relationship enhancement resembles that used for heterosexual couples and can be effective in reducing conflict and enhancing relationship satisfaction (Weisstub and Schoenfeld, 1987).

Communication skills. The need for effective communication skills is equally important for homosexual clients. The principles and methods of intervention are the same as those outlined in Chapter 5, although the situations targeted for treatment may differ. For example, a male homosexual client referred to this author presented with problems of premature ejaculation and extremely poor communication skills. This man had great difficulty forming relationships with either sex and his sexual interactions involved anal sex in local toilet blocks with unknown partners. Part of the focus of attention was to increase communication skills and encourage participation in activities in which he was likely to meet and form relationships. A stop–start method was used successfully during masturbatory activities, in order to increase ejaculatory control. Communication skills training was also successful in increasing ability to initiate and maintain conversations with other men. The client began to attend a local gay community centre where he joined in activities and ultimately formed a series of homosexual relationships.

Although subtle differences in the content of assessment and therapy with gay clients may exist, the point made by Barbach (1980) remains, that the sexual difficulties of homosexual clients are more similar to than different from those of heterosexual clients. Indeed, the cognitive-behavioural approach outlined in Chapters 5 and 6 can be seen to have relevance to all individuals who experience psychosexual difficulties, irrespective of sexual orientation, age, intellectual level, health or physical abilities. Nevertheless, the sexual difficulties of some individuals are influenced by specific factors which make those people 'special' in some way. Understanding the factors which influence their sexual problems should facilitate the assessment and therapy process.

9

Professional issues and conclusions

One of the major points to emerge from this text is the enormous complexity of human sexual responding and the many physical and psychosocial influences that must be taken into account during assessment and intervention. It is clear that a high standard of training of therapists is required and that adherence to a strict code of ethics is important. This chapter discusses the professional issues that should be considered by practitioners who are dealing with psychosexual problems. It emphasizes the many therapist skills which are essential during assessment and intervention with psychosexual difficulties and the need to ensure that a professional approach is taken to the management of clients with such problems.

ETHICAL ISSUES IN THE TREATMENT OF PSYCHOSEXUAL DYSFUNCTIONS

Organizations for those professionals involved in the treatment of sexual problems exist in most countries in Western society. These organizations typically have their own code of ethics and, furthermore, individual professions may also have their own code of ethics with which their members are committed to comply. What follows therefore is a summary of some of the main issues that emerge in relation to the treatment of sexual difficulties. Many of the issues are equally applicable to other forms of psychological disorder. Hence, the importance of ensuring confidentiality of information, seeking informed consent from clients, avoidance of sexual or intimate relationships with one's clients. General standards of ethical behaviour apply equally during the treatment of a sexual problem as they would for any other referral. During the treatment of sexual dysfunctions, however, some ethical issues may be more likely to arise, or may be relevant because of the unique characteristics of sexual behaviour.

Physical contact by the therapist and direct observation of clients' sexual behaviour

The issue of whether the cognitive-behaviour therapist should become involved in any form of physical contact with the client is important to mention, given that many of the exercises involved in the treatment of sexual dysfunctions could easily involve physical contact by a therapist. The content of intervention frequently focuses on education about physical anatomy and techniques for physical contact. It would be very easy for a therapist to demonstrate a particular method, such as the squeeze technique or insertion of dilators, by direct physical contact with the client. For obvious reasons, direct physical contact between the therapist and client should be avoided, unless the practitioner is medically qualified and has a nurse or partner in attendance. The judgment as to what is regarded as acceptable therapist behaviour is primarily determined by social and cultural attitudes. Hence, these values may change over time and differ across different cultures. For example, one current societal value suggests that it is acceptable for medical practitioners to touch a client's genital areas, while other professionals are not permitted to do so. Whether we like this or not, the social convention exists and failure to adhere to this covert regulation may lead to difficulties if the aim is misinterpreted by the client, colleagues or other individuals. Alternative methods are available in order to demonstrate aspects of anatomy or physical techniques. Pictures, films, verbal descriptions or anatomical models may be used for instruction purposes and evidence suggests that these methods are effective in communicating the necessary information. Direct physical contact is not therefore necessary and Brown and Sollod (1988) have suggested that therapists should question their motives if they consider using such methods.

These same points apply with regard to the direct observation of clients' sexual behaviour. Given the alternative methods available for data collection, and the questionable validity of any sexual behaviour that occurs in the presence of an observer, the use of direct behavioural observation of sexual activities in the clinic cannot be condoned. Again, a socially accepted value is that sexual behaviours should occur in private. The danger of misinterpretation of the therapist's motives therefore exists and many clients would find this aspect of assessment or intervention extremely distressing. The possible voyeuristic desires of the therapist must be questioned, given that satisfactory alternative methods for assessment and therapy are available. These points are not made with respect to those academics who are actively involved in research into sexual behaviour. Hopefully the codes of ethics which apply to the institutions in which these individuals are employed will regulate to produce an acceptable standard of behaviour. The importance of such research cannot be underestimated and the work of researchers, such as Masters and Johnson (1966), has played a vital role in the provision of knowledge about sexual behaviour and provides the basis for the treatments of sexual dysfunction today.

Sexual relationships with clients

Sexual or intimate relationships with clients during and after therapy are typically outlawed in the ethical standards of most professions and sex therapy organizations. The issue is mentioned here as it seems likely that the desire or opportunity to engage in sexual activities may occur more frequently during the treatment of a sexual problem in comparison to the treatment of non-sexual disorders. This point is made purely on the basis of subjective opinion and there does not appear to be any empirical evidence either to support or reject the proposition. It seems sensible to suggest that the frequent conversations about sexual issues during assessment and therapy are likely to provide a stimulus for the triggering of sexual arousal for both the therapist and clients. The stimulus conditions which may result in sexual desire may therefore be present more often during the treatment of a sexual problem. It would not be surprising then to find that the temptation to take part in sexual activities with a client occurs more frequently for therapists involved in the treatment of sexual dysfunctions.

Of particular concern regarding sexual activity between therapist and client is the possible negative impact upon the client as the result of the relationship. The position of power, trust and influence of the therapist with respect to the client is frequently stressed, implying that there is no such thing as informed consent when it comes to an intimate relationship between therapist and client (Brown and Sollod, 1988). Violation of this trusting relationship is typically viewed as exploitation of the client's vulnerable position. As with any form of therapy, sexual involvement with a client is highly disregarded amongst professions generally.

Use of sexual surrogates

The use of sexual surrogates during the process of therapy has been a highly controversial issue over the past twenty years. The issue reflects societal values that sexual activity should occur within the context of close, loving and long-term relationships. Furthermore, the fact that therapy typically involves payment leads to questions regarding prostitution of those involved as surrogates, or those who organize the facility.

The attitude of professionals to the use of sex surrogates for the treatment of sexual dysfunctions is variable. Kaplan (1987) suggested that the risk of AIDS in today's society makes the use of sex surrogates highly questionable and unjustified. Whilst this point is acknowledged, it should be pointed out that there are ways around this problem, such as the use of condoms and regular medical checks.

The use of surrogates has generally been limited to those who do not have partners available, willing or able to participate in therapy. The limited research available suggests that outcome of therapy can be highly successful using surrogates. Dauw (1988) reported the results for 501 heterosexual male clients who were treated involving trained surrogates. The surrogates were all masters level graduates with 100 hours of intensive training. All surrogates worked under the guidance of a supervisor, with weekly communications between surrogates and therapist. The surrogates participated in sexual skill assignments, with clients attending regular sessions based on a cognitive-behaviour therapy approach. The outcome of therapy at three-month follow-up was extremely positive, with success rates of 98.2% for primary erectile failure, 85% for secondary erectile failure, 96% for premature ejaculation, 85% for ejaculatory incompetence and 94% for inhibited sexual desire.

Despite the suggestions of positive results for the use of sexual surrogates, the practice is associated with so many ethical difficulties that its use is not recommended for those working in general settings. The intimate nature of assignments places the client at risk of developing emotional feelings for the surrogate which will not be reciprocated. Difficulties may also be experienced by the partner whose spouse is involved as a client in a surrogate therapy progamme (Brown and Sollod, 1988). This point is particularly important for those couples whose relationships are troubled and where one partner refuses to attend for treatment of the sexual problem. Brown and Sollod suggested that the use of a surrogate may exacerbate the marital conflict and proposed that the client should be advised to return for therapy with his partner once the marital conflict is resolved.

The Dauw programme attempts to overcome these difficulties through careful training and supervision of surrogates. No matter how carefully the surrogate programme is managed, however, its use is not recommended, given that the training and supervision requirements are far beyond the resources of the vast majority of practitioners. Legal problems are likely to exist in many countries or states and the possibility that the service may be open to abuse makes the use of surrogate therapy inadvisable.

Alteration of sexual values

Therapists and clients commence their relationship with their own set of values and attitudes about sexual activities and relationships. The situation frequently occurs in which the values of the therapist are different from those of the client(s). In some instances, the views of the therapist may be somewhat more accepting of certain activities than the client's (e.g. regarding oral sex, male–female roles in the sexual relationship). On other occasions the situation may be reversed and some therapists may find themselves with a relatively conservative attitude towards some aspect of the client's sexual relationship in comparison to the client's view (e.g. regarding anal intercourse during homosexual behaviour). The point needs to be made that all individuals have a right to hold particular views. This applies equally to the therapist as to the client. For the most part the discrepancies between therapist and client attitudes are sufficiently minor as not to interfere with the therapy process. If significant discrepancies exist, action is needed if therapy is to progress successfully. For this reason, it is essential that adequate information is obtained during assessment about the client's values and attitudes. These can be taken into account in the development of an appropriate intervention programme.

Several authors have highlighted the ethical implications of attempting to change client values during the therapy process (Brown and Sollod, 1988; Jonsen, 1980). These authors suggest that attempts should not be made to change the client's values and attitudes unless they are actively contributing to the maintenance of the sexual problem and therapy cannot be effective unless they are changed. This point is particularly important in an approach that involves cognitive restructuring. It is important to be able to discriminate between client attitudes that are interfering with the therapy process and those that are not. If the clients attitudes are not interfering with therapy, alternative therapy approaches should be used, where available, which leave the client's attitudes and values unaffected. An example to illustrate this point is the reluctance of some clients to engage in oral sex. Brown and Sollod (1988) suggested that therapy can frequently progress successfully without the therapist focusing specifically upon attempts to encourage the client to change his or her views about this activity. Information may be provided about the normality of the behaviour and lack of adverse side effects, but the client should then be permitted to retain a value system that rejects the use of oral sex if he or she desires. What then of the client who holds negative attitudes about nudity and foreplay? If the client requests help for the treatment of arousal and orgasm difficulties, it would seem that cognitive restructuring of such attitudes would be an essential component of intervention.

It is equally important that the therapist is aware of his or her own attitudes and values with regard to sexuality. There may be some instances in which the therapist feels that his or her attitudes will make the conduct of intervention very difficult and it may be in the client's interests to refer on to a therapist whose values are more in line with those of the client. This factor needs to be discussed in the training of therapists and is frequently overlooked. Generally, it is assumed that the information and education about sexuality provided to therapists will result in a shift towards greater acceptance of liberal sexual values. Whilst this may be the case, it may be very difficult for some therapists with entrenched religious or moral views concerning certain aspects of sexuality to change their views.

ISSUES IN THE TRAINING OF THERAPISTS

The position taken in the present text is that a cognitive-behavioural approach, which takes into account the interactive aspects of the couple's relationship, is most appropriate for the treatment of psychosexual dysfunctions. It is also suggested that adequate background knowledge and skill in cognitive-behavioural assessment and therapy are important in order to tackle the many psychosocial factors which influence sexual functioning. Generally, postgraduate training in therapist skills is required in order to reach a satisfactory level of competence in these prerequisite skill areas. The sex therapist–practitioner who acts as a technician in implementing package approaches is not considered adequately skilled to deal with the complex issues involved in the sexual dysfunctions of many clients.

Although prerequisite skills of competence in the principles and practice of cognitive-behaviour therapy and assessment are stressed, these on their own are not considered to be sufficient for competent management of sexual dysfunctions. The following suggestions are made with regard to the training of therapists in those skills which are more specifically related to the treatment of sexual problems. This outline is based upon the approach used by the author in the training of clinical psychology masters level students in the skills of assessment and intervention with psychosexual dysfunctions.

Sexual knowledge

There is an assumption that students and in particular students in the medical or psychological professions will have an extensive knowledge of human sexual behaviour. In practice this is often not the case and any person who is going to be dealing with a client with a sexual difficulty requires a thorough knowledge of what responses normally occur during sexual activity.

Attitude evaluations

The initial stage of lectures and discussion about sexual responding often brings to light the anxiety that many students have about open discussion of sexual topics. This point is also made by Freeman (1989), who described her approach to training postgraduate students to deal with sexual problems. Freeman makes use of discussion and the opportunity for anonymous questions, so that students are able to obtain answers to questions that they do not feel confident enough to ask in class. The process at this stage is often one of gradual desensitization to the discussion of sexual topics.

It is important for students to examine their own sexual attitudes and explore possible difficulties that they may have in the future in being able to enquire about client's sexual difficulties. Many students initially feel that clients have the right to privacy and that the therapist does not have the right to ask about sexual functioning during client contact related to referral for some other problem. Difficulties relating to negative attitudes towards certain activities such as masturbation or oral sex are also discussed. It is often useful for trainees to complete assessment questionnaires and score up their own results on evaluations such as the Sexual Knowledge and Attitude Test (Lief and Reed, 1972). This may produce some valuable discussion material.

Specific information

The next phase of training focuses upon the provision of information about the aetiology of sexual problems, assessment and intervention. Topics include:

- Organic and psychogenic causes of sexual problems;
- Types of sexual dysfunctions and their characteristics;
- Placing the sexual dysfunction in the context of the general relationship;
- Assessment of sexual dysfunctions (including taking a sexual history);
- Formulating a treatment plan;
- Marital therapy techniques;
- Cognitive therapy techniques;
- Specific skill assignments;
- Dealing with special populations;
- Evaluating treatment outcome.

Methods used during training include lectures, videotaped case examples, role-play using pre-prepared vignettes, written handouts and set readings from texts. The focus is on the practical conduct of assessment and intervention as well as the academic information about methods and effectiveness. The use of role-play at this point provides a valuable means of providing feedback on therapist or interviewer skills and also a desensitizing experience for the trainees. Where the opportunity is available, students may benefit from observing sessions conducted by an experienced practitioner.

Once this aspect of training has been completed, it is important for trainees to commence their own case work under close supervision. In our clinic this typically involves preparation sessions between trainee and supervisor, observation of sessions through a one-way screen and post-session feedback. In some instances, the supervisor may act as co-therapist, with an opposite-sex trainee. Weekly meetings between small groups of trainees and the supervisors also provide a valuable opportunity for case presentation and discussion and a continued learning experience for all involved.

For those therapists who are already involved in clinical practice but who rightly feel a need to accept clients with sexual dysfunctions for therapy, rather than referring them on elsewhere, a variety of training opportunities exist. Workshops are generally available through professional organizations or local associations of persons who have specific interests in the treatment of sexual dysfunctions. A great deal of literature is also available on the subject, which provides the academic knowledge required. Careful assessment and preparation of treatment programmes under supervision of an experienced therapist is then suggested for initial cases.

CONCLUSIONS

Given that an increasing number of individuals and couples are seeking help for sexual dysfunctions, it is important that effective treatment methods are developed. Although a great deal of success has been achieved in the development of psychological treatment programmes, research studies suggest that traditional therapy approaches are not effective for a significant proportion of couples, particularly for certain types of sexual dysfunction. There is therefore a need to continue our attempts to understand the nature and aetiology of psychosexual dysfunctions and to design new and more effective ways of treating such problems. Hopefully, the present text has gone some way towards meeting this goal.

Consideration of the nature and determinants of sexual behaviour revealed the great complexity of the human sexual response and the enormous array of organic and psychosocial factors which play a role in the development and maintenance of sexual dysfunctions. It was suggested that sexual behaviour consists of cognitive/affective, physiological and overt components which may present in different ways for different individuals. The cognitive-behavioural approach to assessment outlined here stresses the need to clarify the nature of each of these aspects of sexual behaviour for each individual and couple.

To complicate matters further, sexual behaviour is influenced by a wide range of biological and psychological factors, which need to be thoroughly assessed if the presenting problem is to be fully understood. Given the interaction between biological and psychosocial variables, there is a need for a combined medical and psychological approach to therapy. Even where aetiology is predominantly organic, secondary psychological influences may result which must be dealt with if treatment is to be successful.

Within the area of psychosocial variables, the importance of cognitive factors was highlighted more strongly than has been the case in previous literature. Cognitive factors must be considered not only as an aspect of the sexual response, but also as factors which act as antecedents or consequences of sexual behaviour and which may thereby play an important role in the generation and maintenance of sexual dysfunction. A model was outlined which summarizes the way in which psychogenic and biogenic factors interact to influence the responses of sexual desire, arousal and orgasm. In particular, an emphasis was placed on the role of cognitive events in the interpretation of stimuli and events, thereby influencing sexual responsiveness at various points of the sexual response cycle. The model assumes that past life experiences act through the processes of learning to determine our current memories, knowledge, attitudes and beliefs. These constructs can be suggested to influence our interpretation of incoming stimuli, which occur in the form of erotic physical, auditory or visual stimulation or fantasy. Current life events such as one's marital relationship also impinge upon our knowledge, attitudes and beliefs and thereby affect our interpretation of events. The way in which incoming stimuli are interpreted is suggested to determine whether the physiological responses of sexual arousal and ultimately orgasm will occur. In summary, it is proposed that the interaction between cognitive and biological factors in the determination of sexual desire, arousal and orgasm must be understood for each couple or individual who present with sexual dysfunction.

This type of approach to sexual dysfunction emphasizes the need for modification of cognitive, relationship and other psychosocial influences during intervention. Where cognitive factors such as maladaptive attitudes or thoughts are found to be maintaining a sexual problem, it is important that cognitive restructuring forms part of the intervention programme. Previous authors have emphasized the importance of cognitive restructuring in the treatment of psychosexual disorders (e.g. Steger, 1978; Walen and Perlmutter, 1988). To date, however, there has been little attempt to provide practical details about how cognitive restructuring methods can be used with clients who present with sexual difficulties. The present book has commenced this task and hopefully future texts will provide further insights into the application of cognitive therapy approaches within the treatment of psychosexual problems.

The quality of the couple's general relationship was also given considerable attention within this book. A case was made to demonstrate that the sexual aspect of a relationship is closely related to the quality of the general relationship for many couples. The direction of influence between satisfaction with the sexual relationship and satisfaction with the relationship generally was proposed to be two-way. Sexual difficulties are likely to result in marital disharmony and, similarly, general relationship problems are likely to interfere with sexual functioning. The approach taken to intervention emphasized the many skills which are common to both satisfactory sexual and general relationships. For example, communication skills, problem-solving skills and frequency of positive interactions of the couple are likely to be important determinants of both sexual and non-sexual aspects of the relationship. Given that many couples who seek help for sexual difficulties also demonstrate problems within other areas of their relationship, a strong case was made for an integrated approach which routinely tackles sexual and non-sexual aspects of the relationship simultaneously. In the past, there has been a tendency to separate out the treatment of marital and sexual difficulties. This book illustrates ways in which marital and sexual therapies can be integrated. Although this suggestion is not new, the present text provides a practical description of how such integration might be achieved.

Given the complexity of sexual behaviour and the wide range of factors that need to be considered during assessment and therapy, the therapist requires considerable skill in the areas of marital and cognitive therapies, in addition to the skills required for implementation of traditional behavioural approaches to the treatment of sexual dysfunctions. It was suggested that the skills of the sex therapist who operates as a technician are inadequate for the treatment of many complex cases of psychosexual dysfunction.

Finally, consideration of special populations revealed that the cognitive-behavioural approach to assessment and therapy outlined here is equally applicable to the management of sexual problems amongst elderly, physically ill or disabled and homosexual clients. Although the special characteristics of each of these populations need to be taken into account by the therapist in designing and implementing the intervention programme, the basic approach to assessment and therapy remains the same.

References

Abrahamson, D.J., Barlow, D.H. and Abrahamson, L.S. (1989) Differential effects of performance demand and distraction on sexually functional and dysfunctional males. *Journal of Abnormal Psychology*, *98*, 241–7

Abramowitz, S.I. and Sewell, H.H. (1980) Marital adjustment and sex therapy outcome. *Journal of Sex Research*, *16*, 325–37

American Psychiatric Association (1987) *Diagnostic and Statistical Manual of Mental Disorders*, 3rd edn, revised. APA, Washington DC

Andersen, B.L. (1981) A comparison of systematic desensitisation and directed masturbation in the treatment of primary orgasmic dysfunction in females. *Journal of Consulting and Clinical Psychology*, *49*, 568–70

Andersen, B.L., Broffitt, B., Karlsson, J.A. and Turnquist, D.C. (1989) A psychometric analysis of the sexual arousability index. *Journal of Consulting and Clinical Psychology*, *57*, 123–30

Andersen, B.J. and Wolf, R.M. (1986) Chronic physical illness and sexual behaviour: Psychological issues. *Journal of Consulting and Clinical Psychology*, *54*, 168–75

Andron, L. (1983) Sexuality counselling with developmentally disabled couples. In *Sex Education and Counselling for Mentally Handicapped People* (eds. A. Craft and M. Craft). Costello, Tunbridge Wells

Annon, J.S. (1975) *The Sexual Pleasure Inventory*. Enabling Systems, Honolulu

Ansari, J.M.A. (1976) Impotence: Prognosis (a controlled study). *British Journal of Psychiatry*, *128*, 194–8

Ansbacher, R. and Adler, J.P. (1988) Infertility work-up and sexual stress. *Medical Aspects of Human Sexuality*, *22*, 55–63.

Bahen-Auger, N., Wilson, M. and Assalian, P. (1988) Sexual response of the Type 1 diabetic woman. *Medical Aspects of Human Sexuality*, *22*, 94–100

Baker, C.D. and De Silva, P. (1988) The relationship between male sexual dysfunction and belief in Zilbergeld's myths: An empirical investigation. *Sexual and Marital Therapy*, *3*, 229–38

Balducci, L., Phillips, M., Gearhart, J.G., Little, D.D., Bowie, C. and McGehee, R.P. (1988) Sexual complication of cancer treatment. *American Family Physician*, *37*, 159–72

Barbach, L. (1980) *Women Discover Orgasm* Free Press, New York

Barlow, D.H. (1986) Causes of sexual dysfunction. The role of anxiety and cognitive interference. *Journal of Consulting and Clinical Psychology*, *54*, 104–48

Barlow, D.H., Sakheim, D.K. and Beck, J.G. (1983) Anxiety increases sexual arousal. *Journal of Abnormal Psychology*, *92*, 49–54

Barrios, B.A. (1988) On the changing nature of behavioural assessment. In *Behavioural Assessment: A Practical Handbook*, 3rd edn (eds A.S. Bellack and M. Hersen). Pergamon, New York

Beck, A.T., Rush, A.J., Shaw, B.G. and Emery, G. (1979) *Cognitive Therapy of Depression*. Wiley, London

Beggs, V.E., Calhoun, K.S. and Wolchik, S.A. (1987) Sexual anxiety and female sexual arousal: a comparison of arousal during sexual anxiety stimuli and sexual pleasure stimuli. *Archives of Sexual Behaviour*, *16*, 311–19

Bell, A.P. and Weinberg, M.S. (1978) *Homosexuality: a Study of Diversity among Men and Women*. Simon & Schuster, New York

Bellack, A.S. and Hersen, M. (eds) (1988) *Behavioural Assessment: A Practical Handbook*, 3rd edn. Pergamon, New York

Bennett, A.H. (1989) Nonprosthetic surgical treatment for vasculogenic impotence. *Medical Aspects of Human Sexuality*, *23*, 54–8

Bentler, P.M. (1967) Heterosexual behaviour assessment – I. Males. *Behaviour Research and Therapy*, *5*, 21–5.

Bentler, P.M. (1968) Heterosexual behaviour assessment – II. Females. *Behaviour Research and Therapy*, *6*, 27–30

Bernstein, G. (1989) Counselling the male diabetic patient with erectile dysfunction. *Medical Aspects of Human Sexuality*, *23*, 45–53

Bishay, N.R. (1988) Cognitive therapy in psychosexual dysfunctions: A preliminary report. *Sexual and Marital Therapy*, *3*, 83–90

Boller, F. and Frank, E. (1982) *Sexual Dysfunction in Neurological Disorders: Diagnosis, Management and Rehabilitation*. Raven Press, New York

Brechner, E.M. (1984) *Love, Sex and Ageing*. Little, Brown & Co., Boston

Bretschneider, J.G. and McCoy, N.L. (1988) Sexual interest and behaviour in healthy 80- to 102-year-olds. *Archives of Sexual Behaviour*, *17*, 109–29

Brown, R.A. and Sollod, R. (1988) Ethical and professional issues in sex therapy. In *Treatment of Sexual Problems in Individual and Couples Therapy* (eds R.A. Brown and J.R. Field). PMA, New York

Butler, R.N. and Lewis, M.L. (1977) *Sex after Sixty: A Guide for Men and Women in their Later Years*. G.K. Hall, Boston

Butler, R.N. and Lewis, M.L. (1987) Sound prescription for your ageing patient: Tips for lifelong sexual fitness. *Medical Aspects of Human Sexuality*, *21*, 96–102

Carney, A., Bancroft, J. and Mathews, A. (1978) Combination of hormonal and psychological treatment for female sexual unresponsiveness: a comparative study. *British Journal of Psychiatry*, *132*, 339–46

Chambless, D.L., Stern, T., Sultan, F.E., Williams, A.J., Hazzard-Linberger, M., Lifshitz, J. and Kelly, L. (1982) The pubococcygens and female orgasm: A correlational study with normal subjects. *Archives of Sexual Behaviour*, *11*, 479–90

Chambless, D.L., Sultan, F.E., Stern, T.E., O'Neill, C., Garrison, S. and Jackson, A. (1984) Effects of pubococcygeal exercises on coital orgasm in women. *Journal of Consulting and Clinical Psychology*, *52*, 114–18

Chapman, R. (1982) Criteria for diagnosing when to do sex therapy in the primary relationships. *Psychotherapy: Theory, Research and Practice*, *19*, 359–67

Clement, U. and Schmidt, G. (1983) The outcome of couple therapy for sexual dysfunctions using three different formats. *Journal of Sex and*

Marital Therapy, 9, 67–78

Comfort, A. (1980) Sexuality in later life. In *Handbook of Mental Health and Aging* (eds J.E. Birren and R.L. Sloane). Prentice-Hall, Englewood Cliffs, New Jersey

Comfort, A. (ed.) (1980) *Sexual Consequences of Disability*. Stickley, Philadelphia

Conte, H.R. (1986) Multivariate assessment of sexual dysfunction. *Journal of Consulting and Clinical Psychology, 54*, 149–157

Craft, A. (1983) Sexuality and mental retardation: A review of the literature. In *Sex Education and Counselling for Mentally Handicapped People* (eds A. Craft and M. Craft). Costello, Tunbridge Wells

Craft, A. (1987) Mental handicap and sexuality: Issues for individuals with a mental handicap, their parents and professionals. In *Mental Handicap and Sexuality: Issues and Perspectives* (ed. A. Craft). Costello, Tunbridge Wells

Croft, L.H. (1982) *Sexuality in Later Life: A Counselling Guide for Physicians*. J. Wright, Boston

Crowe, M.J., Gillan, P. and Golombok, S. (1981) Form and content in the conjoint treatment of sexual dysfunction: A controlled study. *Behaviour Research and Therapy, 19*, 47–54

Dauw, D.C. (1988) Evaluating the effectiveness of the SECS' surrogate-assisted sex therapy model. *Journal of Sex Research, 24*, 269–75

Dawkins, S. and Taylor, R. (1961) Non-consummation of marriage: A survey of seventy cases. *Lancet, ii*, 1029–30

DeAmicis, L.A., Goldberg, D.C., LoPicollo, J., Friedman, J. and Davies, L. (1985) Clinical follow-up of couples treated for sexual dysfunction. *Archives of Sexual Behaviour, 14*, 467–89

DeHaan, C.B. and Wallander, J.L. (1988) Self-concept, sexual knowledge and attitudes, and parental support in the sexual adjustment of women with early- and late-onset physical disability. *Archives of Sexual Behaviour, 17*, 145–61

Dekker, J. and Everaerd, W. (1983) A long-term follow-up study of couples treated for sexual dysfunctions. *Journal of Sex and Marital Therapy, 9*, 99–113

Derogatis, L.R. (1975) *Derogatis Sexual Functioning Inventory*. Clinical Psychometrics Research, Baltimore

Derogatis, L.R. (1983) Retarded ejaculation. In *Clinical Management of Sexual Disorders* (eds J.K. Meyer, C.W. Schmidt and T.N. Wise), pp. 334–39. Williams & Wilkins, Baltimore

Derogatis, L.R. and Meyer, J.K. (1979) A psychological profile of the sexual dysfunctions. *Archives of Sexual Behaviour, 8*, 201–23

Derogatis, L.R., Fagan, P.J., Schmidt, C.W., Wise, T.N. and Gilden, K.S. (1986) Psychological subtypes of anorgasmia: A marker variable approach. *Journal of Sex and Marital Therapy, 12*, 197–210.

Derogatis, L.R., Lopez, M.C. and Zinzeletta, E.M. (1988) Clinical application of the DSFI in the assessment of sexual dysfunctions. In *Treatment of Sexual Problems in Individual and Couples Therapy* (eds R.A. Brown and J.R. Field). PMA, New York

Dhabuwala, C.B., Kumar, A., and Pierce, S.W. (1986) Myocardial infarction and its influence on male sexual function. *Archives of Sexual*

Behaviour, *15*, 499–504

Dow, M.G.T. and Gallagher, J. (1989) A controlled study of combined hormonal and psychological treatment for sexual unresponsiveness in women. *British Journal of Clinical Psychology*, *28*, 201–12

D'Zurilla, T.J. and Goldfield, M. (1971) Problem solving and behaviour modification. *Journal of Abnormal Psychology*, *78*, 107–26

Earls, C.M., Quinsey, V.L., and Castonguay, L.G. (1987) A comparison of three months of scoring penile circumference changes. *Archives of Sexual Behaviour*, *16*, 493–500

Ellis, A. (1958) Rational psychotherapy. *Journal of Genetic Psychology*, *59*, 35–49

Ellis, A. (1977) The basic clinical theory of rational-emotive therapy. In *Handbook of Rational Emotive Therapy*, pp. 3–34 (eds A. Ellis and R. Greiger). Springer, New York

Ellis, E.M. (1983) A review of empirical rape research: Victim reactions and response to treatment. *Clinical Psychology Review*, *3*, 473–90

Ersner-Herschfield, R. and Kopel, S. (1979) Group treatment of preorgasmic women: Evaluation of partner involvement and spacing of sessions. *Journal of Consulting and Clinical Psychology*, *47*, 750–9

Everaerd, W. and Dekker, J. (1982) Treatment of secondary orgasmic dysfunction: A comparison at systematic desensitization and sex therapy. *Behaviour Research and Therapy*, *20*, 269–74

Felstein, I. (1983) Dysfunction: origins and therapeutic approaches in *Sexuality in the Later Years: Role and Behaviour* (ed. R.B. Weg). Academic Press, New York

Fennell, M.J.V. (1989) Depression. In *Cognitive Behaviour Therapy for Psychiatric Problems: A Practical Guide* (eds K. Hawton, P.M. Salkovskis, J. Kirk and D.M. Clark). Oxford University Press, Oxford

Fichten, C.S., Libman, E., Takefman, J. and Brender, W. (1988) Self-monitoring and self-focus in erectile dysfunction. *Journal of Sex and Marital Therapy*, *14*, 120–8

Fordney, D. (1978) Dyspareunia and vaginismus. *Clinical Obstetrics and Gynaecology*, *21*, 205–21

Frank, E., Anderson, C. and Rubinstein, D. (1978) Frequency of sexual dysfunction in 'normal' couples. *New England Journal of Medicine*, *299*, 111–15

Freeman, S.T. (1989) Issues in training therapists to deal with clients' sexual performance problems. *Teaching of Psychology*, *16*, 24–6

Freund, K. and Blanchard, R. (1981) Assessment of sexual dysfunction and deviation. In *Behavioural Assessment: A Practical Handbook* (eds M. Hersen and A.S. Bellack). Pergamon Press, New York

Friedman, J.M., Weiler, S.J., LoPiccolo, J. and Hogan, D.R. (1982) Sexual dysfunctions and their treatment: Current status. In *International Handbook of Behaviour Modification and Therapy* (eds A.S. Bellack, M. Hersen and A.E. Kazdin). Plenum, New York

Fritz, G.S., Stoll, N. and Wagner, N. (1981) A comparison of males and females who were sexually molested as children. *Journal of Sex and Marital Therapy*, *I*, 54–9

Fuchs, K., Abramovici, H., Hoch, Z., Timor-Tritsch, I. and Kleinhaus, M. (1975) Vaginismus: The hypno-therapeutic approach. *Journal of Sex*

REsearch, 11, 39–45

Garde, K. and Lunde, I. (1980a) Female sexual behaviour: A study in a random sample of 40 year old women. *Maturitas, 2*, 225–240

Garde. K. and Lunde, I. (1980b) Social background and social status: Influence on female sexual behaviour. A random sample study of 40-year-old Danish women. *Maturitas, 2*, 241–6

Geboes, K., Steeno, O. and De Moor, P. (1975) Primary anejaculation: Diagnosis and therapy. *Fertility and Sterility, 26*, 1018–20

Gillan, P.W. (1977) Stimulation therapy for sexual dysfunction. In *Progress in Sexology*, pp. 167–71 (ed. E. R. Wheeler). Plenum, New York

Golden, J.S., Price, S. P., Heinrich, A.G. and Lobitz, W.C. (1978) Group vs. couple treatment of sexual dysfunctions. *Archives of Sexual Behaviour, 7*, 593–602

Golombok, S. and Rust, J. (1988) Diagnosis of sexual dysfunction: Relationships between DSM-III-R and the GRISS. *Sexual and Marital Therapy, 3*, 119–124

Gottman, J., Notarius, C., Gonso, J. and Markman, H. (1976) *A Couples Guide to Communication*. Research Press, Champaign, Illinois

Gould, L.A. (1989) Impact of cardiovascular disease on male sexual function. *Medical Aspects of Human Sexuality, 23*, 24–27

Grafenberg, E. (1950) The role of the urethra in female orgasm. *International Journal of Sexology, 3*, 145

Gurian, B. (1988) Loss of father's libido after childbirth. *Medical Aspects of Human Sexuality, 22*, 58–62

Halgin, R.P., Hennessey, J.E., Statlender, S., Feinman, J. and Brown, R. A. (1988) Treatment of sexual dysfunction in the context of general psychotherapy. In *Treatment of Sexual Problems in Individual Couples' Therapy* (eds R. Brown and J.R. Field). PMA, New York

Harbison, J.M., Graham, P.J., Quinn, J.T., McAllister, H. and Woodward, R. (1974) A questionnaire measure of sexual interest. *Archives of Sexual Behaviour, 3*, 357–66

Hawton, K. (1985) *Sex Therapy: A Practical Guide*. Oxford University Press, Oxford

Hawton, K. and Catalan, J. (1986) Prognostic factors in sex therapy. *Behaviour Research and Therapy, 24*, 377–85

Hawton, K., Catalan, J., Martin, P. and Fagg, J. (1986) Long-term outcome of sex therapy. *Behaviour Research Therapy, 24*, 665–75

Heiman, J.R. and LoPiccolo, J. (1983) Clinical outcome of sex therapy. *Archives of General Psychiatry, 40*, 443–9

Heiman, J.R., LoPiccolo, J., Hogan, D. and Roberts, C. (1985) Effectiveness of single therapist versus co-therapy teams in sex therapy. *Journal of Consulting and Clinical Psychology, 53*, 287–94

Heiman. J., LoPiccolo, L, and LoPiccolo, J. (1976) *Becoming Orgasmic: A Sexual Growth Programme for Women*. Prentice-Hall, Englewood Cliffs, New Jersey

Hite, S. (1976) *The Hite Report: A Nationwide Study of Female Sexuality*. Dell, New York

Hof, L. (1987) Evaluating the marital relationship of clients with sexual complaints. In *Integrating Sex and Marital Therapy: A Clinical Guide*

G.R. Weeks and L. Hof). Bruner/Mazel, New York

Hoon, E.F., Hoon, P.W. and Wincze, J.P. (1976) An inventory for the measurement of female arousability: The SAI. *Archives of Sexual Behaviour*, *5*, 291–301

Hotvedt, M. (1983) The cross-cultural and historic context. In *Sexuality in the Later Years*, pp. 13–39 (ed. R.B. Weg). Academic Press, New York

Jacobson, N.S. and Margolin, G. (1979) Marital Therapy: Strategies Based on Social Learning and Behaviour. Bruner/Mazel, New York

Jacobson, N.S., Waldron, H. and Moore, D. (1980) Toward a behavioural profile of marital distress. *Journal of Consulting and Clinical Psychology*, *48*, 696–703

Janda, L.H. and O'Grady, K.E. (1980) Development of a sex anxiety inventory. *Journal of Consulting and Clinical Psychology*, *48*, 169–75

Jehu, D. (1979) *Sexual Dysfunction: A Behavioural Approach to Causation, Assessment and Treatment*. Wiley, London

Jehu, D. (1989) Sexual dysfunction among women clients who were sexually abused in childhood. *Behavioural Psychotherapy*, *17*, 53–70

Jonsen, A.R. (1980) Informed consent. In *Ethical Issues in Sex Therapy and Research*, pp. 206–7 (eds W.H. Masters, V.E. Johnson, R.C. Kolodny and S.M. Weems). Little, Brown & Co., Boston

Julien, E. and Over, R. (1988) Male sexual arousal across five modes of erotic stimulation. *Archives of Sexual Behaviour*, *17*, 131–43

Kantor, H.S. (1977) Sexual effects of oestrogen replacement. *Medical Aspects of Human Sexuality*, *11*, 85–6

Kaplan, H.S. (1974) *The New Sex Therapy: Active Treatment of Sexual Dysfunction*. Brunner/Mazel, New York

Kaplan, H.S (1983) *The Evaluation of Sexual Disorders: Psychological and Medical Aspects*. Brunner/Mazel, New York

Kaplan, H.S (1987) *The Illustrated Manual of Sex Therapy*. Brunner/Mazel, New York

Kaplan, H.S (1988) Intimacy disorders and sexual panic states. *Journal of Sex and Marital Therapy*, *14*, 3–12

Kellet, J.M. (1989) Sex and the elderly. *British Medical Journal*, *299*, 934

Kempton, W. and Caparulo, F. (1983) Sexuality training for professionals who work with mentally handicapped persons. In *Sex Education and Counseling for Mentally Handicapped People* (eds A. Craft and M. Craft). Costello, Tunbridge Wells

Kilmann, P.R. and Auerbach, R.M. (1979) Treatments of premature ejaculation and psychogenic impotence: A critical review of the literature. *Archives of Sexual Behaviour*, *8*, 81–100

Kilmann, P.R. Milan, R.J., Boland, J.P. Nankin, H.R., Davidon, E., West, M.O., Sabalis, R.F., Caid, C. and Devine, J.M. (1987) Group treatment of secondary erectile dysfunction. *Journal of Sex and Marital Therapy*, *13*, 168–82

Kilmann, P.R., Mills, K.J., Caid, C., Davidson, E., Bella, B., Milan, R., Drose, G., Boland, J., Follingstad, D., Montgomery, B. and Wanlass, R. (1986) Treatment of secondary orgasmic dysfunction: An outcome study. *Archives of Sexual Behaviour*, *15*, 211–29

Kinder, B.N. and Curtiss, G. (1988) Specific components in the etiology, assessment and treatment of male sexual dysfunctions: Controlled outcome studies. *Journal of Sex and Marital Therapy*, *14*, 40–8

Kinsey, A.C., Pomeroy, W.B. and Martin, C.E. (1948) *Sexual Behaviour in the Human Male*. Saunders, Philadelphia

Kinsey, A.C., Pomeroy, W.B., Martin, C.E. and Gebhard, P.H. (1953) *Sexual Behaviour in the Human Female*. Saunders, Philadelphia

Kolodny, R.C. (1981) Evaluating sex therapy: Process and outcome at the Masters and Johnson Institute. *Journal of Sex Research*, *17*, 301–18

Kotin, J., Wilbert, D., Verburg, D. and Soldinger, S. (1976) Thioridiazine and sexual dysfunction. *American Journal of Psychiatry*, *133*, 82–85

Lamont, J.A. (1977) Vaginismus. In *Progress in Sexology* (eds R. Gemme and C.C. Wheeler). Plenum Press, New York

Lazarus, A.A. (1963) The treatment of chronic frigidity by systematic desensitization. *Journal of Nervous and Mental Disorders*, *136*, 272–82

Libman, E., Fichten, C.S., Brender, W., Burstein, R., Cohen, J. and Binik, Y. (1984) A comparison of three therapeutic formats in the treatment of secondary orgasmic dysfunction. *Journal of Sex and Marital Therapy*, *3*, 147–59

Libman, E., Fichten, C.S. and Brender, W. (1985) The role of therapeutic format in the treatment of sexual dysfunction: A review. *Clinical Psychology Review*, *5*, 103–17

Lief, H.I. (1981) Self evaluation of sexual behaviour and gratification. In *Sexual Problems in Medical Practice*, pp. 389–99 (ed. H.I. Lief). American Medical Association, Monroe, Wisconsin

Lief, H.I. (1985) Evaluation of inhibited sexual desire: Relationship aspects. In *Comprehensive Evaluation of Disorders of Sexual Desire* (ed. H.S. Kaplan). American Psychiatric Association, Washington DC

Lief, H.I. and Reed, D.M. (1972) *Sexual Knowledge and Attitude Test (SKAT)* 2nd edn. Centre for the Study of Sex Education in Medicine, University of Pennsylvania

Lipsius, S.H. (1987) Prescribing sensate focus without proscribing intercourse. *Journal of Sex and Marital Therapy*, *13*, 106–16

Lobitz, W.C. and Lobitz, G.K (1978) Clinical assessment in the treatment of sexual dysfunctions In *Handbook of Sex Therapy* (eds J. LoPiccolo and L. LoPiccolo). Plenum Press, New York

Lobitz, W.C. and LoPiccolo, J. (1972) New methods in the behavioural treatment of sexual dysfunction. *Journal of Behaviour Therapy and Experimental Psychiatry*, *3*, 265–71

Locke, H.J. and Wallace, K.M. (1959) Short marital adjustment and prediction tests: their reliability and validity. *Marriage and Family Living*, 251–5

LoPiccolo, J. and Lobitz, W.C. (1972) The role of masturbation in the treatment of orgasmic dysfunction. *Archives of Sexual Behaviour*, *2*, 163–71

LoPiccolo, J. (1977) Direct treatment of sexual dysfunction in the couple. In *Handbook of Sexology*, pp. 1227–1244 (eds J. Money and H. Musaph). Elsevier/North-Holland Biomedical Press, Amsterdam

LoPiccolo, L. and Heiman, J.R. (1978) Sexual assessment and history interview. In *Handbook of Sex Therapy* (eds J. LoPiccolo and L. LoPiccolo). Plenum Press, New York

LoPiccolo, J. and Steger, J.C. (1974) The sexual interaction inventory: A new instrument for assessment of sexual dysfunction. *Archives of Sexual Behaviour*, *3*, 585–95

LoPiccolo, J., Heiman, J.R., Hogan, D.R. and Roberts, C.W. (1985) Effectiveness of single therapists versus cotherapy teams in sex therapy. *Journal of Consulting and Clinical Psychology*, *53*, 287–94

Lowe, J.C. and Mikulas, W.L. (1975) Use of written material in learning self-control of premature ejaculation. *Psychological Reports*, *37*, 295–8

Maatman, T.J., Montague, D.K. and Martin, L.M. (1987) Erectile dysfunction in men with diabetes mellitus. *Urology*, *29*, 589–92

Malloy, G.L. and Herold, E.S. (1986) Factors related to sexual counseling of physically disabled adults. *Journal of Sex Research*, *24*, 200–27.

Margolin, G., Michelli, J. and Jacobson, N. (1988) Assessment of marital dysfunction. In *Behavioural Assessment: A Practical Handbook*, 3rd edn (eds A.S. Bellack and M. Hersen). Pergamon Press, New York

Marshall, S. (1989) Evaluation and management of simple erectile dysfunction in office practice. *Medical Aspects of Human Sexuality*, 4–8

Masters, W.H. and Johnson, V. (1966) *Human Sexual Response*. Little, Brown and Co., Boston

Masters, W.H. and Johnson, V.E. (1970) *Human Sexual Inadequacy*. Little, Brown and Co., Boston

Masters, W.H. and Johnson, V.E. (1979) *Homosexuality in Perspective*. Little, Brown and Co., Boston

Mathews, A., Bancroft, J., Whitehead, A., Hackman, A., Julier, D., Bancroft, J., Gath, D. and Shaw, P.(1976) The behavioural treatment of sexual inadequacy: A comparative study. *Behaviour, Research and Therapy*, *14*, 427–36

Mathews, A., Whitehead, A. and Kellet, J.(1983) Psychological and hormonal factors in the treatment of female sexual dysfunction. *Psychological Medicine*, *13*, 83–92

McCarthy, B. (1984) Strategies and techniques for the treatment of inhibited sexual desire. *Journal of Sex and Marital Therapy*, *10*, 97–104

McClure, R.D. (1988) Men with one testicle. *Medical Aspects of Human Sexuality*, *22*, 22–32

McGovern, K.B., Stewart, R.C. and LoPiccolo, J.(1975) Secondary orgasmic dysfunction. Analysis and strategies for treatment. *Archives of Sexual Behaviour*, *4*, 265–75

McMullen, S. and Rosen, R.C. (1979) Self-administered masturbation training in the treatment of primary orgasmic dysfunction. *Journal of Consulting and Clinical Psychology*, *47*, 912–18

McWhirter, D. and Mattison, A. (1980) Treatment of sexual dysfunction in homosexual male couples. In *Principles and Practice of Sex Therapy* (eds S. Leiblum and L. Piervin). Guilford Press, New York

Melzack, R. and Wall, P.D. (1965) Pain mechanisms: A new theory. *Science*, *150*, 971–9

Messe, M.R. and Geer, J.H. (1985) Voluntary vaginal musculative contractions as an enhancer of sexual arousal. *Archives of Sexual Behaviour*, *14*, 13–28

Meyer, J.K. (1983) Training for the treatment of sexual disorders. In *Clinical Management of Sexual Disorders*, pp. 368–379 (eds J.K. Meyer, C.W. Schmidt and T.N. Wise). Williams & Wilkins, Baltimore

Milan, R.J., Kilmann, P.R. and Boland, J.P. (1988) Treatment outcome of secondary orgasmic dysfunction: A two- to six-year follow-up. *Archives of Sexual Behaviour*, *27*, 463–80

Monat, R.K. (1982) *Sexuality and the Mentally Retarded*. College-Hill Press, San Diego

Mooney, T.O., Cole, T.M. and Chilgren, R.A. (1975) *Sexual Options for Paraplegics and Quadriplegics*. Little, Brown & Co., New York

Morokoff, P.J. and LoPiccolo, J.(1986) A comparative evaluation of minimal therapist contact and 15-session treatment for female orgasmic dysfunction. *Journal of Consulting and Clinical Psychology*, *54*, 294–300

Mulligan, T. (1989) Impotence in the older man. *Medical Aspects of Human Sexuality*, *23*, 32–6

Mulligan, T., Retchin, S.M., Chinchilli, V .M. and Bettinger, C.B. (1988) The role of ageing and chronic disease in sexual dysfunction. *Journal of the American Geriatric Society*, *36*, 520–4

Munjack, D.J., Schlaks, A., Sanchez, V.C., Usigli, R., Zulueta, A. and Leonard, M. (1984) Rational emotive therapy in the treatment of erectile failure: An initial study. *Journal of Sexual and Marital Therapy*, *10*, 170–5

Nadig, P. and Becker, R. (1984) A new, non-invasive device for the treatment of impotence in diabetes. *Diabetes*, *33*, 76

Nathan, S.G. (1986) The epidemiology of the DSM-III psychosexual dysfunctions. *Journal of Sex and Marital Therapy*, *12*, 267–81

Neidigh, L. and Kinder, B.N. (1987) The use of audiovisual materials in sex therapy: A critical overview. *Journal of Sex and Marital Therapy*, *13*, 64–72

Nellans, R.E., Ellis, L.R. and Kramer-Levien, D. (1987) New treatment for impotence: Pharmacologic erection. *Medical Aspects of Human Sexuality*, *21*, 20–8

Nelson, J.E. (1987) Counselling the female partner of a man with psychogenic impotence. *Medical Aspects of Human Sexuality*, *21*, 90–101

Nemetz, G.H., Craig, K.D. and Reith, G. (1978) Treatment of female sexual dysfunction through symbolic modelling. *Journal of Consulting and Clinical Psychology*, *46*, 62–73

Nettelbladt, P. and Uddenberg, N. (1979) Sexual dysfunction and sexual satisfaction in 58 married Swedish men. *Journal of Psychosomatic Research*, *23*, 141–7

Newcomb, M.D. and Bentler, P.M. (1988) Behavioural and psychological assessment of sexual dysfunction: An overview. In *Treatment of Sexual Problems in Individual and Couples' Therapy* (eds R.A. Brown and J.R. Field). PMA, New York

Nutter, P. and Condron, M. (1983) Sexual fantasy and activity patterns of females with inhibited sexual desire versus normal controls. *Journal of Sex and Marital Therapy*, *9*, 276–82

Osborn, M., Hawton, K. and Gath, D. (1988) Sexual dysfunction among middle aged women in the community. *British Medical Journal*, *296*, 959–62

O'Sullivan, K. (1979) Observations on vaginismus in Irish women. *Archives of General Psychiatry*, *36*, 824–6

Palmeri, B.A. and Wise, T.N. (1988) Sexual dysfunction in the medically ill. In *Treatment of Sexual Problems in Individual and Couples Therapy* (eds R.A. Brown and J.R. Field). PMA, New York

Patterson, D.G. and O'Gorman, E.C. (1986) The SOMA: A questionnaire measure of sexual anxiety. *British Journal of Psychiatry*, *149*, 63–7

Perelman, M.A. (1977) Group treatment of premature ejaculation 2 years later: Success or failure? Paper presented at the Association for Advancement of Behaviour Therapy Convention, Atlanta, Georgia

Perry, B.A. and Weiss, R.L. (1983) *Interactive Couples Therapy: A Couple's Guide*. Eugene, Oregon

Petrie, W.M. (1980) Sexual effects of antidepressants and psychomotor stimulant drugs. In *Modern Problems of Pharmacopsychiatry*, pp. 77–99 (eds T.A. Ban and P. Pichot). Karger, Basel

Pfeiffer, E. and Davis, G.C. (1972) Determinants of sexual behavior in middle and old age. *Journal of the American Geriatric Society*, *20*, 151–8

Pietropinto, A. and Arora, A. (1988a) Dermatological disorders and sexual functioning. *Medical Aspects of Human Sexuality*, *22*, 86–92

Pietropinto, A. and Arora, A. (1988b) Epilepsy and sexual functioning: Survey analysis. *Medical Aspects of Human Sexuality*, *22*, 78–82

Pietropinto, A. and Arora, A. (1989) Sexual functioning in diabetics. *Medical Aspects of Human Sexuality*, *23*, 74–6

Porte, K.L., Olivieri-Sulo, D. and Wood, W.S. (1987) Thyroid disease and sexual dysfunction. *Medical Aspects of Human Sexuality*, *21*, 39–45

Prather, R.C. (1988) Sexual dysfunction in the diabetes female: A review. *Archives of Sexual Behaviour*, *17*, 277–84

Quadagno, D.M. (1988) Update on the G-Spot. *Medical Aspects of Human Sexuality*, *22*, 93–4

Quadland, M.C. (1980) Private self-consciousness, attribution of responsibility and perfectionist thinking in secondary erectile dysfunction. *Journal of Sex and Marital Therapy*, 1, 47

Reece, R. (1988) Special issues in the etiologies and treatments of sexual problems amongst gay men. *Journal of Homosexuality*, *15*, 43–57

Renshaw, D.C. (1983) Sexuality in old age, illness and disability. In *Psychopharmacology and Sexual Disorders* (ed. D. Wheatley). Oxford University Press, Oxford

Renshaw, D.C. (1988) Sexual problems in later life: A case of impotence. *Clinical Gerontologist*, *8*, 73–6

Riley, A.J. and Riley, E.J. (1978) A controlled study to evaluate directed masturbation in the management of primary orgasmic failure in women. *British Journal of Psychiatry*, *133*, 404–9

Robinson, C.H. and Annon, J.S. (1975) *The Heterosexual Behaviour Inventory*. Enabling Systems Inc., Honolulu

Rosen, R.C. and Beck. J.G. (1988) *Patterns of Sexual Arousal: Psycho-*

physiological Processes and Clinical Applications. Guilford Press, New York

Roth, S.H. (1989) Arthritis and impotence. *Medical Aspects of Human Sexuality*, *23*, 28–31

Rousseau, P.C. (1986) Sexual changes and impotence in elderly men. *American Family Physician*, *34*, 131–6

Rust, J. and Golombok, S. (1986) The GRISS: A psychometric instrument for the assessment of sexual dysfunction. *Archives of Sexual Behaviour*, *15*, 157–65

Sandberg, G. and Quevillon, R.P. (1987) Dyspareunia: An integrated approach to assessment and diagnosis. *Journal of Family Practice*, *24*, 66–9

Sanders, G.L. and Cairns, K.V. (1987) Loss of sexual spontaneity. *Medical Aspects of Human Sexuality*, *21*, 37–43

Sanders, J.D. and Sprenkle, D.H. (1980) Sexual therapy for the post coronary patient. *Journal of Sex and Marital Therapy*, *6*, 174–86

Schellen, M.C. (1968) Further results with induction of ejaculation by electrovibration. *Bulletin Society. Republic Belgium Gynaecology and Obstetrics*, *38*, 301–5

Schiavi, R.C., Schreiner-Engel, P., White, D. and Mandeli,J. (1988) Pituitary–gonadal function during sleep in men with hypoactive sexual desire and normal controls. *Psychomatic Medicine*, *50*, 304–18

Schmaling, K.B., Fruzzetti, A.E. and Jacobson, N. (1989) Marital problems. In *Cognitive Behaviour Therapy for Psychiatric Problems: A Practical Guide* (eds K. Hawton, P.M. Salkovskis, J. Kirk and D.M. Clark). Oxford University Press, Oxford

Scholl, G.M. (1988) Prognostic variables in treating vaginismus. *Obstetrics and Gynaecology*, *72*, 231–5

Schover, L.R. and Jensen, S.B. (1988) *Sexuality and Chronic Illness: A Comprehensive Approach*. Guilford Press, New York

Schover, L.R. and LoPiccolo, J. (1982) Treatment effectiveness for dysfunctions of sexual desire. *Journal of Sex and Marital Therapy*, *8*, 179–97

Schover, L.R., Friedman, J.M., Weiler, S.J. Heiman, J.R. and LoPiccolo, J. (1980) *A Multi-Axial Descriptive System for the Sexual Dysfunctions: Categories and Manual*. Stony Brook, New York

Schover, L.R. Friedman, J.M. Weiler, S.J., Heiman, J.R. and LoPiccolo, J. (1982) Multi-axial problem-oriented system for sexual dysfunction. *Archives of General Psychiatry*, *39*, 614–19

Schreiner-Engel, P. and Schiavi, R.C. (1986) Lifetime psychopathology in individuals with low sexual desire. *Journal of Nervous Mental Disorders*, *174*, 646–51

Scull, G.R. and Sprenkle, D.H. (1980) Retarded ejaculation reconceptualization and implications for treatment. *Journal of Sex and Marital Therapy*, *6*, 234–46

Scrignar, C.B. (1987) Post-traumatic stress disorder and sexual dysfunction. *Medical Aspects of Human Sexuality*, *21*, 102–12

Segraves, K.A. Segraves, R.T. and Schoenberg, H.W. (1987) Use of sexual history to differentiate organic from psychogenic impotence. *Archives of Sexual Behaviour*, *16*, 125–37

Segraves, R.T. (1988) Psychiatric drugs and inhibited female orgasm. *Journal of Sex and Marital Therapy*, *14*, 202–7.

Segraves, R.T., Schoenberg, H.W., Zairns, C.K., Camic, P. and Knoff, J. (1981) Characteristics of erectile dysfunction as a function of medical care system entry point. *Psychosomatic Medicine*, *43*, 227–34

Silverstone, T. and Turner, P. (1982) *Drug Treatment in Psychiatry*, 3rd edn. Routledge & Kegan Paul, London

Smolev, J. (1983) Urological surgery. In *Clinical Management of Sexual Disorders*, pp. 123–33 (eds J.K. Meyer, C.W. Schmidt and T.N. Wise). Williams & Wilkins, Baltimore

Sotile, W.M. and Kilmann, P.R. (1978) Effects of group systematic desensitization on female orgasmic dysfunction. *Archives of Sexual Behaviour*, *7*, 477–92

Spanier, G.B. (1976) Measuring dyadic adjustment: New scales for assessing the quality of marriage and similar dyads. *Journal of Marriage and the Family*, 15–23

Spector, K.R. and Boyle, M. (1986) The prevalence and perceived aetiology of male sexual problems in a non-clinical sample. *British Journal of Medical Psychology*, *59*, 351–8

Spence, S.H. (1983) The training of heterosexual social skills. In *Developments in Social Skills Training* (eds S.H. Spence and G. Shepherd). Academic Press, London

Spence, S.H. (1985) Group versus individual treatment of primary and secondary female orgasmic dysfunction. *Behaviour Research and Therapy*, *23*, 539–48

Spiess, W.F., Geer, J.H. and O'Donohue, W.T. (1984) Premature ejaculation: An investigation of factors in ejaculatory latency. *Journal of Abnormal Psychology*, *93*, 242–5

Stanislaw, H. and Rice, F.J. (1988) Correlation between sexual desire and menstrual cycle changes. *Archives of Sexual Behaviour*, *17*, 499–508

Steger, J. (1978) Cognitive behavioural strategies in the treatment of sexual problems in *Cognitive Behaviour Therapy Research and Application* (eds J. Foreyt and D. Rathjen). Plenum, New York

Stone, J.D. (1987) Marital and sexual counselling of elderly couples. In *Integrating Sex and Marital Therapy: A Clinical Guide* (eds G.R. Weeks and L. Hof). Brunner/Mazel, New York

Starr, B.D. and Weiner, M.B. (1981) *On Sex and Sexuality in the Mature Years*. Stein & Day, New York

Strassberg, D.S., Kelly, M.P., Carroll, C. and Kircher, J.C. (1987) The psychophysiological nature of premature ejaculation. *Archives of Sexual Behaviour*, *16*, 327–336

Stuart, F.M., Hammond, D.C. and Pett, M.A. (1987) Inhibited sexual desire in women. *Archives of Sexual Behaviour*, *16*, 91–106

Stuart, R.B. (1980) *Helping Couples Change: A Social Learning Approach to Marital Therapy*. Guilford Press, New York

Stuntz, R.C. (1988) Assessment of organic factors in sexual dysfunctions. In *Treatment of Sexual Problems in Individual and Couples Therapy* (eds R.A. Brown and J.R. Field). PMA, New York

Takefman, J. and Brender, W. (1984) An analysis of the effectiveness of two components in the treatment of erectile dysfunction. *Archives of Sexual Behaviour*, *13*, 321–40

Thase, M.E., Reynolds, C.F., Jennings, J.R., Frank, E. and Howell, J.R. (1988) Nocturnal penile tumescence is diminished in depressed men. *Biological Psychiatry*, *24*, 33–46

Thienhaus, O.J. (1988) Practical overview of sexual function and advancing age. *Geriatrics*, *43*, 63–7

Treat, S.R. (1987) Enhancing a couple's sexual relationship. In *Integrating Sex and Marital Therapy: A Clinical Guide* (eds G.R. Weeks and L. Hof). Brunner/Mazel, New York

Trimmer, E. (1978) Reducing the side-effects of the pill. *British Journal of Sexual Medicine*, *5*, 62–70

Tripet-Dodge, L.J. Glasgow, R.E. and O'Neill, K.O. (1982) Bibliotherapy in the treatment of female orgasmic dysfunction. *Journal of Consulting and Clinical Psychology*, *50*, 442–3

Trudel, G. and Laurin, F. (1988) The effects of bibliotherapy on orgasmic dysfunction and couple interactions: An experimental study. *Sexual and Marital Therapy*, *3*, 223–8

Trudel, G. and Proulx, S. (1987) The treatment of premature ejaculation by bibliotherapy: An experimental study. *Sexual and Marital Therapy*, *2*, 163–7

Tsai, M., Feldman-Summers, S. and Edgar, M. (1979) Childhood molestation: Variables related to differential impacts on psychosexual functioning in adult women. *Journal of Abnormal Psychology*, *88*, 407–17

Tsitouras, P.D. (1987) Effects of age on testicular function. *Endocrinology and Metabolism Clinics of North America*, *16*, 1045–59

Turk, D.C. Meichenbaum, D. and Genest, M. (1983) *Pain and Behavioural Medicine: A Cognitive Behavioural Perspective.* Guilford Press, New York.

Twentyman, C.T. and McFall, R.M. (1975) Behavioural training of social skills in shy males. *Journal of Consulting and Clinical Psychology*, *43*, 384–95

Vikram, B. and Vikram, R.K. (1988) Prevention of impotence in patients with prostate cancer. *Medical Aspects of Human Sexuality*, *22*, 83–5

Virag, R., Bouilly, P. and Frydman, D. (1985) Is impotence an arterial disorder? A study of arterial risk factors in 440 impotent men. *Lancet*, i, 181–4

Wakefield, J.C. (1987) The semantics of success: Do masturbation exercises lead to partner orgasm? *Journal of Sex and Marital Therapy*, *13*, 3–14

Walbroehl, G.S. (1988) Effects of medical problems on sexuality in the elderly. *Medical Aspects of Human Sexuality*, *22*, 56–66

Walen, S.R. and Perlmutter, R.(1988) Cognitive behavioural treatment of adult sexual dysfunctions from a family perspective. In *Cognitive-Behavioural Therapy with Families* (eds N. Epstein, S.E. Schlesinger, and W. Dryden). Brunner/Mazel, New York

Wallace, D.H. and Barbach, L.G. (1974) Preorgasmic group treatment. *Journal of Sex and Marital Therapy*, *1*, 146–54

Weeks, G.R. (1987) Systematic treatment of inhibited sexual desire. In

Integrating Sex and Marital Therapy: A Clinical Guide (eds G.R. Weeks and L. Hof). Brunner/Mazel, New York

Weg, R.B. (1983a) Introduction: Beyond intercourse and orgasm. In *Sexuality in the Later Years: Roles and Behaviour* (ed. R.B. Weg). Academic Press, New York

Weg, R.B. (1983b) The physiological perspective. In *Sexuality in the Later Years: Roles and Behaviour* (ed. R.B. Weg). Academic Press, New York

Weisstub, E.B. and Schoenfeld, H. (1987) Brief goal-limited couple therapy in the treatment of homosexuals. *American Journal of Psychotherapy*, *41*, 95–103

Weizman, R. and Hart, J. (1987) Sexual behaviour in healthy married elderly men. *Archives of Sexual Behaviour*, *16*, 39–44

Wheeler, D. and Rubin, H.B. (1987) A comparison of volumetric and circumferential measures of penile erection. *Archives of Sexual Behaviour*, *16*, 289–99

Whitehead, A. and Mathews, A. (1986) Factors related to successful outcome in the treatment of sexually unresponsive women. *Psychological Medicine*, *16*, 373–378

Whitehead, E.D., Klyde, B.J., Zussman, S., Wayne, N., Shinbach, K. and Davis, D. (1983) Male sexual dysfunction and diabetes mellitus. *New York Journal of Medicine*, *83*, 1174–9

Whitlatch, C.J. and Zarit, S.H. (1988) Sexual dysfunction in an aged married couple: A case study of a behavioural intervention. *Clinical Gerontologist*, *8*, 43–62

Wilcox, D. and Hager, R. (1980) Toward realistic expectations for orgasmic response in women. *Journal of Sex Research*, *16*, 162–179

Williams, G. (1987) Erectile dysfunction: Diagnosis and treatment. *British Journal of Urology*, *60*, 1–5

Wilson, P., Spence, S.H. and Kavanagh, D.J. (1989) *Cognitive Behavioural Interviewing for Adult Disorders*, Routledge, London

Wincze, J.P. (1971) A comparison of systematic desensitization and vicarious extinction in a case of frigidity. *Journal of Behavioural Therapy and Experimental Psychiatry*, *2*, 285–9

Wincze, J.P. and Caird, W.K. (1976) The effects of systematic desensitization and video desensitization in the treatment of essential sexual dysfunction in women. *Behaviour Therapy*, *7*, 335–42

Wincze, J.P., Bansal, S., Malhotra, C., Balko, A., Susset, J.G. and Malamud, M.(1988) A comparison of nocturnal penile tumescence and penile response to erotic stimulation during waking states in comprehensively diagnosed groups of males experiencing erectile difficulties. *Archives of Sexual Behaviour*, *17*, 333–48

Wise, T.N. (1983) Sexual problems in the aged and incapacitated. In *Clinical Management of Sexual Disorders* (eds J.K. Heyer, C.W. Schmidt and T.N. Wise). Wiliams and Wilkins, Baltimore

Wyatt, G.E., Peters, S.D. and Guthrie, D. (1988) Kinsey revisited, Part 1: Comparisons of the sexual socialization and sexual behaviour of white women over 33 years. *Archives of Sexual Behaviour*, *17*, 201–39

Zeiss, R.A. (1977) Self directed treatment for premature ejaculation:

Preliminary case reports. *Journal of Behaviour Therapy and Experimental Psychiatry*, *8*, 87–91

Zeiss, A.M., Rosen, R.A. and Zeiss, R.A. (1977) Orgasm during intercourse: a treatment strategy for women. *Journal of Consulting and Clinical Psychology*, *45*, 891–5

Zilbergeld, B. (1975) Group treatment of sexual dysfunction in men without partners. *Journal of Sex and Marital Therapy*, *3*, 443–52

Zilbergeld, B. (1978) *Men and Sex.*, Fontana, London

Zimmer, D. (1987) Does marital therapy enhance the effectiveness of treatment for sexual dysfunction? *Journal of Sex and Marital Therapy*, *13*, 193–209

Author index

Subject index